T0132445

In the Secret Place
of the Most High

In the Secret Place of the Most High

✦

Ultimate Living for God's people in a difficult world

King's Kid Series

Expanded Second Edition

Ephrain Tristan Ortiz, MCEd.

iUniverse, Inc.
New York   Bloomington

In the Secret Place of the Most High
Expanded Second Edition

iUniverse books may be ordered through booksellers or by contacting:

iUniverse
1663 Liberty Drive
Bloomington, IN 47403
www.iuniverse.com
1-800-Authors (1-800-288-4677)

Because of the dynamic nature of the Internet, any Web addresses or links contained in this book may have changed since publication and may no longer be valid.

ISBN: 978-1-4401-9256-2 (pbk)
ISBN: 978-1-4401-9257-9 (ebook)

Printed in the United States of America

iUniverse rev. date: 12/18/2009

Special Dedication

For any of Jesus' children who are willing to say, "Yes, Lord!"
instead of "Yes, but…"

Contents

An Introduction from the Author

Living in the "Secret place of the Most High" – that is possibly the ultimate in living for Christians in today's world. Living in such a place (and its existence is more real than just about anyone realizes) means to live without frustration, anxiety, depression, worry, fear, stress, disorder – to live instead the abundant life Jesus came to give us all – this should be the desire of all of us.

The key to living in the secret place of the Most High is to be stewards in everything instead of being owners in anything, which means to surrender all our "rights" to ourselves over to Him. Jesus is *Melek*, which is Hebrew for "King". Jesus is the King, and we are His kids – instruments in His masterful hands to do with as He sees fit. The Bible says:

> **For none of us lives for himself and none of us dies for himself;**
> **while we are alive, we are living for the Lord, and when we die, we**
> **die for the Lord: and so, alive or dead, we belong to the Lord. It**
> **was for this purpose that Christ both died and came to life again:**
> **so that he might be Lord of both the dead and the living. (Romans**
> **14: 7 – 9)**

Only by living as stewards will we reach our full potential in this life, free from disappointments, broken hearts, and anger, because we know that in all things He works together for good to those who love Him and are called according to His purpose. (Romans 8: 28) As His kids, we know He wants His best for us in all things, not just in some things, but in all things.

To see everything in our lives as being of Him and for Him means to stop struggling to hang onto things (only to lose them along with a lot more) and to be thankful that He is able to care for that which is His own. After all, the only real function of a Christian is to be a container for the Lord. It's all about Jesus. There isn't a single good thing in any of us apart from Him.

> **I am the vine, you are the branches. Whoever remains in me, with me in him, bears fruit in plenty; for cut off from me you can do nothing. (John 15: 5)**

We do not seek to win in a situation or circumstance simply for victory's sake. Instead, we seek Jesus who is our victory. This is the highest victory, one which we achieve in the secret place of the Most High, a spiritual stronghold that makes victory total and complete. In Christ, we receive all that His name implies. We become joint heirs with Jesus to all the kingdom of God. To experience this means to enter into the rest of faith – the Lord's faith. There is no need of stressing or struggling to occupy our energies, but simply resting in His finished work and just allowing Him to be all He wants to be in us and through us.

We can have perfect confidence in God's love for us, never taking offense at Him for His way of molding us into His image and likeness; instead we are convinced that He is achieving His purpose in us and that His perfect will is being done.

The end result is an incredible win, many true examples of which are found in this book. These examples are inspiring and stunning enough to have recently made quite an impression on inmates at a maximum security prison. They were unable to put the book down as their hearts burned with hope in the heavenly Father. This is impossible for an author to do, but for God it was no problem. Just like it will be no problem for Him to take whatever it is you're going through and use it to glorify Himself and accomplish a win for you that will make your life better through this "problem" than had the "problem" never occurred to begin with!

God has the power to bring more goodness out of your difficulty than if it had never existed. Not only does He have this power, He is willing to use it on your behalf. Such a victory from God, expressed in constant praise, assures us of His continual presence, for He says He lives in the praises of His people.

> **Yet you, the Holy One, who make your home in the praises of Israel, in you our ancestors put their trust, they trusted and you set them free. To you they called for help and were delivered; in you they trusted and were not put to shame. (Psalm 22: 3 – 5)**

The Bible in Hebrew calls God "Elyon", meaning "Highest" or "Exalted One". This emphasizes that He is the highest in every realm of life. He is "Adonai" or "My Lord", fully in control and "Shaddai" or "Almighty" which means He is able and willing to act in your best interests in every situation imaginable. The Bible says:

You who live in the secret place of *'Elyon*, who spend your nights in the shadow of *Shaddai*, who say to *ADONAI*, "My refuge! My fortress! My God, in whom I trust!" (Psalm 91: 1 – 2) CJB

In some Bible translations, the word "dwell" is used instead of "live". Webster's Dictionary defines the word "dwell" as not only "to live in"; it also defines "dwell" as "to keep the attention directed on someone or something". When we live in the Lord's "secret place" spending our nights in His "shadow", we are keeping our attention directed totally on Him. By doing this, we will experience a peace, comfort, safety and purpose well beyond what anyone or anything else in this world could possibly give us. Scripture says:

Never worry about anything; but tell God all your desires of every kind in prayer and petition shot through with gratitude, and the peace of God which is beyond our understanding will guard your hearts and your thoughts in Christ Jesus. (Philippians 4: 6 – 7)

As we will read in this book, when we live our lives in praise and thanksgiving, regardless of how a situation looks, we are magnifying God, not the problem. As human beings we were designed to magnify Him, giving Him honor and glory in everything. When we keep our focus upon our Father we find an inner peace, a safe resting place (refuge) and inner strength (fortress) that truly become for us "the secret place of the Most High" in which we can live or "dwell." He becomes for us our "Migdal-Oz", which is Hebrew for "Strong Tower."

Now let's be practical. (The Lord wants that of us, believe it or not!) How can focusing more on the Lord instead of a difficult circumstance help us, practically speaking? And assuming it does help us, how can we even keep this focus, especially if we are going through trials that seem to be mercilessly pushing us over the edge? How can we keep our focus on the Lord when our pain is so great that even making it through an hour is a life and death struggle?

We can keep this life – saving focus on the Lord through God's mighty power and love for us, all of which we can tap into with proper prayer and the many resources God provides us with, which we will be covering in the chapters ahead. Don't worry; this book is filled with real life examples of God's resources saving people going through some of the worst case scenarios imaginable. I promise to be practical in this book. Know that God says:

Come to me all you who labour and are overburdened, and I will give you rest. Shoulder my yoke and learn from me, for I am gentle

and humble in heart, and you will find rest for your souls. Yes, my yoke is easy and my burden light. (Matthew 11: 28 – 30)

And:

If you call to me in trouble I will rescue you and you will honour me. (Psalm 50: 15)

We will learn how to defeat any worry and get through any situation victorious through proper prayer and petition. This is the key! You will see how this works well beyond you can imagine! And this will indeed guard our hearts and thoughts in Jesus' love so we can experience this incredible joy, strength and peace, which take us to live safely "under the shadow of the Almighty".

No longer will we be tormented by the difficult circumstances, anxieties, anger, depression, fear, etc. that this world and everything in it may hurl at us. These things can't enter God's secret place for us.

God's shelter and rest from these torments are available now to all who are willing to seek a personal relationship with Him through His Son, Jesus Christ. In this loving relationship, the Christian will find many hidden rights and privileges that go along with being a child of God. These rights and privileges are gifts to us, all detailed throughout His Word, the Holy Bible. Most often, however, they are completely overlooked, even by experienced Christians. God says:

About the gifts of the Spirit, brothers, I want you to be quite certain. (1 Corinthians 12: 1)

The Lord has many gifts for us in His Word. Many of His followers are unaware of these treasures and although they eventually stumble into heaven at the end of their earthly lives, it often is after living defeated, tired lives on this earth. If God's children learned to use these overlooked gifts, they would experience an extraordinary intimacy with God, a heaven on earth, a victory over the circumstances of their lives, and an incredible refuge from any challenge this world sends their way.

By using and sharing these gifts, believers would experience a tremendous growth in their trust of the Heavenly Father, an incredible enjoyment from letting Him masterfully manage the small and large details of their lives and a satisfaction from helping others that is literally "out of this world"! The richness in Christian lives needs to be so evident to others that it attracts many people to seek God and obtain the peace and joy they have. The Lord says:

Give thanks to *ADONAI*! Call on his name! Make his deeds known among the peoples. Sing to him, sing praises to him, talk about all his wonders. Glory in his holy name; let those seeking *ADONAI* have joyful hearts. Seek *ADONAI* and his strength; always seek his presence. (Psalm 105: 1 – 4) CJB

"Adonai" (a do NAI) is the Hebrew word for "My Lord." Teaching you about the great things Adonai does for us in love and out of a desire to enter into a relationship with us, is the purpose of this book. The Lord said to me at the beginning of this writing:

My people are destroyed for lack of knowledge. (Hosea 4: 6)

The Lord impressed upon me that many of His people are suffering and dying, both physically and spiritually, for not knowing what His Word says about living "in the secret place of the Most High". It's time that ended!

All God's people need to know about the many privileges, gifts, blessings and treasures to be found in His Word. As you'll read in this book, we put way too many limits on the Lord's power, and His love and power are limitless, as is His desire to use His power for our behalf. Too often people pray in such a way that they are actually telling God they don't believe in, or want His intervention! In chapters ahead we will discover how people do this and how to keep from doing this ourselves.

The Lord Jesus alone is our strength, our comforter and our victory, and it's time His people learned to pray so this truth becomes fulfilled in their lives. By doing so, we will dwell on Him in everything, so that in everything, we can dwell in the peace and safety of the Lord's secret, loving shelter. Jesus is the Christ, a term coming from the Greek word "Christos" meaning "Anointed One". In Hebrew the term "Messiah" is used. Jesus or Yeshua, as He is known in Hebrew is the Anointed One, the One empowered by God's Spirit to deliver His people from sin, death and all the problems that come along with those.

Kings and priests have been anointed with olive oil since ancient times, receiving authority in a special ceremony. So Jesus, being the "Anointed One" or the "Messiah" or "Christ" carries the truth that He holds God's special priestly and kingly authority. His priestly authority He uses to save us and His kingly authority He uses to rule over all things.

If we are children of the King Jesus, we don't need to live as victims and slaves of all the circumstances we find ourselves surrounded by in this world. As His children we can live above the circumstances instead of below them.

We can live as God's friends, free and victorious over everything! Great is God's mercy and compassion for us!

Please ask God to guide you, speak to you, and teach you through this book. My prayer is that you grow closer to this awesome Heavenly Father who is inviting you into a loving relationship with His Son Jesus Christ (Yeshua Messiah). I pray that you experience His love, forgiveness, peace, joy and other great things in abundance. May your life lead others to Him as well. I ask all these things in Jesus' name. Amen.

Chapter 1

God's Heroic Rescue Plan

Let's pray before we begin:

Heavenly Father, we praise You and thank You for your kindness and goodness. How great You are and how worthy You are to be praised! Thank You for your everlasting love and compassion. Please bless the reader of this book with your awesome care and favor. It is no accident or coincidence, but your Spirit has drawn him/her to read about how You provide for us so well. Thank You! Speak to this special reader in this book and touch his/her heart.

Thank You for all the details and circumstances of this reader's life. Use them all as part of your perfect, loving plan to draw him/her closer to you. Take especially any difficult circumstances in this reader's life and use them for good, so much good in fact, that more good comes into this reader's life from these difficulties than if these difficulties hadn't happened at all. Lead this good to overflow and bless anyone else You wish, and in doing so, glorify your holy name. Yes, Lord, glorify it, and glorify it again in the wonderful work You are doing in the life of this reader. Thank You in Jesus' name. Amen.

Dear reader, you have a loving Creator, a God in heaven who cares for you and loves you far more than you can imagine. He is "El Roi" (El raw EE), which is Hebrew for "The God who sees me."

Yes He sees you indeed. He even knows how many hairs are on your head! Scripture says:

Can you not buy two sparrows for a penny? And yet not one falls to the ground without your Father knowing. Why, every hair on your head has been counted. So there is no need to be afraid; you are worth more than many sparrows. (Matthew 10: 29 – 31)

Yes His eyes are on you. His eyes are on you because He loves you and desires a personal relationship with you. In fact, He loves you so much He sent His only Son to give His life for you on a cross. His Son, Jesus Christ became one of us, a human being and lived perfectly among us as directed by the Word of God. He became the living Word of God in human form. In fact, Jesus was and still is the Word; He always will be.

Jesus came to free us from sin and death. What is sin? God's definition of sin is "everything that does not come from faith" in the Bible book of Romans 14: 23. This faith is an unwavering belief in God that brings us to trust in His love for us and His willingness and ability to provide for all our needs. The Bible says,

May the God of hope fill you with all joy and peace in your faith, so that in the power of the Holy Spirit you may be rich in hope. (Romans 15:13)

When we act against this faith in God, we sin. Many people think of sin as committing an obvious moral evil like murder, dealing drugs, kidnapping or grand theft. It is true that sins are moral evils and a personal rebellion against God and His law. They also involve a lack of faith in His power and a lack of faith in how God will judge such things. But anytime we distrust God and run to something in this world to fill the inner emptiness only He can fill, we sin. An example of this would be the people who drink, go through many lovers, buy toys or spend endless hours at work or in spending sprees to find temporary relief from depression, inner emptiness and other pain instead of trusting in God to satisfy them and/or heal their hurts.

Sin, or a lack of faith in God brings many painful things in this world such as anxiety, depression, pain, rejection, loneliness, mental illness, disease, disappointments, hurts, evil actions and injustices of all kinds. To put it bluntly, the best man has a sick, depraved heart and has no hope for survival apart from Christ.

Without Jesus, man has a corrupted condition that will bring a guilty standing from God, a standing leading to condemnation. Only Jesus offers us His righteousness, a "not guilty" standing before the heavenly Father, and a freedom and healing from all the effects of the corrupt human heart. The Bible says:

> **For his sake I have suffered the loss of all things and count them as rubbish, in order that I may gain Christ and be found in him, not having a righteousness of my own that comes from the law, but that which comes through faith in Christ, the righteousness from God that depends on faith. (Philippians 3: 8 – 9)**

Yes, Christ saves us from our inherent sinful nature that causes nothing but death for us at the end of our earthly life. Why? Because we don't have the ability to save ourselves after we die. We don't have the power to keep ourselves alive, and all the sins we've committed will not even allow us to remain in God's holy presence when our life on this earth ends. Without God we are doomed to eternal separation from Him after we die. This is condemnation, or hell.

We can rejoice though, because Jesus has the ability and willingness to give us eternal life after we die. He did this by His death on the cross. He died as a sacrifice for all the sin in the world and paid the price of our condemnation. Through Him and the work He does in us, we become righteous and accepted in God's eyes.

Jesus also defeated death, and in His rising from the dead, promised those who are His children to also rise and live with Him forever.

Beginnings

We don't need to debate the fact that most people in this world don't even come close to enjoying life as abundantly or fulfilling their life's purpose as much as they were meant to. Anxiety, depression, fear, anger, confusion, broken hearts and broken dreams are all too common in both the young and old.

Addictions to drugs, alcohol, sensuality, money making, shallow relationships, career, life in the fast lane, etc. all fall short of filling the inner emptiness most people have.

As if all that weren't enough, beautiful oceans and valleys reek of pollution, disease and destruction from war. Crime, illness, and poverty are at an all – time high as the family unit continues to weaken and the murders of dozens of innocents occur on a single school ground.

What happened? According to the Bible, the world was once perfect and good. (See Genesis 1: 31) Man lived a peaceful, joyous life in close friendship with the world's Creator in a garden paradise called Eden. (See Genesis 2: 4 – 25)

All too was peaceful in heaven once as God's wonderful angels worshipped and served the Lord. What is an angel? The Bible says this of them:

Are they not all ministering spirits sent forth to minister to those who will inherit salvation? (Hebrews 1: 14)

Angels are invisible to our human eyes but they work secretly to help us and serve us in our walk with God. Heaven was full of these beautiful spirits in the beginning. One of the highest classes of angels is the cherubim. Psalm 18:10 states that God actually mounts on top of them and flies. They enjoy constant closeness to God.

One of the cherubim, a guardian named Lucifer, which means "the morning star," was full of beauty and wisdom. He was given high privilege and authority with that. The 18th verse of Chapter 28 of the Bible book of Ezekiel says that sanctuaries were under Lucifer, which means he was involved greatly in the worship of God.

The beauty, power, wisdom, and authority the Lord lovingly gave this creature weren't enough for him though. Out of pride and jealousy, Lucifer began to desire God's throne and to become God himself. He rebelled against God, attempting to ascend to the throne. One third of God's angels joined him in starting a war in heaven, and we read in Revelation 12: 7 – 9 that the angel Michael and the rest of God's faithful angels defeated Lucifer and his evil angels, casting them out of heaven, where they descended down to earth.

The name of Lucifer was changed to Satan, which means "the accuser." The angels who joined him lost their beauty and much of their power, becoming evil, disembodied spirits, or demons. (Sin makes everyone weaker, not stronger.) Removed from heaven, Satan and his demons settled on the earth, which at the time was under the authority of Adam, God's first created human being.

Now the Bible says God made this earth and all that is in it.

In the beginning God created the heaven and the earth. (Genesis 1: 1)

God also created man in His image.

God created man in the image of himself, in the image of God he created him, male and female he created them. (Genesis 1: 27)

Being made in God's image means we humans are privileged to act as God's representatives on this earth, being sub-rulers over God's creation, subduing the creatures of the earth and in this becoming a reflection of God's good rule over us. Beyond this function, we are to be like God in other ways, being spiritual, rational, and relational beings who communicate with others. Like God, our souls live on eternally. This divine purpose for humanity has been struck with the effect of the sin of Adam and Eve.

Expelled from heaven and now on the earth, Satan saw a way to continue his hateful rebellion of God by targeting the first human couple, Adam and Eve. Through his cleverness and smooth speech, Satan, disguised as a serpent-- then a beautiful creature-- convinced Adam and his mate Eve to rebel against God. He convinced the couple to believe that God lied to them and hid information from them to keep them from being gods themselves.

Satan even convinced them to willingly disobey the Lord by eating from the tree of life, a special tree that gave immortality. God had forbidden Adam and Eve to eat from this tree. When the Lord asked the couple about their actions, neither of them accepted responsibility. Adam blamed Eve, and Eve blamed the serpent.

As a result of this decision to reject God, Adam lost his authority over the earthly paradise, and was forced out of Eden. Scripture says:

He banished the man, and in front of the garden of Eden he posted the great winged creatures and the fiery flashing sword, to guard the way to the tree of life. (Genesis 3: 24)

Adam couldn't stay with the tree of life; he would live forever in a state of rebellion toward God. So he was left on his own, to be his own god. Left to his own power, though, his body began to age and get weaker as he toiled and strained against the crops and animals of the earth to provide for Eve and himself. (See Genesis 3: 17 – 19.) Instead of being God's servant, Adam was now Satan's slave.

The earth itself became polluted with death, pain, disease, violence, and many other consequences of this fall from grace. In fact, Adam's son Cain became the first murderer, killing his brother Abel in jealousy. (See Genesis chapter 4.) We can see how Adam's choice to sin against God by following Satan was already beginning to corrupt the world.

The Bible says there is an actual curse in the ground. No matter where we go, no matter how much we try to control our environment and situation, eventually the curse finds us.

Accursed be the soil because of you! Painfully will you get your food from it as long as you live. (Genesis 3: 17)

So we suffer from this fall. We die or succumb to illness too soon. We struggle to make a living or to keep our families together. We live in confusion, disorder and in a state of making foolish decisions we could kick ourselves afterwards for having made. God does not cause these things; He permits them, all so we will come to Him as we were originally intended to. The curse in the ground was designed to lead us to Him. Otherwise, if everything was always a "bed of roses" we would not think we had any need of the Lord. So our world was damaged as a result of man's rebellion against God.

Satan and his demonic army used and continue to use, the damaged world as a place to continue their hateful rebellion against God by warring on his most prized creature: man.

Generations later, the same spirit of inherent evil from Adam lives on in humanity, bringing with it sickness, wars, violence, crime, and death. There is hope though!

God could have destroyed all the evil in the earth, or even forced man to obey Him. Adonai, who desires our love, does not work that way though, for taking away our free will would not allow us to respond to Him in real love.

In an incredible act of love, God's Son descended to Earth to come to us in the form of a man, Jesus Christ or Yeshua Messiah. He took on the same temptations Adam did, facing Satan's smooth speech and temptations, but unlike Adam, He was victorious over the devil, defeating him in the desert and through the cross. Jesus, or Yeshua lived the Word of God perfectly in humility, obedience, and compassion. The Lord says,

> **If death came to many through the offense of one man, how much greater an effect the grace of God has had, coming to so many and so plentifully as a free gift through the one man Jesus Christ! (Romans 5: 15)**

Through the offense of this one man (Adam), people legally lost the world's ownership; it had to be legally won back by one man. This man was Jesus Christ. He undid the damage Adam caused. God says:

> **For if, because of one man's trespass, death reigned through that one man, much more will those who receive the abundance of grace and the free gift of righteousness reign in life through the one man Jesus Christ. (Romans 5: 17)**

And:

> **For this is how God loved the world: he gave his only Son, so that everyone who believes in him may not perish but may have eternal life. For God sent his Son into the world not to judge the world, but so that through him the world might be saved. (John 3: 16 – 17)**

How did God give us His Son? Well God couldn't just act as if all the sins of man had never happened. There had to be atonement. The death of Jesus on the cross accomplished this. Jesus offered Himself as a living sacrifice for all the past, present, and future sins of the world. He took the wrath and punishment God was to give us and took it upon Himself. Jesus, or Yeshua now works as a priest on our behalf, drawing people to Him. Scripture says:

> **But he holds his priesthood permanently, because he continues forever. Consequently, he is able to save to the uttermost those who draw near to God through him, since he always lives to make intercession for them. (Hebrews 7: 24 – 25)**

On the third day after His crucifixion, Yeshua was raised from the dead by God. This occurrence demonstrated God's acceptance of Yeshua's intercession for us and His acceptance of the Messiah's sacrifice for all those who would repent and believe.

> **It concerns his Son – he is descended from David physically; he was powerfully demonstrated to be Son of God spiritually, set apart by his having been resurrected from the dead; he is Yeshua the Messiah, our Lord. (Romans 1: 4) CJB**

Yes, Yeshua/Jesus then ascended to heaven where He is our priest permanently, interceding for us and will come again in the same way as people saw him go into heaven. (Acts 1: 11) When this happens, the heaven and the earth which have literally been groaning from their corruption (which is why we see the increase in bizarre fires, earthquakes, dry lightning, viruses, etc.) will "pass away" and will be transformed in an incredibly wonderful, radical way. (2 Peter 3: 7 – 13; Revelation 21: 1) God's people, those redeemed by faith in Yeshua will be brought into God's presence and live life as it was meant to be lived.

So everyone in this world has to pick one of two choices. The first choice is the way of Adam, which is to continue to live in sin as Satan's slave and gamble on this corrupt, unstable world to (maybe) give you temporary comfort at times, eventually finding yourself dead and awaiting a terrible fate for rejecting God's salvation plan for you through the Messiah. The second choice is to follow the way of Jesus the Messiah and experience His love, comfort, and joy now, in spite of whatever the world may bring you, and enjoy the many gifts His children are blessed with, one of which is to have the assurance of someday living eternally with God.

Our Heavenly Father truly is "Adonai Yireh" (a do NAI yir EH), or our "Lord who provides".

Chapter 2

Becoming a Child of God

You can enjoy an incredibly fulfilling relationship with the Heavenly Father and, as one of His children, enter His shelter and rest. He desires that nothing come between you and Him, whether it be worry, stress, disease, fear, anxiety, depression, hurt, poverty, imprisonment, guilt, anger, resentment, danger, overwhelming circumstances or anything else.

God can and will take on any of these problems for you and *fully* free you from the hold they bring you. If you've gotten yourself into a mess out of your own foolishness or bad choices He can restore you and even use your mistakes to bring you to a place in life better than you could have imagined. He does this in love. How do you know this is all not just some fairy tale? It's easy. Try being one of His kids! Enter into a personal relationship with Him and see!

If you're not willing to enter into this relationship with the Lord at this point, I encourage you to continue reading this book to find out about all the wonderful treasures and privileges God offers those who enter into a personal relationship with His Son Jesus. You will also read of many real life accounts of God's intervention in people's situations at many levels of seriousness. Should you have a change of heart, you can always come back to this chapter and pray as directed at the end of it.

If you are already willing to enter into this relationship with Jesus, then your position as one of God's children will now be established. *We are all God's creations, but we only become His special children by our choice.* The Lord says:

> **But to those who did accept him he gave power to become children of God, to those who believed in his name who were born not from human stock or human desire or human will but from God himself. (John 1: 12 – 13)**

The name of the One we are to accept into our hearts and believe in is Jesus, the Son of God, also known as the Lord Yeshua. When we invite Him into our hearts we don't start a religion, rather we begin a wonderful relationship that brings us great love, joy, healing and peace, along with many special rights and privileges. We can stand on the promises Jesus gives us in His Word and see the results.

What are some of these promises for His kids? His Word says:

VICTORY OVER WORLDLY CHALLENGES:
Nor are his commandments burdensome, because every child of God overcomes the world. And this is the victory that has overcome the world – our faith. Who can overcome the world but the one who believes that Jesus is the Son of God? (1 John 5: 3 – 5)

A FULFILLING LIFE WITH PURPOSE (Jesus says): **"I came that they may have life, and have it abundantly." (John 10: 10)**

For we are his workmanship, created in Christ Jesus for good works, which God prepared beforehand, that we should walk in them. (Ephesians 2: 10)

A PURPOSE FILLED LIFE AFTER REPENTING FROM MAKING BAD CHOICES: **'For I know what plans I have in mind for you,' says *ADONAI*, 'plans for well – being, not for bad things; so that you can have hope and a future. When you call to me and pray to me, I will listen to you. When you seek me, you will find me, provided you seek for me wholeheartedly; and I will let you find me,' says *ADONAI*. 'Then I will reverse your exile.' (Jeremiah 29: 11 – 14) CJB**

PEACE: **Never worry about anything; but tell God all your desires of every kind in prayer and petition shot through with gratitude, and the peace of God which is beyond our understanding will guard your hearts and your thoughts in Christ Jesus. (Philippians 4: 6 – 7)**

PROTECTION: **He rescues you from the snare of the fowler set on destruction; he covers you with his pinions, you find shelter** under his wings. His constancy is shield and protection. (Psalm 91: 3 – 4)

PROSPERITY: Beloved, I pray that you may prosper in all things and be in health, just as your soul prospers. (3 John 1: 2)

COMFORT: Blessed be the God and Father of our Lord Jesus Christ, the merciful Father and the God who gives every possible encouragement; he supports us in every hardship, so that we are able to come to the support of others, in every hardship of theirs because of the encouragement that we ourselves receive from God. (2 Corinthians 1: 3 – 4)

WISDOM: Any of you who lacks wisdom must ask God, who gives to all generously and without scolding; it will be given. (James 1: 5)

CONFIDENCE: There is nothing I cannot do in the One who strengthens me. (Philippians 4: 13)

HEALING/FORGIVENESS: Bless *ADONAI*, my soul! Everything in me, bless his holy name! Bless *ADONAI*, my soul, and forget none of his benefits! He forgives all your offenses, he heals all your diseases, he redeems your life from the pit, he surrounds you with grace and compassion, he contents you with good as long as you live, so that your youth is renewed like an eagle's. (Psalm 103: 1 – 5) CJB

ABILITY TO REJOICE DURING TROUBLE: **And so I will sing of your strength, in the morning acclaim your faithful love; you have been a stronghold for me, a refuge when I was in trouble. (Psalm 59: 16)

ETERNAL LIFE: This is the testimony: God has given us eternal life, and this life is in his Son. Whoever has the Son has life, and whoever has not the Son of God has not life. (1 John 5: 11 – 12)

And these are just some of the promises Jesus offers us when we receive Him into our hearts as our Lord and Savior! What does "Lord" mean? It means allowing Jesus to have first place in managing all the affairs of your life. He'll take over the scrambled messes you've made and turn them into great things. God says:

> **We are well aware that God works with those who love him, those who have been called in accordance with his purpose, and turns everything to their good. (Romans 8: 28)**

> **Unless *ADONAI* builds the house, its builders work in vain. Unless *ADONAI* guards the city, the guard keeps watch in vain. (Psalm 127) CJB**

As the Lord straightens out all the areas of your life, you'll find yourself drawn closer to Him in the process, and find great peace, strength, happiness and more. Other people will notice this and be drawn to the name of Jesus too, which is what the Lord wants.

What does having Jesus as our "Savior" mean? It means He saves us from sin and death. He, and He alone, was able to resist every temptation and trial He faced in his human life on earth, and He fulfilled every requirement for a human to be righteous in the eyes of God. He then offered himself as an unstained sacrifice to God as payment for all the sins of the world, past, present, and future. The Bible says:

> **He was bearing our sins in his own body on the cross, so that we might die to our sins and live for uprightness; through his bruises you have been healed. (1 Peter 2: 24)**

> **As it is, he has made his appearance once and for all, at the end of the last age, to do away with sin by sacrificing himself. Since human beings die only once, after which comes judgment, so Christ too, having offered himself only once to bear the sin of many, will manifest himself a second time, sin being no more, to those who are waiting for him, to bring them salvation. (Hebrews 9:26 – 28)**

With Jesus standing in our place to take the punishment of our sins for us, we become reconciled to God and able to live eternally with Him after our earthly life. God's Word says:

> **For this is how God loved the world: he gave his only Son, so that everyone who believes in him may not perish but may have eternal life. For God sent his Son into the world not to judge the world, but so that through him the world might be saved. (John 3: 16 – 17)**

Not only did He conquer sin's hold over us, He also conquered death by rising from the dead. By believing in His sacrifice and resurrection as the Son of God we know we too will rise from the dead, as He did.

> **As it was by one man that death came, so through one man has come the resurrection of the dead. Just as all die in Adam, so in Christ all will be brought to life. (1 Corinthians 1: 21 – 22)**

> **God raised up the Lord and he will raise us up too by his power. (1 Corinthians 6: 14)**

So Jesus, as Savior, frees us from sin and death, as well as everything in this world that would enslave us by distracting us from the life and peace – giving presence of our Heavenly Father. The Word says:

> **Now this Lord is the Spirit and where the Spirit of the Lord is, there is freedom. (2 Corinthians 3: 17)**

What must you do to receive these promises? You must become born again, by believing in Jesus as the Son of God and receive Him into your heart. Invite Jesus Christ to take over your life as Savior and Lord of all of it, knowing that apart from Him, you can do nothing nor can you have anything to offer. Jesus says:

> **"I am the vine, you are the branches. He who remains in me, with me in him, bears fruit in plenty; for cut off from me you can do nothing." (John 15: 5)**

The Bible also says:

> **Jesus said: "I am the Way; I am Truth and Life. No one can come to the Father except through me." (John 14: 6)**

When you think of all God has done for you, such as offering you His incomparable love, healing, forgiveness of sins, peace, strength, protection, wisdom and eternal life, is asking His Son Jesus to be your Lord and Savior really too much to ask?

After inviting Jesus into your heart as Lord and Savior, ask God to give you His gift of the Holy Spirit, who is given to those who believe in Him. This Spirit will guide you, strengthen you, and reprogram you mind to think the thoughts of God instead of the second best alternative. God promises to give you this for the asking. God says:

If you then, evil as you are, know how to give your children what is good, how much more will the heavenly Father give the Holy Spirit to those who ask him! (Luke 11: 13)

Then the Spirit of *ADONAI* will fall on you; you will prophesy with them and be turned into another man! (1 Samuel 10: 6) CJB

As we will read in some chapters ahead, Jesus' Holy Spirit comforts us, teaches us, counsels us and gives us strength and protection. The Holy Spirit in this way draws us into a deeper relationship with Jesus Christ. If you'd like to ask Jesus into your heart I'd like to encourage you to pray the following:

Prayer to Accept Jesus as my personal Lord and Savior

Dear Heavenly Father,

I come to You in the name of your Son Jesus. Your Word says in John 6:37 that "whoever comes to Me I will never drive away." So I come to You now admitting that I'm a sinner and I need You in my life. Your Word says if I confess with my mouth that Jesus is Lord and believe in my heart that You raised Him from the dead, I shall be saved.

I believe this with my heart and I confess with my mouth that Jesus now is my Lord. Come Lord Jesus. Come into my heart and be Lord of my life right now. I believe You are the Son of God. You took the penalty for my sins by dying on the cross. I believe You conquered death by rising on the third day so I could someday have eternal life.

*Father, thank You for forgiving all of my sins. (Name them._____)
I repent of them, turning away from them. Jesus, You are my Lord and Savior; I am a new creation in You. Old things have passed away. Now send me Your Holy Spirit to fill me and live in me. Come Holy Spirit. Come and live in me. Give me the desire to pray unceasingly and praise God unceasingly. Grant me the strength to love and forgive. Grant me your peace and healing. Grant me the wisdom to live as a child of God in heaven while I'm still on earth. Thank You Heavenly Father. I pray all these things in your Son Jesus' name. Amen.*

Welcome! You are now one of Jesus' children with all the many rights and privileges that go along with it! You may have felt something dramatic take place inside you when you prayed this prayer, or you may have not. Have faith in the fact that you have received all you have prayed for. God says you have. Trust Him at His Word, not on your feelings, which are affected by food, times of day, weather, your last sleep and other things. The Lord says:

> **God is no human being that he should lie, no child of Adam to change his mind. Is it his to say and not to do, is it his to speak and not fulfill? (Numbers 23: 19)**

> **So it is with the word that goes from my mouth: it will not return to me unfulfilled or before having carried out my good pleasure and having achieved what it was sent to do. (Isaiah 55: 11)**

So if you prayed the above prayer in faith, believe that you are adopted by God as one of His children. You are a "King's kid"! Please don't assume that Jesus comes into your heart as Lord and Savior just because you completed a Christian initiation or new member class at your church. You have to personally invite Him in!

Remember, if you won't decide at this point to invite Jesus into your heart, I encourage you to read the rest of the book and consider this invitation again and return to this chapter at the end. This book dedicates itself to revealing to you the incredible treasures and privileges God gives to help His children stay true to Him. May you be blessed to learn how Jesus expresses His love toward you and protects you.

Chapter 3

Praise and the Power of Loosing to God

Praise and thanksgiving prayers release more of God's power in all situations more than any other form of petitions. If we look at how Jesus prayed, we will see that this is how he communicated with the Father. The gospel of Mark tells of when Jesus fed five thousand people with just two fish and five loaves of bread:

> **Then he took the five loaves and the two fish, raised his eyes to heaven and said the blessing; then he broke the loaves and began handing them to his disciples to distribute among the people. He also shared out the two fish among them all. They all ate as much as they wanted. (Mark 6: 41)**

Do you see how Jesus kept His eyes focused on the Father (by looking up to heaven) and gave thanks (the blessing) for the situation? Those were the first things He did! Can you imagine Jesus praying in this way: "Oh God, what am I going to do? Look at this crowd! There are thousands of people here and I don't have near enough to feed them all. Help me out here please!"

Of course not! But I can imagine Jesus praying like this:

"Heavenly Father, my eyes are on You as I praise You and thank You for the awesome ways You provide for us. You are Adonai Yireh (My Lord who provides). Thank You for bringing all these people to us. I praise You for the food we do have. Thank You that humanly speaking, the food we have seems so insufficient. Thank You because You will be our provider then, blessing us and bringing the glory You

deserve. You bring plenty where man has little. You bring the visible out of the invisible, so I trust You to use this food for the good of everyone here as part of your loving plan for us all. Provide for us all, oh all powerful God, El Shaddai, and do so that your holy name be glorified. Praise to You, Heavenly Father!"

Which prayer indicates a trust in God? Which prayer magnifies God much more than the problem? The second prayer does, of course. Yet many people say prayers like the first one all the time. They worship the problem more than they do God when they pray. They whine, they fearfully beg and talk about the problem with such worry and a lack of confidence in God that He seems like nothing more than a small, ineffective part of the prayer scenery.

When people pray in this way, they actually make an idol of the problem through all the worry, negative attention and energy they give it. What is an idol? Nelson's New Illustrated Bible Dictionary (Thomas Nelson Publishers 1986) says that an idol is "a representation or symbol of an object of worship." It can also be "anything that stands between us and God or something we substitute for God."

When we allow something to block us from God's joy and peaceful presence in our lives through the energy and attention we give it, we have created an idol, or false god. We then must repent immediately and give the problem or circumstance over to the Lord, thus destroying this false god.

When Jesus' friend Lazarus died, he wept and was deeply moved in spirit and troubled. (See this in John 11: 33 – 35.) Why did the Lord cry even though He knew He would be resurrecting Lazarus? He was probably grieved over all the suffering brought about by man's rebellion against God. Even so, Jesus gave the situation over to God by openly giving thanks and praise to God as He prayed over the situation. John says:

> So they took the stone away. Then Jesus lifted up his eyes and said: 'Father, I thank you for hearing my prayer. I myself knew that you hear me always, but I speak for the sake of all these who are standing around me, so that they may believe it was you who sent me.' (John 11: 41 –b 42)

What resulted from praying this way was one of the greatest miracles in the gospels. Lazarus came back to life!

> When he had said this, he cried in a loud voice, 'Lazarus, come out!' The dead man came out, his feet and hands bound with strips

of material, and a cloth over his face. Jesus said to them, 'Unbind him, let him go free.' (John 11: 43 – 44)

Whenever we pray in praise and thanksgiving, as Jesus did, we loose the power of God to work a miracle in us, and/or the situation. In doing so we are worshipping God and God alone. This is the very thing we are called to do. The Bible says:

You shall worship the Lord your God, and only him shall you serve. (Luke 4: 8)

Praising and giving thanks to God in everything, is a form of prayer that shows the highest faith and trust in God. Praying in this way looses all emotional attachment to the situation and gives the problem to Him, creating a prayer that worships God by its very nature, and in so doing, pleases our Father in Heaven. It then frees us to allow His power to enter into our lives.

Only faith can guarantee the blessings that we hope for, or prove the existence of realities that are unseen. It is for their faith that our ancestors are acknowledged. (Hebrews 11: 1)

In Matthew 18:18 we are told that whatever we loose on earth we loose in Heaven. When we loose a problem on earth by entrusting it completely to God and giving up our emotional attachment to it, the situation becomes loosed in Heaven, Loosing the situation to the throne of Heaven allows God's power to work powerfully in it. We stop focusing on our "giant" of a problem, and focus faithfully instead on God's loving presence and power.

Do you have a family member or friend going through a crisis, addiction, disease, sinful lifestyle or other prayer need? The Lord says:

Always be joyful; pray constantly; and for all things give thanks; this is the will of God for you in Christ Jesus. (1 Thessalonians 5: 17)

So we are to give thanks in *all* circumstances, not just the easy or "the good ones". Are you willing to thank God for allowing what has happened to you, or your friend or family member no matter how tragic it seems to your natural senses? Will you believe He permitted the problem as a loving means for all of you to run to Him and let Him take over? Will you believe He permitted it to show you His great love, power and grace? What is grace? Merriam - Webster's Collegiate Dictionary Tenth Edition defines it as being "Unmerited divine assistance given humans for their regeneration or sanctification". It also describes grace as being "special favor" and "an act or instance of kindness".

Will you trust that the Lord will use this problem for good? He permitted it (and the reasons go way back to the fall we talked about in Chapter One) so He could draw you to Him through the special favor, the kindness, the divine help He wants to give you, a goodness which will not only draw you, and others closer to Him, but will also loose forth God's blessings in a way you never thought possible. In fact, you will benefit more from the "problem" than if it never had occurred to begin with! You will be regenerated, or made into a much more alive human being, one who is right with God! Such blessings will glorify our Heavenly Father's name.

I suffered a serious fall a couple of years ago. My thigh bone, or femur got pulled slightly out of place and I walked several months with it this way. It was adjusted back properly but not before osteoarthritis set in. I was diagnosed with severe advanced osteoarthritis by two doctors and was notified I would need a hip and partial femur replacement. In other words, I'd have a plastic hip and part plastic thigh bone. For someone having been active in Martial Arts, sports, dance, running, hiking, etc. such news was pretty devastating.

One doctor looked at me straight in the eye and said, "You WILL get this hip replacement procedure someday. It is unavoidable." A nurse in the emergency room one dark night said to me, "This hip arthritis you have will not go away." Minutes later, I watched a middle aged man hobble painfully through the halls of the emergency room; his back was misshapen and his legs were distorted from walking under hips that no longer functioned as they used to. I began to see myself in him. How long would it be before I looked like that? Is that what I had to look forward to? I felt a cold heaviness and sadness seep into my ribs as if they were some powerfully bad medicine.

As if these gloomy medical predictions and imaginings regarding my hip and femur weren't enough, I was also suffering from a sciatic nerve that was tangled up in my hip joint somehow, getting pinched regularly as I stepped or moved. I went to a circus with some friends in San Jose a short time later, and as we walked to the tent entrance, my leg froze. The sciatic nerve cut so painfully into my hip bone that all I could do was hang on to a metal sign post. I had to call someone to pick me up and I let my friends know I couldn't walk any further. They wanted to cancel the circus trip but I insisted they still go since they had children who wanted to see it. So they went ahead, but the whole afternoon ended up being a sad experience for everyone.

I had recently lost my job and the medical benefits along with it, so I had no means of affording the hip surgery. Walking continued being excruciatingly painful because I no longer had cartilage in my hip socket to keep my hip bone from rubbing against my femur. I needed rest after walking 100 feet, but my leg continued to lock on me as it had at the circus. I put on a lot of extra weight and even sleep became difficult because of the hot inflammation I'd feel. An MRI I had done on me showed that I even had small lumps, or cysts growing around the hip bone.

The pain went all the way from my hip and lower back all the way down to below my knee. The muscles in the left leg, the arthritic one, were shrinking noticeably too. It concerned me how flabby the left leg was beginning to feel in comparison to the right one. It got so I was required to use a cane. Even that didn't help much; a cane assists a weak leg. It can't do much for a leg that is useless.

One afternoon I went for a walk with my dad. I had the cane and as we passed some children, my leg froze. The nerve got caught in my hip so badly that a gritted my teeth in a guttural growl; it was all I could do to keep from screaming. My dad held me by the arm and I noticed how the children turned their faces away politely and quietly looked away as we passed by slowly. I found it interesting how instinctively they knew to turn away as a way of respecting my indignity and embarrassment.

As the months passed I prayed and prayed and prayed for healing in a "woe is me" sort of way, and naturally the condition didn't improve. It wasn't until several brothers in the Lord prayed for me, and we praised the Lord together for the condition, and for the improvement the Lord would bring it, glorifying His holy name.

As the days passed, I continued to praise and thank God for allowing my leg to deteriorate, knowing He was somehow going to use this situation for good. I thanked Him for even having a leg. It was better than no leg. I thanked Him for the pain in each step, for it reminded me of being alive. For that I was thankful. I praised and thanked God that He was going to use this severe osteoarthritis for the glory of His name somehow.

On one Saturday, the one right before Palm Sunday I was walking outside the church talking with a Christian pastor friend of mine when I felt the inflammation in my hip joint leave my body. The rubbing sensation I'd felt in between the hip and femur joint left. I shared my joy with my pastor friend and he reminded me how we had prayed about my condition the Tuesday before.

As of this writing, all of my osteoarthritis symptoms are gone. I still struggle with the nerve at times, but it doesn't pinch or freeze me anymore. I once asked the Lord what to do about the pinch and I got two visions. One was of me performing Tae Kwon Do kicks in a routine I used to do as a kid; another vision was of an exercise I'd never seen before: I was sitting sideways on a bench and leaning back while performing bicycling motions with my legs. I asked the Lord to confirm these visions so I would know they were from Him. I immediately felt a strong inner urge to open my Bible up to the eighth and eleventh chapters of the gospel of Matthew. They said the following:

> **When John had heard in prison what Christ was doing and he sent his disciples to ask him, 'Are you the one who is to come, or are we to expect someone else?' Jesus answered, 'Go back and tell John what you hear and see; the blind see again, and the lame walk, those suffering from virulent skin – disease are cleansed, and the deaf hear, the dead are raised to life and the good news is proclaimed to the poor; and blessed is anyone who does not find me a cause of falling. (Matthew 11: 2 – 6)**

> **That evening they brought him many who were possessed by devils. He drove out the spirits with a command and cured all who were sick. This was to fulfill what was spoken by the prophet Isaiah: He himself bore our sicknesses away and carried our diseases. (Matthew 8: 16 – 17)**

I saw these scriptures as confirmation of the visions being from the Lord, so I've been performing these exercises daily in faith. As a result of these exercises, my leg does not freeze anymore nor does the nerve get pinched like it did. I have a slight limp when I haven't been moving for a while. It disappears once I warm up with movement like running and walking long distances, lifting heavy weights, practicing Martial Arts and stretching. The joy I feel is beyond words. I sleep comfortably, I can sit without pain, and my two legs are the same size again with equal muscle tone on both sides.

I enjoy all the compliments from people about how I look the most fit I've ever been; I've lost 60 pounds from these exercises and a few others I believe the Lord has guided me in doing. It ends up being an intense two hour exercise regimen I follow daily. I have self defense and fitness students now. I have a very physically active life. This is all quite "impossible", humanly speaking for someone once diagnosed with no cartilage in one hip. Bare bones rubbing against each other can permit very little movement whatsoever, let alone exercise for two hours a day.

Can the Lord actually lead one to exercise a certain way? There may be those who scoff at this. Well, Scripture says the following about Yeshua Messiah (Jesus Christ):

It is in him that all the treasures of wisdom and knowledge are hidden. (Colossians 2: 3) CJB

Since all wisdom and knowledge are in Yeshua, He would know best in how to exercise my body and yours. Yes, Yeshua is Lord of lords, King of kings and Coach of coaches. Amen? Amen!!! (I answer with a strong amen in case you didn't.) Besides, if you're ever in the Santa Clara County in California I could lead you to quite a few witnesses who can testify how radically the Lord has transformed me physically. I actually have kiddos half my age regularly ask what they could do to have a body like mine. That's not bad for one who used to be a seriously fat arthritic guy with an "irreversible bone disease", a cane and one leg.

God has blessed me by allowing me to be living proof that He still heals. Not only that, He has shared with me that anyone willing to go to Him in faith can be healed from the bone disease as I was. God says:

We are well aware that God works with those who love him, those who have been called in accordance with his purpose, and turns everything to their good. (Romans 8: 28)

Notice that God says "everything" not "some things" or even "most things". He says that He turns EVERYTHING to good in the lives of those who love Him. He surely took my disease and used it for good as He promised in the verse above. I am a living testimony to His healing power. I also enjoy hearing the Lord talk to me in His Word. I learned that as a result of the injury. Had I only whined and complained about the osteoarthritis I'm sure I'd be laid up in a bed somehow, leg throbbing. I probably wouldn't even be able to walk.

We bind problems to ourselves and restrict God's power from working when we gripe, whine, complain or give the devil control.

Even using words like "my this" and "my that" also can prevent us from loosing problems to God. I once suffered from painful memories of a lifestyle very removed from God. Whenever a memory of this would pop into my mind, I would say, "Heavenly Father, I give you my thought, my memory. I put it at the foot of your holy cross, Jesus."

Praying this way brought some relief, but the memories kept returning, and the pain of them would not subside. Unwittingly, I was binding the pain of each memory to me by constantly referring to them as "my this" or "my that."

The Lord finally called me on that. I seemed to hear Him say: "My child, I have a problem with the way you're asking me to help you. If you want me to heal you of this memory, why do you keep holding on to it by calling it yours? When you use 'my this' or 'my that' you are binding it to yourself. I won't be able to do much for you in this way. So loose it to Me! Give it to me!"

I then praised and thanked God for teaching me this and I thanked him for allowing *the* memory as part of his wonderful plan for my good. I then gave *it* to him, placing *it* at the foot of his cross for him to take. Tremendous healing came after this.

So instead of asking God to heal "your" son or daughter, give them to Him as His children in prayer. This will boost the power of your prayer since it will magnify God instead of something negative or soul draining. Say things like, "Lord, thank You for this child of yours you've lent me to care for. Use this illness in your child for his good as part of your wonderful plan for him. Heal him in the name of Jesus for the glory of your holy name!"

So turn everything over to Him and get great results, whether it is *the* job situation, the injury/illness, the divorce, court case, problem, every circumstance, etc. He can handle it much more effectively than you can. Magnify Him in it, praise Him and thank Him for allowing it. Thank Him that you know He'll turn it into good for you and show off His power in a way that's personal for you, so you won't miss the miracle as being from Him. He'll do this for you! Praise be to God!

You can easily test the power of praise prayer by undergoing a 90-day praise training program. For 90 days, start out the day by thanking Jesus for taking over your life for the next 24 hours. Acknowledge Him as your Lord, Savior, Motivator, and the One who will renew your mind. You are to trust Him by praising and thanking Him for everything that happens throughout the day regardless of how it may appear to your natural senses. Do this in big things and little things. Scripture says:

And whatever you say or do, let it be in the name of the Lord Jesus, in thanksgiving to God the Father through him. (Colossians 3: 17)

Be persevering in your prayers and be thankful as you stay awake to pray. (Colossians 4: 2)

Sing psalms and hymns and inspired songs among yourselves, singing and chanting to the Lord in your hearts, always and everywhere giving thanks to God who is our Father in the name of our Lord Jesus Christ. (Ephesians 5: 19 – 20)

Thank him for the slow driver in front of you. It's better than not being able to drive behind anybody. Thank Him for the hot weather that teaches you patience. Thank Him for the cold weather that strengthens you. Thank Him for giving you a foot that feels pain when you've bumped it on a table. It's better than having no foot! Thank Him you even have a table! Thank Him for ears that hear all the noise when you want peace and quiet. It's better than having no ears! Thank Him for all of these things, trusting that He is using each one for your good, and the glory of His awesome name.

Do this again the following day and so on. Persist! As Jewish people say, pray with "hutzpah" or perseverance and determination! You are guaranteed to experience a strength, joy, peace and power unlike any you've experienced before. This is not to mention the many miracles you'll see since prayer not only changes us for good, often times the circumstances change for good too. Amen? Ah, so you answered my amen this time. Praise Adonai!

Here are several examples of prayers using praise to help you learn the language of giving God thanks and praise in everything. Remember to ask for God's help in teaching you to trust Him by praising Him and thanking Him in all things. I encourage those who prefer using the name "Yeshua" for "Jesus" to do so.

Praise Prayer for a Special Need

Precious Jesus, You are my Lord and Savior. How great it is to praise your holy name and give thanks to You. I am sorry when I don't use praise as a channel through which You can send me all the blessings You died for, to give me.

Thank You Jesus for your forgiveness; thank You for giving me the power to pray to You confidently. I know You hear me.

Thank You for giving me the obedience to praise You with every breath of my being. Thank You my Lord and my God for all that You are to me. I now praise You Lord for the very thing in my life that would be nothing more than a source of concern and trouble to me were it not for You. Jesus, I thank You and praise You for the good You plan to bring out of _____(Name the concern for which you have never praised Him for and thank Him for allowing it). I know You'll work great blessings and good in my life through it. Thank You for using this concern to draw me closer to You. Thank You for your loving plan for me and for setting me free from all anxiety about this problem.

I transfer ownership of this problem to You. It is now yours. Thank You for taking it. Work in it for the glory of your awesome name. In Jesus' name I pray. Amen.

For those times when it is difficult to praise God, doing so will not only help you survive or stand firm in a crisis, but you will actually thrive in it.

Prayer for When You Find it Hard to Praise God

Father in heaven, I come to You today bringing to You my praise. I hurt today. I don't feel like praising You, but I will do so because in 1 Thessalonians 5:16 – 18, You said to do so. In all circumstances, whether they seem good or bad to me, I thank You and praise You for this is your will for me in Christ Jesus.

Because of my sacrifice of continuous praise, I look forward to the day when You say to me, "Well done good and faithful servant. You've been faithful to praise me in the face of adversity. Now I can put you in charge of a few more things or maybe many things."

Lord, I give you feelings of _____ _____. I give You the concern of _____. I place them at the foot of your holy cross so You may deal with them in your great love.

Thank You for taking them. Come Lord Jesus, send me your Holy Spirit, the great comforter to me. Dwell in me oh Holy Spirit of peace, love, healing, and inner joy. I love You, my Lord and my God. I am grateful to You for this moment and for all that You've allowed to happen to bring me to where I am now in my relationship with You.

Thank You for using this concern to draw me closer to You. I trust in You to use this concern and all the details of my life for my good and the good of anyone else You wish. Thank You for using this concern as part of your loving plan for me and for the glory of your name. In fact, I'm going to miss this problem when it's gone. It has been a real friend because it has drawn me to a greater closeness to You, which can only be good. I love You, my mighty God! Let all creation praise You!

Thank You Lord, for calling me to look above the ordinary, average way of doing things and seeing things. Thank You for allowing your thoughts to begin to become mine so I can see things from your standpoint.

Great is your wisdom and holiness oh God. May You be praised and exalted forevermore. In your Son Jesus' name I pray. Amen.

Prayer for When You Feel Your Praying Was Unsuccessful

Heavenly Father, King of glory, praised be your holy name. Thank You that I am your child since I have confessed your Son Jesus as my Lord and Savior. Since I am your son/daughter, I thank You that I don't have to be impressed by negatives, because You are a miracle – working God who never makes mistakes.

So Holy Spirit of praise, come to my assistance. Lord You promise us the garment of praise for the spirit of heaviness (depression). So Lord I praise You and thank You for permitting _____.

Be glorified in it Lord, as only You can.

If I've made a mistake, You're still the redeeming God. If I've misread You, if I've misread the signs and prayed the wrong thing, well I have faith that You will lead me back to your perfect will. You honor those who take a leap of faith for You.

Please correct me if I've stumbled, and lead me back to You as part of your loving plan for me. Hallelujah! In Jesus' holy name I pray. Amen.

The Bible book of Psalms contains many words of praise you can use when you pray. Here is a praise prayer that includes more special Hebrew names for God and which detail different aspects of his loving character:

Prayer of Adoration and Praise

Let everything that has breath praise ADONAI! Halleluyah! (Psalm 150: 6) CJB

Yet you, the Holy One, who make your home in the praises of Israel, in you our ancestors put their trust, they trusted and you set them free. (Psalm 22:3)

Heavenly Father, Lord of lords, great is your holy name! Let all creation, every creature of the air, sea, and land glorify You. Let every human being in all the corners of the world declare your splendor and awesomeness.

I love You, my light and salvation, my faithful God, Adonai Shammah (a do NAI SHAM mah), (My Lord ever present), who never leaves me. You never forsake or let down those who seek You with all their hearts.

Praise and honor to You, my Adonai Tsidkenu (a do NAI tsi KAY nu), (My Lord my righteousness). When I confess my sins You are faithful and just to forgive me and purify me. Holy are You, oh God!

I adore You, my Adonai Shalom (a do NAI sha LOME), (My Lord my peace). With You in my life, I need not be anxious about anything, but by praising You and thanking You for all of my circumstances, I can approach You in confidence for all my needs and concerns. Then your peace, which surpasses all human understanding, will guard my mind and heart in Christ Jesus.

I exalt You, oh Adonai Yireh (a do NAI yi REH), (My Lord my provider). I thank You for meeting every one of my needs, spiritual, emotional, physical, financial, and all others.

I bless You, Adonai M'kaddesh (a do NAI mkad DESH), (My Lord my sanctifier). I thank You for calling me to be an important part of your kingdom; I am fruitful in every good work You have called me to perform in harmony with your perfect will.

Holy are You, Adonai Nissi (a do NAI nis SEE), (My Lord my banner of love and protection). You are my shield, oh God most high. You are my refuge, my stronghold in times of trouble. Your right hand sustains me. Glory to You Lord!

I worship You, Adonai Rapha (a do NAI ra PHA), (My Lord my health, my wholeness, and my healer). You make all my bitter experiences sweet. You turn my mourning into dancing and exchange my inner heaviness for a garment of praise. Thank You for forgiving me and healing me of all my illnesses.

I bless your holy name, my Adonai Roi (a do NAI row EE), (My Lord my Good Shepherd). Thank You for your wisdom. Thank You for guiding me in paths of righteousness for the sake of your name. I need not fear anything for You are with me. Your rod and your staff, they comfort me.

How awesome You are Lord Yeshua, Aryeh Lammatteh Yehudah (ar YEH la mat THE ye hoo DAH), (Lion of the Tribe of Judah). You have the power to banish all fear, to watch over me with your fierce protecting love.

Thank you, Lord Yeshua, Immanu – El (im ma nu AIL), You are "God with us". You are with me in this prayer and in this situation. Be glorified in it, Immanuel!

Lord Yeshua, You are my peace. You are Sar Shalom (SAR sha LOME) (Prince of Peace). In You I can rest from any trouble.

Praise to You, Yeshua (Jesus)! Barukh, Adonai! (Blessed be the Lord!)

I rejoice in You, Heavenly Father, now and forever more. Great is your holiness and I'll ever praise You in the Name of Lord Yeshua the Messiah! Amen.

As you grow in maturity as a child of God, His Holy Spirit will continue to teach you the language of praise when you pray. Be persistent and your prayers will become much more effective and they will flow naturally and confidently out from you.

Scriptures for meditation

This is what the love of God is: keeping his commandments. Nor are his commandments burdensome, because every child of God overcomes the world. And this is the victory that has overcome the world – our faith. Who can overcome the world but the one who believes that Jesus is the Son of God? (1 John 5: 4 – 5)

I have come so that they may have life, and have it to the full. (John 10: 10)

The heartfelt prayer of someone upright works very powerfully. (James 5: 16)

In truth I tell you, whatever you bind on earth will be bound in heaven; whatever you loose on earth will be loosed in heaven. (Matthew 18: 18)

Always be joyful; pray constantly; and for all things give thanks; this is the will of God for you in Christ Jesus. (1 Thessalonians 5: 17 - 18)

Sing psalms and hymns and inspired songs among yourselves, singing and chanting to the Lord in your hearts, always and everywhere giving thanks to God who is our Father in the name of our Lord Jesus Christ. (Ephesians 5: 19 – 20)

Author's Note

In the eleventh chapter of the gospel of Matthew we read these words of the Lord:

> 'Come to me, all you who labour and are overburdened, and I will give you rest. Shoulder my yoke and learn from me, for I am gentle and humble in heart, and you will find rest for your souls. Yes, my yoke is easy and my burden light.' (Matthew 11: 28 – 30)

These verses could be only rightly said by God Himself revealed in the flesh, Jesus Christ. No man has ever been able to say, nor can any man presently say, nor will any man ever be able to say these things and mean them. It does not matter how intelligent, wise, godly or compassionate, no man can promise this rest that the Lord alone can promise to everyone who comes to Him. The mark of a good priest or preacher is one who points to Christ, not to himself, nor to his culture or religious system. For only Christ can give this rest to all. What is this rest the Lord speaks of? To answer this, let's first address what a "yoke" is. (It's not the "yolk" of an egg!")

In ancient times, a yoke was a heavy, curved device laid on the neck of someone who was defeated. A yoke was designed to curb the will and bring its victim into submission, whether to a slave master, a conquering king or other dominating force. It was a heavy, painful burden. A person coming under Christ's yoke however is blessed and not burdened. His yoke promises this "rest" which has two forms: One, it is the rest of conscience in regard to sin. The distressed soul, burdened with guilt comes to Jesus and finds peace when he trusts in Him as the great sin bearer. The second rest is the rest of heart. Adverse circumstances can arise and fill your heart with fear, doubts and anxiety. But when you take Christ's yoke and learn of Him, you are able to find calm in the midst of the storm, finding perfect rest as you trust all to

Jesus Christ who rules over your life and controls all things. You can have rest in your heart no matter what the circumstances.

> **With the coming of evening that same day, he said to them, 'Let us cross over to the other side.' And leaving the crowd behind, they took him, just as he was, in the boat; and there were other boats with him. Then it began to blow a great gale and the waves were breaking into the boat so that it was almost swamped. But he was in the stern, his head on the cushion, asleep. They woke him and said to him, 'Master, do you not care? We are lost!' And he woke up and rebuked the wind and said to the sea, 'Quiet now! Be calm!' And the wind dropped, and there followed a great calm. Then he said to them, 'Why are you so frightened? Have you still no faith?' They were overcome with awe and said to one another, 'Who can this be? Even the wind and the sea obey him.' (Mark 4: 35 – 41)**

The disciples in this passage were told by the Lord that they'd be crossing over to the other side of the Sea of Galilee, a body of water 696 feet below sea level and positioned between high hills. Such a position often results in violent drafts of winds and sudden storms in this sea. One of these storms hit the disciples' boat, frightening them so much they forgot the Lord said they'd make it to the other side. They lost faith in Jesus' assurance of a safe crossing, which is why He rebuked them after He'd calmed the storm. Hebrews 11: 6 states that it is impossible to please God without faith in Him. Faith would have enabled them to rest in the fact that Jesus was with them. "Let's cross over to the other side," He had said. "I am God the Son. I have seen the future. I know we are going to arrive." This should have been grounds for their confidence and their rest. But it wasn't. Even so, they cried out to Him and He intervened to assure them. It is interesting that the ancient expression Jesus used to say "Be calm" means also "Be muzzled", as in a dog's mouth being clamped shut by its Master. The winds and the sea recognized the voice of their master and they were muzzled. So the Lord can "muzzle" any circumstance in our lives, bringing us His promised rest.

Chapter 4

The Incredible Joy of the Lord!

Finally, brothers, I wish you joy in the Lord. (Philippians 3: 1)

Children, be on your guard against false gods. (1 John 5: 20)

Our Heavenly Father desires for His kids to experience His joy, a kind of calm happiness (although it can burst with excitement too) that's with us always, regardless of the details or circumstances of our lives. We can experience this God – given joy by worshiping our Lord in everything, even those things that appear bad or negative in our lives. By doing so, we turn ownership of any problem or situation over to Him. How? As mentioned in the last chapter, we do this by magnifying the Lord, the solution to everything.

The Lord Yeshua (Jesus) takes the problem for us, and turns it into good as His perfect, loving plan for us. This plan can only draw us near to Him, give us joy and glorify His name. Here is an easy to remember example of this truth. It's found in Acts 1: 8 and Acts 8: 1. Just remember, 1: 8 and 8: 1 in the book of Acts.

Acts 1: 8 reads like this:

> **'But you will receive the power of the Holy Spirit which will come on you, and then you will be my witnesses not only in Jerusalem but throughout Judaea and Samaria, and indeed to earth's remotest end.' (Acts 1: 8)**

Jesus told His disciples they would receive power from God and preach God's great message of salvation to the world. In the Acts chapters that follow, we can read of incredible miracles performed through this Holy Spirit – given power to the disciples. We can also see that the disciples praised God and thanked Him in everything, even when they suffered persecution from Jesus' enemies. Soon after, a man named Saul began to attack the Church, placing believers in jail and even approving the execution of a Christian named Stephen. We read this in Acts 8: 1:

> **That day a bitter persecution started against the church in Jerusalem, and everyone except the apostles scattered to the country districts of Judaea and Samaria. (Acts 8: 1)**

Although at first glance it would appear that evil was triumphing, what was really happening was that God was in control, accomplishing His original plan to spread the gospel of Christ. All that evil did was spread the disciples out to other areas, areas in fact that Christ said they would be witnessing to in the first place! (Acts 1: 8) And soon after, the fanatical Saul would become a Christian himself (Acts 9) and be used by God to write much of the New Testament and spread the gospel to many non – Jewish people. So in the end, more good resulted from that persecution than if the persecution had never taken place. It is because of that good that we have the message of Christ in us today!

So if you're one of God's children and you are complaining or griping over problems and circumstances, your spirituality decreases and you aren't acting better than those who don't even believe in God. You are doing nothing more than becoming a slave to the problem by magnifying the problem instead of magnifying the solution and the Lord of call, who is Jesus.

When you decide to be the owner of some problem you give all your energies and thoughts to it, more so than you give to God. The problem then becomes for you a false idol or god. You are giving to it what you should be giving to God: your total focus. The Lord says:

> **Then God said all these words: "I am *ADONAI* your God, who brought you out of the land of Egypt, out of the abode of slavery. You are to have no other gods before me. You are not to make for yourselves a carved image or any kind of representation of anything in heaven above, on the earth beneath or in the water below the shoreline. You are not to bow down to them or serve them; for I, *ADONAI* your God, am a jealous God, punishing the children for the sins of the parents to the third and fourth generation of those who hate me, but displaying grace to the thousandth generation of those who love me and obey my *mitzvot*. (Exodus 20: 1 – 6) CJB**

"Mitzvot" means "commandments". We can see that our God is very strict regarding whom we are to bow down and serve in worship: Him and Him alone. He is the One we are to give our total devotion, respect, reverence and admiration to. Worship is to be given to God alone, not to what we define as "positive" things (like riches, lovers, fame, careers, etc.) or to what we see as "negative" things (like problems or difficult circumstances).

Our God truly is El Kanna (El kan NAH), which is Hebrew for "Jealous God." His jealousy is not like that of people; His is a burning zeal for our wholehearted response in making Him our total focus. He wants nothing to stand between us and Him. He is also very generous with us, giving blessings for a thousand generations to the family of those who love Him, while only allowing three or four generations to experience the repercussions of those who hate Him.

When you own a problem, your inner peace leaves, you become troubled, and you develop all sorts of disturbances in your spirit, soul, mind and body. Your feelings get hurt and you find yourself giving the problem all you can to protect what you believe are your rights. This will accomplish nothing more than slavery to stress, disorder and poor choices.

I read some Hebrew; it was the original language God expressed Himself with in the Bible. There are many fascinating things about Hebrew and one of them is this: the absence of ownership words such as "my" or "mine". You will read things like this: "there is to me a son" instead of "my son" or "there is to me a house" instead of "my house". "The son that is to me" is read instead of "my son".

Can you imagine speaking this way? "Hi Joe. The son that is to me wants to know if he can play with the son that is to you. What do you think?" Joe could say something like, "Absolutely, Harry. The son that is to me would like that very much. Why don't you bring Rocky to the house that is to us? Shall we say, six o' clock?"

The language God used stresses that we don't "own" anything. We are only to care for it/her/him for a while. We are stewards, not owners. And this we do to magnify Christ. We read the following about Christ in Scripture:

All things were created through him and for him. He exists before all things and in him all things hold together. (Colossians 1: 16b – 17)

Joe and Harry are stewards of sons. They are to train them in the Lord's ways so they may glorify Christ. When Christ is glorified in the circumstances, it brings His children to be above the circumstances rather than under them. For instance, in a nearby county there is an annual financial appeal by the leader of a certain church. Almost all the churches under this leader do everything from car raffles, bingos, lotteries, sales and other human tricks to raise money for this appeal. However, there is one church among them that preaches Christ and praises Him for the financial need and thanks Him ahead of time for using this need for good and for His glory. This church reaches its financial appeal goals long before the rest.

> **Set your hearts on his kingdom first, and on God's saving justice, and all these other things will be given you as well. (Matthew 6: 33)**

So if Harry and Joe put their hearts into raising their children in the path of Christ, they will get much better results than they would by trying to hog their children all to themselves. Hogging things to yourself actually makes you lose the very things you try to "hog". For instance, in the days of Jesus' human ministry, members of the religious establishment rejected Him because of the threat He presented to their corruption, religious legalism and control. They tried to "save" their twisted religious positions by crucifying Christ. Well Jesus rose again, triumphing over their evil plans and their religious positions came to a permanent end when the Romans came and destroyed Jerusalem in AD 70.

So don't try to "save" something or someone. We aren't called to be owners of anything in this life. And we don't "save" anyone or anything. We are called to be stewards for our Lord while on this earth. What is a steward? It's a servant whose only responsibility is to be faithful to God for the things He entrusts to us for a while.

The Lord provides us with a body, spirit, soul and mind to be used for His work. He entrusts us with responsibilities to our families and neighbors, and He provides us with gifts and talents to be used to draw other people to His love. None of these things or people is ours. God's Word says:

> **Do you not realize that your body is the temple of the Holy Spirit who is in you and whom you received from God? You are not your own property, then; you have been bought at a price. So use your body for the glory of God. (1 Corinthians 6: 19 – 20)**

> **Now a long time afterwards, the master of those servants came back and went through his accounts with them. The man who had received the five talents came forward bringing five more. "Sir," he said, "you entrusted me with five talents; here are five more that I have made." His master said to him, "Well done, good and trustworthy servant; you have shown you are trustworthy in small**

things; I will trust you with greater; come and join in your master's happiness." (Matthew 25: 19 – 21)

Whatever you eat, then, or drink, and whatever else you do, do it all for the glory of God. (1 Corinthians 10: 31)

A steward of God has it easier than the owners. She is free from stress, ulcers, and other symptoms of owning things. She only has to report to the Lord for further instructions after carrying out the previous ones. If a problem occurs, she tells the Lord about it, confesses any wrongdoing, and praises and thanks God for allowing the problem to take place for the good it will bring and for the honor it will bring to the Lord.

She is thankful that God will use the problem to draw her closer to the Lord and trusts that God will turn the situation into good.

An owner says, "Look at this problem! How terrible it is! Poor me! I need to do this and that, or this and that will happen. This isn't fair! Why is this happening to me? My rights are being violated!"

A steward says, "Heavenly Father, there is a situation here. I'm counting on You to come to the rescue. Use this situation for good and for the glory of your awesome name. Thank You for using this to bring about the perfect plan You have for me in it and anyone else as well. Praise You Jesus!"

A steward learns to praise Jesus for the day, whether it's cloudy or sunny. A steward praises God for the excessive traffic on the road or for the lack of it. A steward will even praise God for what seems a tragedy to the natural senses. He thanks Jesus for using everything, great or small, positive or "negative" for his good and for the glory of God's name. God says:

"Let thanksgiving be your sacrifice to God, fulfill the vows you make to the Most High; then if you call to me in time of trouble I will rescue you and you will honour Me." (Psalm 50: 14 – 15)

Note the word "sacrifice" in the above verse. There are times when you won't feel like thanking God or praising Him for something. You will be sacrificing, or giving up your "right" to stay a long time in your troubled feelings. When you do this, you are being obedient to God and will experience tremendous healing and deliverance.

This is not to say that it's wrong to experience sadness, grief, or anger. If you'll read the book of Psalms, David often expressed feelings like this to God. The Lord always appreciates our honesty. But David's intimate relationship with God always brought him back to praise and thank God not long after expressing his pain. He knew that sacrifices of praise would be pleasing to

God and would bring him deliverance from his troubles and an increased closeness to God. Read these verses of one of David's psalms:

> **You turned my mourning into dancing! You removed my sackcloth and clothed me with joy, so that my well-being can praise you and not be silent; *ADONAI* my God, I will thank you forever! (Psalm 30: 11 – 12) CJB**

A steward will experience a joy and peace bubbling up from inside, a joy that will be with him no matter how things may appear to his natural senses. It is what Paul referred to as "learning to be content in every circumstance."

A steward is free, as only Jesus can make him free. Amen! Since he owns nothing, he can enjoy all of God's gifts and possessions. All anger, anxiety, fear, depression, and doubt will have no place in his life. He is free to be victorious in Jesus and dwell in "the secret place of the Most High," a special place of comfort, rest and safety:

> **You who live in the secret place of '*Elyon*, who spend your nights in the shadow of *Shaddai*, who say to *ADONAI*, "My refuge! My fortress! My God, in whom I trust!" (Psalm 91: 1 – 2) CJB**

The apostle Paul, in writing the letter to the Philippians, wrote:

> **Not that I speak in regard to need for I have learned in whatever state I am, to be content: I know how to be abased, and I know how to abound. Everywhere and in all things I have learned both to be full and to be hungry, both to abound and to suffer need. I can do all things through Christ who strengthens me. (Philippians 4: 10 – 13)**

God says:

> **Always be joyful in the Lord; I repeat, be joyful. (Philippians 4: 4)**

Author's Note:

"Now all that praising and thanking God for allowing everything may be alright for things that aren't all that bad," I can imagine someone saying. "But what kind of God would expect me to do that in a situation like mine?" Still another one may ask, "How can I thank the Lord for allowing my little child to die in that accident at the hands of a drunk driver? Surely that was an evil thing, a tragic thing and because of this, the command to 'thank God in everything' doesn't apply!"

Are you asking similar questions? Perhaps you or someone has suffered the sudden loss of one or more important people to you in an unexplainable tragedy. Or perhaps you're going through something else that seems impossible to praise God and thank Him in.

Are we expected to praise and thank the Lord in things like these? Well, what did Job ("Iyov" in Hebrew) do when he found out his children died? Scripture says:

> While he was still speaking, another one came and said, "Your sons and daughters were eating and drinking wine in their oldest brother's house, when suddenly a strong wind blew in from over the desert. It struck the four corners of the house, so that it fell on the young people; they are dead, and I'm the only one who escaped to tell you."
>
> Iyov got up, tore his coat, shaved his head, fell down on the ground and worshipped; he said,
>
> "Naked I came from my mother's womb,
> And naked I will return there.
> ADONAI gave; ADONAI took;
> Blessed be the name of ADONAI."
>
> In all this Iyov neither committed a sin nor put blame on God. (Job 1: 18 – 22) CJB

37

This all comes down to two simple questions. One is this: Does God have the power to take what you are going through and bring more goodness and blessings for you and everyone involved than had this tragedy never occurred to begin with? The other question is this: Is He willing to use this power on your behalf and on behalf of those involved?

If you answered "yes" to these or you're at least willing to believe it as much as possible while asking the Lord for the power to overcome any unbelief in you, then rest assured that if you trust God in this, you will not be disappointed. *Our God promises that if we have faith in His power and willingness to bring more goodness out of this tragedy than had it never happened we will be satisfied with the end results.* Scripture says:

> **Calling to you, none shall ever be put to shame, but shame is theirs who groundlessly break faith. (Psalm 25: 3)**

> **No one who relies on this will be brought to disgrace. (Romans 10: 11)**

In Jewish expression, being "put to shame" or "brought to disgrace" refers to putting all your trust in something only to suffer a humiliating disappointment. In certain English Bible translations the word "disappointment" is used instead of the original Jewish expression for this. By calling out to the Lord in your pain and being obedient to His words, you never have to worry about disappointed. You will be satisfied at the end result of having put your trust in Him.

Francisco, a brother at my church knows what it is like to lose a child. He lost a young daughter several years ago. He and his wife trusted in God's strength and peace in this loss. They experienced a peace and strength which surprised those who visited them to express their condolences. The Lord spoke to them through scripture verses that suddenly came alive to them in how they spoke to them specifically as to their loss. They had assurance from God that their daughter was in His kingdom, in His care, and the Lord's strength flowed in them, leading them to share the good news of God's peace and power with many people.

Francisco and his wife are used powerfully by the Lord, leading people regularly to Christ and serving as excellent witnesses of God's peace and strength in very difficult times.

How different is another local family I know who lost their young adult son in an accident on the highway. The parents, who were left with three daughters, continue to hold on to anger towards God and have openly told me they willingly refuse to accept what they call a wasteful death and great injustice. They also resent what God says about peace, healing and trusting in Him. "We are no longer a complete family," the mother said to me. A week after saying this she said she wished God would take her life as well; she had no wish to continue living. This she said right in front of two of her daughters.

A year later I ran into them at a church activity and asked them how they were doing. The mother said no one spoke to each other in the home anymore. The three daughters quietly stayed in each of their rooms and interacted with no one. The parents continued to hold onto their anger at God and refused to express any trust in His plan in all this. And it was tearing their family apart.

"When we are with the Lord, what happens around us doesn't matter" says, evangelist Oscar Cuevas. "What matters is that we are with Him." These words he shared on the second day of sharing the gospel with a weekend long assembly of Catholic men. Mr. Cuevas had received word the evening before of the sudden death of one of his sons in a traffic accident. Like Frank, he experienced the Lord's strength and peace in the midst of such tragic news and the group of men he ministered to witnessed it. The Lord comforted him and assured him of his son's presence in His kingdom. "Tend to my vineyard. Your son is safe with me," the Lord said to Mr. Cuevas.

The next day, the evangelist completed sharing his message with the men who broke down in tears at such a display of God's love for them in the middle of such tragedy. Dozens of men's hearts were won for Christ on that day and the number continues into the hundreds and thousands through Mr. Cuevas' continuing personal testimony of how the Lord extended His compassion to him in such a difficult time and continues to bless him in a ministry with tremendous impact in winning hearts for the Lord. "The man who perseveres in the Lord will be saved," says Mr. Cuevas.

Tragedies will continue to be part of this fallen world until our Lord Jesus returns. Expressing our anger, sadness, our pain openly to Him is good and to be expected. We see this throughout the book of Psalms. But we especially must trust in God's power and willingness to take these tragedies and extend His goodness towards us so more blessings come forth than had the tragedy never occurred. Remember, we cannot see what's going on in His kingdom, how beautifully He is ministering to our lost little ones or how He's working on our behalf before we can see it. So we must trust in God taking everything and using it to bring forth good for all His children involved. And in all this, we are to thank and praise Him. King David, who we will read about in the next couple of chapters, lost his baby son. He said this:

"Can I bring him back again? I shall go to him but he cannot come back to me." (2 Samuel 12: 23)

We know then that we will be reunited with our lost children. Let us trust in our God knowing He will never disappoint us when we trust Him in the sadness, knowing He has the power and the willingness to bless us immeasurably, regardless of how difficult the circumstance is.

Chapter 5

Israel's God – Your God!

CBN News Report on the Arab Israeli six day war of 1967:

"The stage was set for war and Israel's enemies prepared for victory. They remained convinced they could 'drive the Jews into the sea.' Israel found itself outnumbered and out – gunned on three fronts: Egypt to the south, Jordan to the west and Syria to the north. The Soviet Union had poured $2 Billion worth of arms into the Arab nations. Israel's enemies brought back twice as many soldiers, three times as many tanks and four times as many airplanes to the battlefield. Rabbis in Jerusalem anticipated so many deaths they actually designated all of the public parks in Jerusalem as cemeteries. . . .

"But what was about to transpire would not only stun Israel's enemies and confound military experts but transfix the world. Many believe what happened in the six days following June 4, 1967 was nothing short of a miracle. In six days, the Jewish people defended themselves, destroyed their enemies, tripled their land; recaptured Jerusalem for the first time in 2,000 years and on the seventh day they rested. . . .

"Moshe Dayan, the commander of the Israeli forces went to visit the Western Wall the day after it was liberated and there's a tradition to put notes to God in the wall. So he put a little note to God in the wall. And of course as soon as he left, the newspaper men in their typical discreet way ran and took the note out and read it. And what did it say? It was a line from Psalm 118: 23 which says, 'The Lord has done this, and it is marvelous in your eyes.'"

Why begin this chapter with a news report of a war that stunned the world? It is so we can know that when God determines to save a person, or a people, and has a special purpose for them to fulfill, there is no one, nor anything, no matter how powerful, numerous, cunning or treacherous, who can stand in the way of His plan for that person or people. The Bible book of Romans, in its 11th chapter, tells us God's prediction of a future generation of Israelis who will repent from their disobedience to Him and accept Yeshua Messiah, or Jesus Christ.

God made the people of Israel His chosen people, a people through whom He would bless the world and share His love and saving grace. We read the following in Scripture:

> Did any other people ever hear the voice of God speaking out of a fire, as you have heard, and stay alive? Or has God ever tried to go and take for himself a nation from the very bowels of another nation, by means of ordeals, signs, wonders, war, a mighty hand, an outstretched arm and great terrors – like all that *ADONAI* your God did for you in Egypt before your very eyes? This was shown to you, so that you would know that *ADONAI* is God, and there is no other beside him. (Deuteronomy 4: 33 – 35) CJB

> For you are a people set apart as holy for *ADONAI* your God. *ADONAI* your God has chosen you out of all the peoples on the face of the earth to be his own unique treasure. (Deuteronomy 7: 6 – 7) CJB

> "I will make of you a great nation, I will bless you, and I will make your name great; and you are to be a blessing. I will bless those who bless you, but I will curse anyone who curses you; and by you all the families of the earth will be blessed." (Genesis 12: 2 – 3) CJB

One might wonder, from reading the Bible books and seeing century after century of Israel's disobedience and rebellion toward God, why God would choose them.

> He came to his own, and his own people did not accept Him. (John 1: 11)

One should rather ask why the Lord would choose to save any of us. We all have been rebellious and disobedient. Many people refuse to accept the Lord. And if one studies the gospels carefully, one can see that Jesus was crucified by Jewish people and Gentiles. All took part. In the second chapter of the book of Acts, Peter is addressing a huge crowd made up of men from all nations. He is addressing Jewish people and Gentiles when he says:

> **This man, who was put into your power by the deliberate intention and foreknowledge of God, you took and had crucified and killed by men outside the Law. But God raised him to life, freeing him from the pangs of Hades; for it was impossible for him to be held in its power. . . (Acts 2: 23 – 24)**

Verses 37 – 41 of the same chapter tell how the crowd was "cut to the heart" (v. 37) and repented, or turned away from their sins and turned to God. Three thousand accepted Christ as their Lord on that day. (v. 41)

Regarding Israel, perhaps the Lord chose one of the least likely, least able people, the "fewest of all peoples" (Deuteronomy 7: 7) to convey His love to the world so people could see His mercy and grace. Through them, He gave us His Son the Messiah. The Bible says:

> **But God chose what is foolish in the world to shame the wise, God chose what is weak in the world to shame the strong, God chose what is low and despised in the world, even things that are not, to bring to nothing things that are, so that no human being might boast in the presence of God. (1 Corinthians 1: 27 – 29)**

Israel will, in the last days turn away from this rebellion and embrace the Heavenly Father through His Son, Jesus Christ. Until that day comes, however, Israel is preserved and held (with most of the world unaware) as a suffering nation on land in which they will be when their hearts turn from disobedience to obedience, from rejection to loving acceptance of Yeshua.

> **I want you to be quite certain, brothers, of this mystery, to save you from congratulating yourselves on your own good sense: part of Israel had its mind hardened, but only until the gentiles have wholly come in; and this is how all Israel will be saved. (Romans 11: 25 – 26)**

Christ speaks of Israel in a couple of parables. Here is one:

> **In the morning, as he was returning to the city, he became hungry. And seeing a fig tree by the wayside, he went to it and found on it nothing but leaves. And he said to it, "May no fruit ever come from you again!" And the fig tree withered at once. (Matthew 21: 18 – 19)**

Among most types of fig trees the fruit comes out before the leaves. So the tree above had the appearance of bearing fruit but it was not. We know from Luke 13: 6 that the fig tree was in a vineyard. A fig tree in a vineyard was a well – known symbol for Judah, the southern Jewish tribe of Israel. When Jesus came, He found a lot of religious rituals, rules and ceremonies, but no fruit for God. Israel rejected Christ, and for the next 30 + years continued rejecting Him through the preaching efforts of His apostles.

Rome came and destroyed Jerusalem in AD 70, destroying or scattering all the Jewish people, crucifying thousands of them outside the city. Survivors were scattered to all corners of the world. So Israel was given up to spiritual fruitlessness until the end of this present age. Despite this, the Lord has not forgotten Israel. He says:

> **"In the past you were abandoned and hated, so that no one would even pass through you; but now I will make you the pride of the ages, a joy for many generations. You will drink the milk of nations, you will nurse at royal breasts and know that I, *ADONAI*, am your Savior, your Redeemer, the Mighty One of Ya 'kov. (Isaiah 60: 15 – 16) CJB**

"Ya'akov" is Hebrew for "Jacob". It's encouraging to see how the Lord chooses to identify Himself with someone who made some pretty bad choices early in life before coming to know Him. This gives us hope. In Psalm 147, the Lord is called the "Builder of Jerusalem". He loves to build us up into new, wonderful creations full of abundant life, as He did with Jacob (Genesis 25 – 35). So will He do for Israel, as He will do for you.

> **He gathers together the exiles of Israel, healing the broken – hearted and binding their wounds. . . (Psalm 147: 2 – 3)**

Christ speaks of Israel in another parable, that of the "hidden treasure" in the gospel of Matthew:

> **'The kingdom of Heaven is like treasure hidden in a field which someone has found; he hides it again, goes off in his joy, sells everything he owns and buys the field.' (Matthew 13: 44)**

Many Christians believe that the man in the above parable represents the believer in Christ. This view is wrong for these reasons. A believer in Christ does not buy Christ as the man buys the field, nor does he hide the treasure as the man does. While the Christian may see his faith in Christ as a treasure, he is not to hide it. He shares it, as he is commanded to do in Scripture verses such as Mark 5: 19, Matthew 28: 20 and Acts 1: 8 to name a few. This treasure in this parable then must be Israel. We can find support in Scripture for this. The Lord is speaking to Israel when He says the following:

> **Now therefore, if you will indeed obey my voice and keep my covenant, you shall be my treasured possession among all peoples... (Exodus 19: 5)**

> **For *Yah* chose Ya'akov for himself, Isra'el as his own unique treasure. (Psalm 135: 4) CJB**

"Yah" is translated as "The Lord". The original Hebrew word for "treasure" in the above Scripture is "Lisgulato" (Lis guh lah toh), which literally means "treasure of Him". Israel is not recognized by the world these days as being this treasure of the Lord, and so it is "hidden" as the parable says. Christ, in His coming to earth and dying for everyone's (Israel and the Gentiles) salvation, gave "everything". Scripture says:

> **Make your own the mind of Christ Jesus: Who, being in the form of God, did not count equality with God something to be grasped. But he emptied himself, taking the form of a slave, becoming as human beings are; and being in every way like a human being, he was humbler yet, even to accepting death, death on a cross. (Philippians 2: 5 – 8)**

Though the world's people may gaze on in amazement at stories such as the Six Day War, their eyes are darkened so much they just can't put two and two together in seeing that Israel is still an important Biblical nation today with a prophetic future. Others believe that Israel in the Old Testament is the Christian Church in the New Testament, and so Israel is pretty much out of any kind of Biblical importance and is God's "special treasure" no more. Such people are ignorant of Israel's future salvation, as can be read in Romans 9 – 11 as well as in the 60th chapter of Isaiah. Isaiah prophecies the following about Jerusalem ("Yerushalayim" in Hebrew):

> **"Arise, shine [Yerushalayim] for your light has come, the glory of *ADONAI* has risen over you. For although darkness covers the earth and thick darkness the peoples; on you *ADONAI* will rise; over you will be seen his glory. Nations will go toward your light and kings toward your shining splendor." (Isaiah 60: 1 – 3) CJB**

Even though God sustains this nation in miraculous deliverance after miraculous deliverance, there are still evil forces who foolishly believe they can come between the Heavenly Father's plan for Israel. God will glorify Himself very visibly through Israel someday and everyone will see it.

On October 6, 1973, during the Yom Kippur War, Israeli planes in both the Sinai and Cuban Heights were destroyed by Soviet missiles. Only three Israeli tanks stood between the Syrian army and Israel's city of Galilee. The Syrian commander, seeing such a tiny force blocking his way, reasoned, "This looks too easy. It must be a trap." So he ordered his forces to stop and analyze the situation. It was no trap, though. Those three tanks were all that stood between the Syrian army and Galilee! While the Syrian troops waited in confusion, Israeli reinforcements arrived and were able to push the Syrian forces back.

God has His protective care over Israel until that day they choose to make things better for themselves by turning to Him as a nation. They will someday, but now as a nation overall, they still have not accepted Jesus. Followers of Christ as a whole, tend to be non – Jewish, or "Gentiles" (although there are communities of Jewish believers). And things will probably go from bad to worse for Israel before they decide to be obedient to God and let Jesus be their Lord. Jesus once said:

> '**Jerusalem, Jerusalem, you that kill the prophets and stone those who are sent to you! How often have I longed to gather your children together, as a hen gathers her chicks under her wings, and you refused! Look! Your house will be deserted, for, I promise, you shall not see me any more until you are saying:** *Blessed is he who is coming in the name of the Lord!*' **(Matthew 23: 37 - 39)**

So the gloom of Israel's rejection of Christ is pierced with a certain ray of hope; when Yeshua Messiah comes again it will be to a generation of Israelis who will welcome Him. What a glorious day that will be!

The Bible warns Gentile Christians not to become proud in the meantime however. As we've read, in the future all Israel will accept Christ. The Bible says the following to the Gentiles as well:

> **You will say, 'Branches were broken off on purpose for me to be grafted in.' True; they through their unbelief were broken off, and you are established through your faith. So it is not pride that you should have, but fear; if God did not spare the natural branches, he might not spare you either. Remember God's severity as well as his goodness; his severity to those who fell, and his goodness to you as**

long as you persevere in it; if not, you too will be cut off. (Romans 11: 19 – 22)

So Gentile believers need to be humble and grateful because they are where they are in Christ because of God's kindness. Perhaps an illustration can explain this a little bit better.

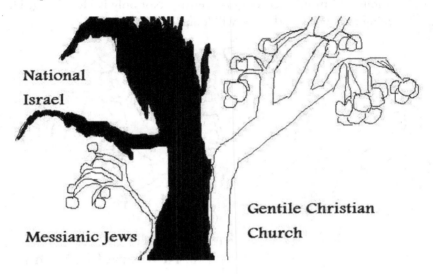

National Israel

Messianic Jews

Gentile Christian Church

We see that national Israel, the dark part of the above tree is currently broken, lifeless and spiritually fruitless because of its unbelief. As we can see on the left though, there is a small remnant of Jewish believers (Messianic Jews) in the Lord Yeshua. The Gentile Church as we can see was "grafted" in and is producing fruitfulness through its belief in Christ and the proclaiming of the gospel. At this time there is a separation between it and the Messianic Jewish community.

We see though, that Israel was the original, natural part of the tree, the "trunk" originally intended for the bearing of spiritual fruit to the world. It is still part of the tree, and will bear fruit again someday, bringing unity to The Christian Gentile Church and Jewish believers.

How true. We read earlier in this book that angels rebelling against God were not spared. Nor have Jewish or Gentile people who have rejected God. So no one should become proud but rather work towards humility and obedience. And referring again to Israel, the Bible says this:

And they, if they do not persevere in their unbelief, will be grafted in; for it is within the power of God to graft them in again. After all,

> **if you, cut off from what was by nature a wild olive, could then be grafted unnaturally on to a cultivated olive, how much easier will it be for them, the branches that naturally belong there, to be grafted on to the olive tree which is their own. (Romans 11: 23 – 24)**

Yes, the Lord is more than willing to restore Israel to their place as a light for all nations and fulfill their original destiny. Not only is He willing, He says it's going to happen so the tree will look like this:

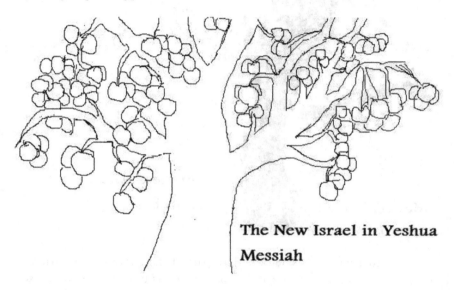

The New Israel in Yeshua Messiah

According to Scripture, Israel will not continue in its unbelief but will be grafted back into their natural tree through their future acceptance of Yeshua.

> **I want you to be quite certain, brothers, of this mystery, to save you from congratulating yourselves on your own good sense: part of Israel had its mind hardened, but only until the gentiles have wholly come in; and this is how all Israel will be saved. As scripture says: *From Zion will come the Redeemer, he will remove godlessness from Jacob. And this will be my covenant with them, when I take their sins away.* (Romans 11: 25 – 27)**

So just as we have been shown mercy, so will Israel be shown mercy when it turns to Christ and resumes its place to bear spiritual fruit for God.

> As regards the gospel, they are enemies, but for your sake; but as regards those who are God's choice, they are still well loved for the sake of their ancestors. There is no change of mind on God's part about the gifts he has made or of his choice. Just as you were in the past disobedient to God but now you have been shown mercy through their disobedience; so in the same way they are disobedient now, so that through the mercy shown to you they too will receive mercy. (Romans 11: 28 – 31)

God has a plan of salvation for the rest of the world too, and it is put in a parable following the one about Israel. Jesus says:

> Again, the kingdom of heaven is like a merchant looking for fine pearls; when he finds one of great value he goes and sells everything he owns and buys it. (Matthew 13: 45)

Many people interpret this parable incorrectly, from a person's point of view instead of God's. They see the merchant as representing someone who finds Christ, the "pearl of great value". While Christ is a treasure, there is much more to be read in this parable. Do you know that the pearl, unlike other precious stones such as diamonds, rubies, sapphires, etc. comes from an animal? It does not come geologically, or from the earth as the valuable stones you'll find in a jewelry store do. It comes from the oyster, a shell – dwelling animal from the sea.

The pearl becomes formed out of a wound that occurs in the oyster's side. The wound, caused by the irritation of the oyster's side against its shell, opens and the pearl is formed from this. We read the following correlation with Christ in Scripture:

> Consequently the soldiers came and broke the legs of the first man who had been crucified with him and then of the other. When they came to Jesus, they saw he was already dead, and so instead of breaking his legs one of the soldiers pierced his side with a lance; and immediately there came out blood and water. (John 19: 32 – 35)

In the same way, Christ's wounds suffered on that cross gave life to us, His children the church. We read these verses in the Bible:

> He was bearing our sins in his own body on the cross, so that we might die to our sins and live for uprightness; through his bruises you have been healed. You had gone astray like sheep but now you

have returned to the shepherd and guardian of your souls. (1 Peter 2: 24 – 25)

For you know that the price of your ransom from the futile way of life handed down from your ancestors was paid, not in anything perishable like silver or gold, but in precious blood as of a blameless and spotless lamb, Christ. (1 Peter 1: 18 – 19)

The pearl, which comes from the wound of the oyster, also reflects light. In the same way, Christians, coming from faith in Christ, reflect light as well. The letter to the Ephesians says:

You were darkness once, but now you are light in the Lord; behave as children of light, for the effects of the light are seen in complete goodness and uprightness and truth. Try to discover what the Lord wants of you, take no part in the futile works of darkness but, on the contrary, show them up for what they are. (Ephesians 5: 8 – 11)

So you are that pearl of great value! And Christ gave all He had, buying your rightness before God as a child to be saved from everything that comes against you and living with God eternally in the next life.

Let's not choose to ignore Christ's offer of eternal life and His saving intervention in all that overwhelms us in this life. Why continue being bombarded by things that take away our peace: inner and outer enemies, health problems, fear, anger, depression, etc. etc.? And without God, things will go from bad to worse or will masquerade as seeming better until the hour of our death. Then things will get worse for sure.

As we can see in all this, there are terrible consequences for rejecting Christ. It doesn't have to be this way, though. As God has a wonderful plan of salvation for Israel, so He has a wonderful plan of salvation for you too. His plan will turn things around for you, whether it is from God changing you and your problematic situation or changing you. You will see great improvement in your life through this plan you can take advantage of immediately, a plan we'll learn about in the next couple of chapters, through the life of a man God Himself called, "a man after My own heart", David, the beloved king of Israel. In the meantime, pray for Israel so you may be blessed in special ways by the Lord. He says:

I will make of you a great nation, I will bless you, and I will make your name great; and you are to be a blessing. I will bless those who bless you, but I will curse anyone who curses you; and by you all the families of the earth will be blessed. (Genesis 12: 2 – 3) CJB

Prayer for Israel – Hosanna ("Please Save Now")

Father, in the name of Yeshua and according to your holy Word, I long for, and pray for, the peace of Israel, that its inhabitants may be born again. I pray that You, Lord, will be a refuge and a stronghold to the children of Israel. Father, Your Word says that "multitudes, multitudes are in the valley of decision" and whoever calls upon your name shall be delivered and saved. Please have mercy upon Israel. Hosanna.

Please be gracious to them, O Lord, and consider that they fight for their land to be restored. You, Lord are their strength and stronghold in their day of trouble. We pray that they are righteous before You and that You will make even their enemies to be at peace with them. Your Word says that You will deliver those for whom we intercede, who are not innocent, through the cleanness of our hands. May they realize that You are their defense and shield. Hosanna.

We thank You, Lord, for your Word. Thank You Lord that You have a covenant with Israel and that You will take away their sin. They are your beloved. Your Word also says that your gifts are irrevocable, that you never withdraw them once they are given, and that You do not change your mind about those to whom You give your grace to or to whom You send your call. Hosanna.

Though they have been very disobedient and rebellious toward You, Lord, we pray that now they will repent and obtain your mercy and forgiveness through your Son. We praise You, Lord, for your compassion and your forgiveness through Yeshua. We praise You, Lord that they are under your protection and divine guidance, that they are your special possession, your peculiar treasure, and that You will spare them, for we have read in your Word that all Israel shall be saved! Hosanna!

Thank You, Father, for delivering us all from every evil work and the authority You have given us with the name of Yeshua. We love You and praise You; every day with its new reasons do we praise You! Hosanna!

I pray for the peace of Jerusalem! May they prosper they who love you, "The Holy City!" Peace be within your walls and prosperity within your palaces! Glory to You, Lord Yeshua Messiah! Hosanna!

Chapter 6

King David –
The Man after God's Own Heart

Are you in an impossible situation? Or one that is overwhelming? Or how about one full of imminent defeat, dread, terror and possibly death? There's hope! There's great blessing and victory behind it all! Learn from David! The beloved king of Israel suffered more than his share of failures, troubles, betrayals, physical danger, tragic deaths and disgraces in the family and more. Despite these things, God was always faithful to powerfully demonstrate His loving presence and intervention in David's life.

David was given a large place in the Bible, probably to give those of us who suffer hope and victory while pointing to our Savior, Jesus. The Lord Jesus Himself would be called "Son of David", a descendent of David, yet perfect and unmatched in greatness. (Matthew 22: 41 – 46)

David was called "a man after my own heart" by God. (Acts 13: 22) God called no other person in the Bible by such a title. Not Abraham. Not Moses. Not Joseph. Not even the apostle John, who was referred to as "the disciple Jesus loved." (John 21: 20) What was so special about this David? Perhaps we can answer such a question when we observe David's fight against Goliath the Philistine ("P'lishti" in Hebrew). Watch how David defeats his giant, and let it guide you toward defeating your own.

> **A champion stepped out from the Philistine ranks; his name was Goliath, from Gath; he was six cubits and one span tall. On his head was a bronze helmet and he wore a breastplate of scale-armour; the breastplate weighed five thousand shekels of bronze. He had bronze**

greaves on his legs and a bronze scimitar slung across his shoulders. The shaft of his spear was like a weaver's beam, and the head of his spear weighed six hundred shekels of iron. A shield-bearer walked in front of him. Taking position in front of the Israelite lines, he shouted, 'Why have you come out to range yourselves for battle? Am I not a Philistine and are you not Saul's lackeys? Choose a man and let him come down to me.' (1 Samuel 17: 4 – 8)

David would seem to be the least likely one to face such a formidable opponent. He was nothing but a simple shepherd boy, caring for sheep 24 hours a day, living out in the field with the creatures. The youngest of eight brothers, he had little of what the world would consider the abilities and experience to take on the 9 foot 9 inch tall giant Goliath, whose breastplate alone (125 lbs.) weighed as much as David. His spear alone weighed 15 pounds! This is not including the armor on his legs or his bronze helmet. I can tell you from my 30 years experience in the Martial Arts, you'd have to be a freak of nature to be strong enough to fight with all of that on.

So naturally, the shepherd boy's countrymen, the army of Israel were completely terrified of the giant, who, for forty days straight, strutted around like some American Wrestling Federation mutant mocking the laughable competition. What does all this have to do with you, you ask? It has everything to do with you.

The same God who took down David's giant and protected Him while giving him an incredible life purpose wants to do the same for you and me. God blessed David in ways unimaginable while saving him from any crisis arising, bringing such delight to him and loving him so much that everyone around David noticed. He wishes to do the same for us.

As the Lord is David's God, so He wants to be yours and have the extraordinary relationship with you that David had on earth. In doing so, He as your loving Father takes on your problems and concerns, freeing you from them while leading you to live a life more fulfilling than you ever thought possible, a life that can, and will last forever.

What giant struts around in your life defying you? It doesn't need to be some nearly ten foot tall Philistine. It can be illness or poverty. Or divorce. Perhaps it is a criminal past, imprisonment or a bundle of legal problems. How about attacks on your reputation? Or are you frustrated from trying to adapt to a new country or other living situation? Maybe you miss someone you loved. Perhaps you battle depression, chronic fatigue or fear.

Possibly you are suffering because of obsessive bullies who love tearing you apart. Maybe you struggle with alcohol, gambling or other unhealthy addictions. Or you might fear for your life and personal safety. Whatever the giant in your life is, you only know that it mercilessly batters at your heart, mind, body and very soul. It parades around, laughing at you, mocking at you, defying you to stand up to it. It seems invincible, unstoppable to your natural senses. Yet God is a supernatural God, and we can experience His supernatural power in our lives.

Let's get back to the story. The Israelite and Philistine armies had drawn battle lines and faced each other. David arrived with bread and cheese for his brothers in the army when he saw the giant Goliath strut around making his usual arrogant challenges to the army of Israel. How did the army and king (Saul) of Israel react?

> **When Saul and all Israel heard these words of the Philistine, they were dismayed and terrified. (1 Samuel 17: 11)**

> **As soon as the Israelites saw this man, they all ran away from him and were terrified. (1 Samuel 17: 24)**

The men of Israel saw the man Goliath, and that was all they saw. They focused on the giant and all that made the giant do is become larger and larger to their natural senses. David, on the other hand, reacted in a whole different way altogether:

> **David asked the men who were standing near him, 'What would be the reward for killing this Philistine and saving Israel from disgrace? Who is this uncircumcised Philistine, to challenge the armies of the living God?" (1 Samuel 17: 26)**

There was only one army out there against the Philistines; at least that is what anybody's natural senses would tell them. Because of his close relationship with God, however, David saw that God had many armies out there against the Philistines. He had angels, the forces of nature, His saints in heaven, His saints on the earth, etc. So He had "armies", just as David said. And because David realized all this, he had no fear in facing this giant and glorifying his God in doing so. There you have it, wisdom that would be written by the apostle Paul centuries later.

> **God did not give us a spirit of timidity, but the Spirit of power and love and self-control. (2 Timothy 1: 7)**

> **So whether you eat or drink, or whatever you do, do all to the glory of God. (1 Corinthians 10: 31)**

David was so focused on God that this wisdom lived in him. If we read verses 23 – 47 of the 17th chapter of 1 Samuel, we'll see that all David talked about was the might of God and how the Lord had given him the power to defeat a lion and bear in the past, and would also give him the power to defeat the Philistine. He faced the giant out of love for his God and his nation of Israel (David's future "sheep" whom someday he would be king over), and he faced the giant with the sound mind that realized that no giant is any match for the living God and a tiny stone. David said these words to the king of the terrified Israelite army, King Saul:

> **"Your servant used to look after the sheep for his father and whenever a lion or a bear came and took a sheep from the flock, I used to follow it up, lay into it and snatch the sheep out of its jaws. If it turned on me, I would seize it by the beard and batter it to death. Your servant has killed both lion and bear, and this uncircumcised Philistine will end up like one of them for having challenged the armies of the living God. (1 Samuel 17: 34 – 36)**

David demonstrates his total focus on the Lord again. He not only is aware of the "armies" the Lord has at His command, but he remembers how the Lord has saved him from dangers in the past:

> **Then David said, "*ADONAI*, who rescued me from the paw of the lion and from the paw of the bear, will rescue me from the paw of this P'lishti!" (1 Samuel 17: 37) CJB**

So David, because of his focus on God, had that "sound mind" mentioned in the Christian walk. It allowed him to see the giant (the Philistine/P'lishti) in the situation while making sure to see the hand of God in the situation even more. What did David do next? Well he received King Saul's blessing and went out and got five stones for his slingshot. He put the stones in his shepherd's bag and with his slingshot in hand, he walked towards the Philistine. (1 Samuel 17: 37 – 40) As we can read afterwards, David's focus on the Lord during his battle with the giant never wavered.

In the meantime what did the giant focus on? He placed all his faith in his own power and resources, which is what ruthless antagonists like to do. After looking over David and seeing he was no more than a kid, he said:

> **The Philistine said to David, 'Am I a dog for you to come after me with sticks?' And the Philistine cursed David by his gods. The**

> Philistine said to David, 'Come over here and I will give your flesh
> to the birds of the air and the wild beasts!' (1 Samuel 17: 43 – 44)

As David and Goliath faced each other, the giant boasted of his own abilities, while David boasted of God's abilities.

> Then the P'lishti said to David, "Come here to me, so I can give your
> flesh to the birds in the air and the wild animals." David answered
> the P'lishti, "You're coming at me with a sword, a spear and a
> javelin. But I'm coming at you in the name of *ADONAI-Tzva'ot*,
> the God of the armies of Isra'el, whom you have challenged. Today
> *ADONAI* will hand you over to me. (1 Samuel 17: 44 – 47) CJB

> > (*Author's note:* "*ADONAI-Tzva'ot*" [*a-do-NAI tse-ba-OATH*] *means*
> > "*My Lord of hosts*". *Hosts can refer to celestial bodies, angelic beings,*
> > *human beings and nature itself. Truly the Lord can summon all these*
> > *as His soldiers, which brings people to often translate "ADONAI-*
> > *Tzva'ot" as "My Lord of armies".)*

It is interesting what happens next.

> No sooner had the Philistine started forward to confront David
> than David darted out of the lines and ran to meet the Philistine.
> (1 Samuel 17: 48)

I like those words, "No sooner had the Philistine started forward…" We see no hesitation on the part of David's trust in God's deliverance. David darted out of the lines. Webster's Dictionary defines "dart" as "to move with sudden speed". And after moving quickly and suddenly from the Israelite lines he ran to face his opponent! Trusting in God's power and willingness to deliver him from the arrogant, murderous giant, he ran. And what resulted next was an incredible victory, the telling of which has captivated and inspired thousands of men, women and children for ages.

> Putting his hand in his bag, he took out a stone, slung it and struck
> the Philistine on the forehead; the stone penetrated his forehead
> and he fell face forwards on the ground. Thus David triumphed
> over the Philistine with a sling and a stone; he hit the Philistine
> and killed him, though he had no sword in his hand. (1 Samuel
> 17: 49 – 50)

Skeptics might say, "The battle between David and Goliath is an old, clever fantasy story designed to teach us spiritual truths. Something like just doesn't happen in real life." People of such weak faith are mistaken, as you've seen from reading my CBN News report in the previous chapter, and as you can read in Luke's story in the next chapter. Those are pretty modern examples for those who are concerned about the age of the David and Goliath battle.

And the six day war was an even more fantastic (but equally as true) account of God intervening to save His people from a "giant". And there's even more. I challenge you to research that war or the Arab Israeli wars of 1948 – 49, 1956, and 1973, all of which were failed attempts of the full power of many determined nations to completely annihilate the tiny country of Israel.

The Lord still works incredible victories for His people. I have seen Him heal people from debilitating illnesses and alcoholism, rescue them from physical danger and deliver them from all types of difficult circumstances. In the chapter entitled, "More victories" you'll read the incredible testimony of a young man who beat 20 felony charges and was freed on the very day his opponents were prematurely congratulating themselves for sending the man to prison for the rest of his life. God wants to take on your giants for you, if you'll let Him.

A young lady called me one morning, asking me to come over and change all the locks in her house. (My dad's a locksmith.) I asked her what was going on, and I found out she was angry with her husband , who was making a habit of leaving for entire weekends and spending hundreds of dollars attending some kind of pyramid business scheme. His trips would not only upset his wife, but his children as well.

This gentleman's activities were tearing up his family as he spent hundreds of dollars each month on some kind of self help book club he was pressured into joining by his business partners. These books would take up hours of his time, confusing him with philosophy, mind meditation techniques and other things instead of reading the Word of God. Such involvement was damaging his marriage and his relationship with his children.

Well I listened to her express her anger and frustration and responded with as kind and loving an ear as I could give her. Thank God she calmed down a little and then I encouraged her to take her concerns to the Lord. Shortly I began leading her to praise God in all this, actually thanking Him for every hour and dollar spent by her husband on this business, as well as thanking God for every weekend he had been away without so much as even a phone call, trusting that the Lord would use it for good and show off in the process.

I guessed she was a little bewildered at me from the silence I heard on the other end of the line. Soon I heard her laugh and say to me, "Oh you and your praises to the Lord," reminding me of the Psalm which says:

> **Many were bewildered at me, but you are my sure refuge. My mouth is full of your praises, filled with your splendor all day long. (Psalm 71: 7 – 8)**

Our conversation became a prayer to God that He would be glorified by working a wonderful change in this man and that He would do so by using the very things that were bothering my friend. Well God's hand intervened since we had loosed the situation over to Him completely. The husband never attended any of these business conferences ever again after that weekend and he voluntarily left the "self help" book club. He even left the business altogether, despite the pressure put on him by relatives who were involved in it. He chose instead to put his family and marriage first, and so my friends are now in peace.

Once you let God take on all those things that concern you, powerful interventions such as the one I just shared with you will become common, the way Christianity was meant to be. We'll continue studying the protocol needed for us to let God's power work in us and in our situations the most fully through magnifying Him within the circumstance, not magnifying the circumstance itself. We can be above the circumstance as He wishes us to be, instead of under it. We'll correctly enter into a closer relationship with God more fulfilling than we could ever believe possible!

Many people, even experienced Christians, often unwittingly cut off God's full intervention in their lives, or at least are ignorant in how to approach Him in a way that pleases Him so He can work the most fully in their lives and take on what concerns them. You'll be happy to know we'll be working on the protocol needed for allowing God to battle for you. David knew this way of approaching the Lord, and it excited God! And so God "showed off" for David in taking down that giant and giving Israel an incredible victory.

David was a master of perfect prayer with wonderful secrets to obtaining the Heavenly Father's divine help. His mastery in petitioning the Father led to God giving him a large voice in the Bible. David's story and writings are found in the two books of Samuel, 1 Chronicles, 1 Kings and the book of Psalms. He is mentioned in many other books as well. David knew the correct protocol in obtaining the powerful intervention from God that He gave him and the nation of Israel. The Lord wants you know this protocol too and draw close to Him so He can "show off" His love for you and the infinite power and goodness He has for you, just as He did for David.

The Lord wants to take on any giants you may have troubling you, if you'll let Him. The central truth I want you to get from this chapter is this: focus on God, as David did in this chapter. Focus on God and your giants will fall. He will take them down so you can see how real He is and how much He wants to be in your life blessing you. If you focus on your giants, however, they will grow in size and you will be the one to fall. You'll fall painfully, and you'll fall hard. I encourage you to meditate upon the following:

> **If I raise my eyes to the hills,**
> **from where will my help come?**
> **My help comes from *ADONAI*,**
> **the maker of heaven and earth.**
>
> **He will not let your foot slip –**
> **your guardian is not asleep.**
> **No, the guardian of Isra'el**
> **never slumbers or sleeps.**
>
> ***ADONAI* is your guardian; at your right hand**
> ***ADONAI* provides you with shade –**
> **the sun can't strike you during the day**
> **or even the moon at night.**
>
> ***ADONAI* will guard you against all harm;**
> **he will guard your life.**
> ***ADONAI* will guard your coming and going**
> **from now on and forever.**
> **(Psalm 121) CJB**

Prayer to be a man or woman after God's heart

Dear Lord, I want to be a person after your own heart, just like David. Help me praise You and thank You in everything, regardless of how it seems to my natural senses. I trust You and know that You'll take everything in my life and use it for my good and the good of anyone else You wish. May You show off in my life so that others may see that You are a wondrous, awesome God, one who is deserving of all our love, honor and praise. Help me delight myself in you so I, as David may receive the desires of my heart, those desires which are yours too, that I may please you in everything. Thank You, Lord Yeshua, for your peace in my life that surpasses all understanding.

Amen.

Chapter 7

Jesus and Jonathan: King of Israel –
Prince of Israel

Salinas is an agricultural city in central California, near the coast. Known for its cool weather, fine produce and excellent evangelical Christian ministries, it nonetheless struggles with high crime and gang violence, often committed in broad daylight in front of witnesses. These violent criminals could care less if anyone sees them, due perhaps to arrogance, drug use, a feeling of invincibility, some kind of devilish power or a combination of these things.

Last year a Salinas business owner and relative of some dear friends of mine attended a business fair, where he had a display booth promoting his health club. We'll call him Luke. The fair was over, Luke was tired and all he wanted to do was nothing more than go home and rest for another big day tomorrow. He was to be godfather for one of his nephews, a wonderful little boy who loved him beyond measure.

As Luke packed up his health club flyers, coupons and other promotional materials, several cars burst onto the scene, screeching to a stop in front of him and numerous witnesses. Ten men burst out of the vehicles and ran toward Luke, mouthing out murderous threats and obscenities. The ten men overwhelmed the lone man in a cowardly attack, beating him mercilessly until he fell to the ground unconscious. They beat him for a few more cruel moments before leaving him for dead or near dead. The ten men arrogantly strutted off to their vehicles with their chests puffed out and their chins thrusting back and forth like overgrown, defiant pigeons. They got back into their cars smugly and proudly and drove away.

Luke was rushed to the hospital where he was listed in critical condition. His family called me and asked me to pray for him. A friend and I held him in intense prayer in the way David often did in the book of Psalms. We expressed our grief and anger honestly, and soon the Holy Spirit led us into praising God for allowing the situation exactly as it was, thanking Him for the good He would work in it, glorifying His name and drawing people closer to Himself.

Other people like his family, prayed for him too, and stayed with him at the hospital around the clock. We also prayed for the ten men who had beaten him and held the whole situation up to the Lord in prayer, asking for His healing, mercy, peace and justice. What drives people like those ten men to such cruel behavior? The answer isn't an easy one even though you've possibly seen such cruelty up close and personal. Perhaps it was directed toward you or someone you know or love. The cruelty may not be in the form of a physical attack; it can be with words, deception or anything else that causes pain. Perhaps the circumstances of your life seem so unfair, merciless and overwhelming that they drive you to cruelty.

Such cruel behavior was directed at David, early in his life. He had been chosen by God as the future king of Israel. The Lord's prophet Samuel had anointed David with oil as a sign and seal of this kingship, and God's hand was with David, giving him victory after victory as a warrior in Israel's army. This special favor from God, along with David's rising popularity didn't sit well with Israel's current king, Saul. We read the following in Scripture:

> **On their return, when David was coming back from killing the Philistine, the women came out of all the towns of Israel, singing and dancing to meet King Saul with tambourines, sistrums and cries of joy; and as they danced the women sang:**

> **Saul has killed his thousands,**
> **and David his tens of thousands.**

> **Saul was very angry; the incident displeased him. 'They have given David the tens of thousands,' he said, 'but me only the thousands; what more can he have except the throne?' And Saul watched David jealously from that day onwards.**
> **(1 Samuel 18: 6 – 9)**

King Saul was already a soul who was "losing it" and David's successes and favor from God added anger and jealousy to his inner problems, leading him to a murderous rage. He soon tried to kill David, twice with a spear.

David played the harp as on other occasions. Saul had a spear in his hand. Saul brandished the spear; he said, 'I will pin David to the wall!' David evaded him twice. (1 Samuel 18: 10 – 11)

The enraged king didn't stop there. Pretending to have given up his murderous plans for David, he tried to trick the young man into getting himself killed by requiring a dangerous dowry (or bride-price) in order to marry his daughter Michal ("Mikhal" in Hebrew).

Saul gave instructions to his servants, 'Have a private word with David and say, 'Look the king is fond of you and all his servants love you – why not be the king's son-in-law?'(1 Samuel 18: 22)

This was nothing but a setup. The king knew David wouldn't have the money or position to afford the bride-price for the daughter of Saul. It was true.

Saul's servants repeated these words to David's ear, to which David replied, 'Do you think that becoming the king's son-in-law is a trivial matter? I have neither wealth nor position.' (1 Samuel 18: 23)

Still, it would not be right for David to refuse the king's "wish" for him to marry Michal either. So David would have to follow the king's suggestion for meeting this bride-price, which was for David to kill one hundred Philistines (and get himself killed in the process).

Saul replied, 'Tell David this: "The king desires no bride-price except one hundred Philistine foreskins, in vengeance on the king's enemies."' Saul was counting on getting David killed by the Philistines. (1 Samuel 18: 25)

Saul's attempt to kill David failed again. In fact, not only did David succeed in obtaining the dowry, he doubled it.

And no time was lost; before David got up to go, he and his men killed two hundred of the Philistines. David brought their foreskins back and counted them out before the king, so that he could be the king's son in law. Saul then gave him his daughter Michal in marriage. (1 Samuel 18: 26 – 27)

It was obvious to Saul ("Sha'ul" in Hebrew) that God was with David, but that didn't change his attitude one bit.

> **Sha'ul saw and understood that *ADONAI* was with David and that Mikhal, Sha'ul's daughter loved him. This only made Sha'ul the more afraid of David, so that Sha'ul became David's enemy for the rest of his life (1 Samuel 18: 28 – 29) CJB**

King Saul then tried to kill David with a spear a couple more times but missed again. Saul's rage must have brought a lot of confusion to David. Hadn't he done nothing but good, assisting the king in defeating the enemies of his kingdom and following all his commands faithfully? Still Saul continued in his murderous vendetta. He even tried to convince his son and his servants to kill David but they refused.

Once again Saul tried to spear David while David was playing music at his house, but the crazed king failed again. David fled from his presence and Saul went on to try involving David's wife Michal in still another murder plot. Michal helped David escape, however, and David left the kingdom of Saul as a fugitive on the run.

Yet Saul continued trying to destroy David's life. He went on to send troops after David in a determined manhunt, one in which the king himself would participate in. As we saw at the beginning of this chapter, there are still Sauls today. Gangs beat a single person to death, dictators torture peaceful citizens, employers seduce hard workers, spiritual leaders molest children, ministers take advantage of others; strong and powerful people torment the vulnerable and innocent.

Sauls still stalk Davids. How does God respond to this? Does He come at the Sauls with lightning and earthquakes? We may want him to. He's been known to do things like this before. In fact I'll tell you about a time he did something like this in my life later in this book. As to how he will treat any Saul in your life, I couldn't tell you. But one thing I can tell you he always does for someone like you is this. He sends you someone very special, a Jonathan.

> **A friend is a friend at all times, it is for adversity that a brother is born. (Proverbs 17: 17)**

Who is Jonathan? Jonathan was the prince of Israel when Saul was attempting to kill David. He was a noble soldier, fighting Philistines when David was still caring for sheep. Being King Saul's son, it was Jonathan's right, humanly and logically speaking, to inherit Saul's kingdom. He had all the reason to dislike David strongly since God had picked David as Israel's next king instead of him. But Jonathan chose to love David strongly instead. God responded to Saul's cruelty with Jonathan's loyalty. Jonathan was gracious because the Heavenly Father, the Master of masters, took his and David's hearts and connected them together in an inseparable bond. We read these verses at the beginning of 1 Samuel 18:

> **When David had finished talking to Saul, Jonathan felt an inward affection for David. Jonathan loved him like his very self. (1 Samuel 18: 1)**
>
> **Jonathan made a pact with David, since he loved him like his very self; Jonathan took off the cloak which he was wearing and gave it to David, and his armour too, even including his sword, his bow and his belt. (1 Samuel 18: 3 – 4)**

Jonathan loved David, replacing David's smelly shepherd (pastor) garments with his own purple robe, the robe of a prince. He gave his sword and bow to David. Jonathan also gave his throne to David, which by human reasoning was his. And after this, he protected David. When Jonathan heard of Saul's evil plots, he informed his new friend. When Saul came after David, Jonathan hid him. He issued warnings like those in 1 Samuel 19: 2 – 3.

> **Saul let his son Jonathan and all his servants know of his intention to kill David. But Jonathan, Saul's son, held David in great affection, and Jonathan warned David, 'My father Saul is looking for a way to kill you, so be on your guard tomorrow morning; go into hiding, stay out of sight. I shall go out and keep my father company in the countryside where you will be, and shall talk to my father about you; I shall see what the situation is and then tell you.' (1 Samuel 19: 1 – 3)**

Wouldn't it be an awesome, yet rare blessing to have a friend like Jonathan, a friend who protects you, remains close to your soul and has nothing but your best interests at heart? He wants nothing but your happiness. He is an ally who lets you be yourself. You feel safe with that person, no need to be careful with words or thoughts. You truly feel like you are in "the secret place of the Most High" when you are with him. You know his faithful hand will separate any gossip, slander, judgments and other nonsense from the genuine, keep what matters, and with a backward throw, toss the worthless stuff away with his hand.

God gave David such a friend and God gives us such a friend. As he gave David the prince of Israel as his friend, so he gives us the King of Israel, Jesus the Christ, Yeshua the Messiah. As Scripture says of Jesus:

> **He will be great and will be called Son of the Most High. The Lord God will give him the throne of his ancestor David; he will rule over the House of Jacob forever and his reign will have no end. (Luke 1: 32 – 33)**

"The House of Jacob" is an expression meaning Israel, for the Israelite people are descendants of Jacob, a patriarch from the Bible. You may remember the name Jacob mentioned from the 11th chapter of Romans Scripture quoted in Chapter 5.

We just read in 1 Samuel 18: 3 – 4 that Jonathan made a pact, or covenant with David. What is this? It's an agreement between people or two groups that involves promises on the part of each one to the other. The Hebrew word for "covenant" means "between", which emphasizes the personal relationship between both parties in the covenant. Has Jesus made a covenant with us? Yes, because Jesus says:

> **"For this is how God loved the world: he gave his only Son so everyone who believes in him may not perish but may have eternal life." (John 3: 16)**

The Lord promises us eternal life with Him if we are willing to accept Jesus in our hearts. We accept Him as our Savior for He saves us from the separation sin puts between us and God. He also saves us from the death that is a result of this separation. Since He has defeated sin and death on the cross, He is Lord over these things, having complete authority over them. So Jesus must be our Lord and Savior. He cannot save us from anything unless He is Lord over it. And He is Lord over everything. The Bible says the following about Christ:

> **He is the image of the unseen God, the first – born of all creation. (Colossians 1: 15)**

Now a Jehovah's Witness says, "Aha! Jesus was born and had a beginning! So he was created and can't be God!" Well such foolishness shows a lack of understanding of the Jewish culture. The "first born" refers to the heir of a family, the one who inherits all the rights from the father. In Jesus' case, He inherits the right to bestow salvation and eternal life from the Father in heaven. He is Lord over all creation. He's Lord over all. It's all about Him. Whereas with people who use the "Jesus was created" argument, they try to make everything about themselves. Further proof of everything existing for Jesus' glory can be found in this verse in Colossians.

> **For in him were created all things in heaven and on earth: everything visible and everything invisible, thrones, ruling forces, sovereignties, powers – all things were created through him and for him. (Colossians 1: 16)**

And Jesus also says:

> **"And look, I am with you always, yes, to the end time." (Matthew 28: 20)**

Jonathan clothed David. Has Jesus clothed us? Yes! He offers us:

> **"white robes, to clothe you and hide your shameful nakedness." (Revelation 3: 18)**

Jesus cloaks us with clothes for Heaven by purifying us from sin. In fact, He actually takes the clothing process a step further than does Jonathan. He not only gives us clothes for Heaven, He puts on the filthy rags we had on. 2 Corinthians 5: 21 says:

> **God made this sinless man be a sin offering on our behalf, so that in union with him we might fully share in God's righteousness. (2 Corinthians 5: 21) CJB**

By becoming sin for us and dying on the cross, Jesus took the punishment that was going to be given to us, death and eternal separation from God, for all the sins and offenses we have committed. He also defeated death itself by rising from the dead on the third day. By believing in our heart that He did all these things, we too can be saved from the death our sinful life brings. Our Heavenly Father is a holy God. His holiness is so pure that we, in our weak, naturally evil nature fall short of the glory of God. Scripture says,

> **No distinction is made: all have sinned and lack God's glory. (Romans 3: 23)**

Only Jesus can bridge this gap between the Heavenly Father and us. The Lord Jesus says:

I am the way, I am Truth and Life. No one can come to the Father except through me. (John 14: 6)

And once we come to the Heavenly Father by accepting Jesus as this bridge, our Savior from sin and death and Lord of our lives, He equips us and strengthens us. He knows we will have problems and difficulties in this life. We will also be subject to attacks from the devil, the fallen angel who rebelled against God long ago and attempts to steer people away from the Lord. One can easily see this evil spirit's presence in the blindness of the hateful aggressors mentioned in this book so far. But, as I said, Jesus equips us to defeat this enemy whose strength does not even come close to the Lord's. Jesus gives us many tools and weapons. In Ephesians 6, we read:

> **That is why you must take up all God's armour, or you will not be able to put up any resistance on the evil day, or stand your ground, even though you exert yourselves to the full. So stand your ground, with truth a belt round your waist, and uprightness a breastplate, wearing for shoes on your feet the eagerness to spread the gospel of peace, and always carrying the shield of faith so that you can use it to quench the burning arrows of the Evil One. And then you must take salvation as your helmet and the sword of the Spirit, that is, the word of God. (Ephesians 6: 13 – 17)**

We will cover the use of this armor in detail later in the book. Just know for now that the Lord equips us with everything to live abundantly and in victory over giants, Sauls and anything else.

> **No; we come through all these things triumphantly victorious, by the power of him who loved us. (Romans 8: 37)**

And just as Jonathan promised to protect David, Jesus vows to protect you. Jesus says in John's gospel:

> **I give them eternal life; they will never be lost and no one will ever steal them from my hand. (John 10: 28)**

And we read the following in the book of Romans:

> **For I am certain of this: neither death nor life, nor angels, nor principalities, nothing already in existence and nothing still to come, nor any power, nor the heights nor the depths, nor any created thing whatever, will be able to come between us and the**

love of God, known to us in Christ Jesus our Lord. (Romans 8: 38 – 39)

We have a true friend in Christ. And because we do, we can choose to focus on our "Jonathan", our Lord Jesus instead of our Sauls. We can meditate on His kindness and make our Sauls shrink. Scripture says:

This is the revelation of God's love for us, that God sent his only Son into the world that we might have life through him. (1 John 4: 9)

Or should we instead focus on our Sauls and make them grow? As Paul says, "By no means!" Do you remember Luke, from the beginning of this chapter? Well the Lord brought peace to the situation for us. He answered our prayers. On the day after the assault Luke was in a coma and doctors anticipated he would be in this for weeks or longer. We continued to praise God for the situation and thank Him for allowing it. We thanked Him for blessing each blow that struck Luke and I praised Him for the good He would do in the situation.

I even praised the Lord for allowing the attackers to live such perverted lives, praying that He would use their violent lifestyle to defeat them so they would realize how they were destroying themselves, thus repenting and drawing closer to God. I prayed for the Lord to be glorified in the situation. I asked Him to bless the attackers and bring good out of even actions such as theirs.

That same day Luke came out of the coma. Not only that, he was healed from alcohol addiction, a problem since his youth. And all ten men were captured by the police and put in jail. For men to be blessed by the Lord they often have to be defeated first! And guess who does the defeating? You bet it's the Lord! Praise Yeshua! So it is good to bless enemies. Jesus says:

But I say this to you who are listening: Love your enemies, do good to those who hate you, bless those who curse you, pray for those who treat you badly. (Luke 6: 27 – 28)

We pray that the Lord touch these ten men's hearts so they may leave their lives of violence and live for Jesus. Luke is on his feet and has fully recovered. His business is also prospering very well too.

Yes, we have a true friend in Christ. He brings us peace and victory in each and every circumstance. And anything that takes away our peace is not from Him. So what else can we do but let Him come into our heart? David writes:

Lift up your heads, you gates! Lift them up, everlasting doors, so that the glorious king can enter! Who is he, this glorious king? *ADONAI-Tzva'ot* – he is the glorious king. (Psalm 24: 7 – 10) CJB

Remember that "ADONAI-Tzva'ot" means "Lord of Hosts" or "Lord of Armies". He does go to war for you. And He always wins. Jesus also says:

"Look, I am standing at the door knocking. If one of you hears me calling and opens the door, I will come in to share a meal at that person's side. (Revelation 3: 20)

What more can we do but open the "gates" of our hearts so this King can enter us and live within us? He guarantees us His loving presence always in our life, as well as His peace, protection, guidance, cleansing from any sin we've ever committed, and a right relationship with God. He also gives us eternal life, life forever, by believing in Him, Jesus, the King of Israel, your "Jonathan." I encourage you to take the following psalm to heart:

> ***ADONAI* is my shepherd; I lack nothing.**
> **He has me lie down in grassy pastures,**
> **he leads me by quiet water,**
> **he restores my inner person.**
>
> **He guides me in right paths**
> **for the sake of his own name.**
> **Even if I pass through death-dark ravines,**
> **I will fear no disaster; for you are with me;**
> **your rod and staff reassure me.**
>
> **You prepare a table for me,**
> **even as my enemies watch;**
> **you anoint my head with oil**
> **from an overflowing cup.**
>
> **Goodness and grace will pursue me**
> **every day of my life;**
> **and I will live in the house of *ADONAI***
> **for years and years to come.**
> **(Psalm 23) CJB**

Author's Note:

Do you know that everything in the world is pretty much made of space? It's true. If you take a powerful microscope and look at any creation, whether it be a piece of wood, metal or even the Israeli cactus growing in my back yard, you'll see atoms of whatever you're looking at, with space in between them and all around them. What's holding these atoms up? They're not connected to anything; they're just floating. And the strange part of it is that there is more space in all these creations than there are atoms. The atoms aren't connected to anything so there is no explanation for what holds them up into the shapes of these things.

Years ago, geeky individuals who were puzzled at all these atoms floating around with no reason why they shouldn't fall apart came up with a solution. "Let's magnify the atom! When we do, we'll know why things in nature don't simply fall apart! Ha!" Well they magnified the atom all right, and found it to be made up of electrons going around a nucleus made up of protons and neutrons. (No, croutons go in salads.) And you know what? There's even space in between the parts of an atom! If anything, these geeky fellows became even more puzzled. There is absolutely no reason why everything in nature doesn't fall apart.

Well according to the Bible, there is a reason. Jesus holds everything together. If we go to the same place in Colossians where we were earlier, we read the following about Jesus:

He exists before all things and in him all things hold together. (Colossians 1: 17)

So every rock, tree, fruit, vegetable, etc. glorifies Christ's power by its very existence. Even you and every human being or living creature, upon close examination is pretty much made of small particles with space in between. Christ's power holds all of us together. Without Him we'd fall apart, literally.

We are pretty much empty space as well! When we were kids and made a mistake we'd say things like "I am such an air head" or "I am so scatter brained". We were declaring profound spiritual truths and not even realizing it!

Chapter 8

Kuma Adonai! (Arise, oh Lord!) Victory over Dangerous Enemies

King David, the "man after God's own heart" once prayed the following in Psalm 35: "Contend, O Lord, with those who contend with me; fight against those who fight against me! Take hold of shield and buckler and rise for my help! Draw the spear and javelin against my pursuers! Say to my soul, 'I am your salvation!'"

Wow. Can you sense the need, the desperation? Can you see the sheer will –power to keep an unwavering focus on God in the midst of extremely dangerous enemies and crisis in his prayer? I can. And the Lord is still the same God the psalmist was intimate with! He has the power and the willingness to save us, His children from anything that would come attempt to come between us and Him. What we need to do is trust Him and keep our focus on Him regardless of how the situation looks like around ourselves. Another king of Israel prayed in this way:

> **"Our God, will you not pass sentence on them, since we are helpless against this vast horde about to attack us? Because we do not know what to do, we look to you." (2 Chronicles 20: 12)**

God does deliver us from enemies if we are willing to let Him do so, and if we're honest in our involvement regarding the enemies, which means we're not out there provoking people. One of the best stories in the Bible of how God works in this type of deliverance is the account of King Jehoshaphat's

Battle in 2 Chronicles 20: 1 – 30. It is an excellent example of how God's full power is unleashed to help those who trust in Him through effective prayer and praise. He goes to battle for His children!

Jehoshaphat was ruler over a little kingdom called Judah. ("Y'hudah" in Hebrew) One day King Jehoshaphat found out that powerful armies from the territories of Ammon, Moab and Mount Seir surrounded his small land. Their intention: to attack Judah, destroy its people and take its land.

The Bible says that Judah's king was alarmed and went to inquire of the Lord. He proclaimed a fast throughout his country and he and all of his people came together to ask for God's help.

King Jehoshaphat's prayer is in verses 6 – 12 of the 20th chapter of 2 Chronicles and has been studied carefully by many Bible scholars over the years. We can read the king's prayer and see that he began with praise:

> **"*ADONAI*, God of our ancestors, you alone are God in heaven. You rule all the kingdoms of the nations. In your hand are power and strength, so that no one can withstand you." (2 Chronicles 20: 6) CJB**

By praying in this way, King Jehoshaphat took his eyes off the threatening circumstances and focused on God. In doing so, he turned the fear – producing situation into a trusting act of worship of God instead. This is a crucial step in the protocol we discussed earlier in approaching God for help in crisis. The next lines of Jehoshaphat's prayer continued with thanksgiving by remembering the goodness God had shown before:

> **"You, our God, drove out those living in the land ahead of your people Isra'el and gave it forever to the descendants of Avraham your friend. They lived in it, built you a sanctuary in it for your name and said, 'If calamity strikes us, such as war, judgment, disease or famine, we will stand before this house – that is, before you, since your name is in this house – and cry to you in our distress; and you will hear us and rescue us.' (2 Chronicles 20: 7 – 9) CJB**

Judah's king was very aware of the serious danger the tiny nation was in. Verse three told us King Jehoshaphat was "alarmed" when he found out about the surrounding armies. But the king didn't dwell on the problem, he recognized it, realized he didn't have the ability to deal with it, and he went to God for help:

"Now see, the Ammonites and Moabites and the people of Mount Seir, whom you would not allow Israel to invade when they came out of Egypt – on the contrary, Israel avoided them and did not destroy them – see how they reward us, by coming to drive us out of your possession which you allotted to us! Our God, will you not pass sentence on them, since we are helpless against this vast horde about to attack us? Because we do not know what to do, we look to you." (2 Chronicles 20: 10 – 12)

The king took an honest look at Israel's past treatment of these attackers, and saw that Israel had been obedient to the Lord in the mercy they showed to them in the past. There was no unconfessed wrongdoing on Israel's part. This was an important self examination because unconfessed sin before God forms a barrier between His intervention and us. We'll discuss this in more detail in Chapter 13.

King Jehoshaphat saw the real danger and his nation's helplessness in the face of it. He chose to direct his focus on the Lord and on His mighty power and willingness to help them. This is exactly how we are to be in our own lives. We don't allow ourselves to be blind to the evil and threats around us. Nor do we let the evil cause us to give in to fear. The Lord says to us who trust in Him:

Do not be afraid, for I am with you; do not be alarmed, for I am your God. I give you strength; truly I help you, truly I hold you firm with my saving right hand. (Isaiah 41: 10)

Instead, we allow this opposition to give us greater cause to praise and thank God for working in these things with His control and authority. We focus our hearts most on God and trust He will use what appears evil or negative to our natural senses and use it for our good, as part of His perfect, loving plan to bless us, draw us closer to Him and glorify His holy name.

After King Jehoshaphat prayed, God responded immediately:

"Do not be afraid or daunted by this vast horde, for the war is not your affair but God's." (2 Chronicles 20: 15)

What a great promise for us! We don't need to let anything in this world bring us fear, intimidation or discouragement because we aren't the ones with the power to deal with it, God is. He will fight for us. Rest assured that you, being a child of God have been paid for. God sent His Son Jesus to die for you on that cross many years ago.

You are not your own property, then; you have been bought at a price. (1 Corinthians 6: 20)

Jesus died for you; the Lord "invested" in you being one of His children. And if we trust Him, God will ALWAYS protect His investment. In Jehoshaphat's case, the Lord gave the king these instructions next:

> **"Tomorrow go down against them. They will be coming up by the ascent of Tzitz, and you will find them at the end of the vadi, before the Yeru'el Desert. You won't even need to fight this battle! Just take your positions, Y'hudah and Yerushalayim, stand still and watch how *ADONAI* will deliver you! Don't be afraid or distressed; tomorrow, go out against them; for *ADONAI* is with you." (2 Chronicles 20: 16 – 17) CJB**

The next morning, Jehoshaphat followed the Lord's instructions by sending out his army to the desert. In front of his army he appointed men to lead the march by singing praises to God saying,

> **"Give thanks to *ADONAI*, for his grace endures forever!" (2 Chronicles 20: 22) CJB**

Yes it does. God is truly "El Olam" (EL o LAM), "the Everlasting God," whose love endures forever. As Jehoshaphat's men praised God, the Bible states that the Lord caused the enemy armies to turn on each other, slaughtering themselves completely:

> **Then, during the time they were singing and praising, *ADONAI* brought a surprise attack against the people of 'Amon, Mo'av and Mount Se 'ir who had come to fight Y'hudah; and they were defeated. What happened was that the people of 'Amon and Mo'av began attacking those people who lived by Mount Se 'ir, to kill and destroy them completely; and when they had finished off the people from Se 'ir, they set to work slaughtering each other. So when Y'hudah reached the watchtower overlooking the desert, they looked toward the horde; and there in front of them were corpses fallen to the ground; none had escaped. (2 Chronicles 20: 22 – 24) CJB**

Little Judah was safe. The Lord delivered them from trouble, which is what He promises to do for His children many times throughout the Bible.

God doesn't promise to keep us out of trouble, but He promises to deliver or save us from it.

Now someone may choose to ignore all that was mentioned earlier in this book concerning the nation Israel's deliverances, the personal testimonies and 2 Chronicles, choosing to say that King Jehoshaphat's battle is just a clever story meant to teach us praise and thanksgiving (or perhaps something else); we aren't to be ridiculous and believe something like that could actually happen. Just praising God and sending people out to sing thanks to God in front of their army could not save a country from a military attack today. "God helps those who help themselves," is a popular saying.

"May God help those who help themselves," is what I would say and pray in response to that. I believe with all my heart that it is possible for modern day Jehoshaphat – type victories to take place. In fact it is more than possible; it is a certainty.

A few years ago I became a leader in a certain church prayer group. I'll call it prayer group X. Within about five months I had built a web site for this prayer group and was leading evangelizing trips to churches in other nearby towns, inviting hundreds of people to attend this group. I was running an information table on the prayer group outside after the services, and had made various flyers, signs and other promotional material for the prayer group. I was also beginning to preach before hundreds of people. Attendance in the prayer group increased dramatically and prayer group X gained a high visibility in the church. As one of the leaders said to me, "You've done very much in very little time." I am reminded of the following scripture regarding Joseph ("Yosef" in Hebrew), the son of Jacob:

> **ADONAI was with Yosef, and he became wealthy while he was in the household of the Egyptian. His master saw how ADONAI was with him, that ADONAI prospered everything he did. His master saw how ADONAI was with him, that ADONAI prospered everything he did. Yosef pleased him as he served him, and his master appointed him manager of his household; he entrusted all his possessions to Yosef. (Genesis 39: 2 – 4)**

I worked as a greeter during the beginning of services at the prayer group X's church, using this work as an opportunity to invite more people to the prayer group. Its attendance increased dramatically. I even began to design t shirts for them and also served as a translator for its leaders who didn't speak English very well. I began to coordinate fundraisers and published the first edition of this book and was invited to present my experiences as a writer to a writing class at a local college.

Along with all this activity came required attendance at meetings and councils that dealt more with money and activity schedules than spiritual matters. I became a representative for the prayer group in these as well. Soon I began to feel jealousy coming at me from various members in the group. One of the leaders began tell them to stop being jealousy over my successes. I felt confused. Wasn't I doing everything to help their ministry increase and become more effective? I didn't understand why people would dislike how well I was helping.

Shortly thereafter, gossip started arising about this "new guy who has come out of nowhere" and after some digging around, a couple of individuals found out I'd been convicted of a battery misdemeanor occurring during a self defense class years back, when I was not walking with the Lord. I had been given a week of work program for this offense but I'd also been in the news concerning books I'd written about a conspiracy in public education; the news stated the district attorney would be filing charges on various illegal investigative activities I was accused of. Years of prison time were mentioned also.

Although the charges on me regarding my books were never filed, I had been given a week of work program service by the county court for the misdemeanor which I pleaded no contest to. Reading about certain details of the case stirred strong feelings in the prayer group X people who were investigating my past. These individuals took various internet articles that they'd downloaded and attempted to show them to the prayer group leaders. A couple of them refused to look at them because of the following scriptures:

> **So for anyone who is in Christ, there is a new creation: the old order is gone, and a new being is there to see. (2 Corinthians 5: 17)**

> **The punishment already imposed by the majority was quite enough for such a person; and now by contrast you should forgive and encourage him all the more, or he may be overwhelmed by the extent of his distress. (2 Corinthians 2: 6 – 7)**

A couple of other leaders read them, though and soon the pastor at the prayer group X's church received the internet downloads from these individuals. They also went to the local college. It wasn't long before I received a letter from the pastor through a third person. The letter demanded I cease all my activities assisting the prayer group.

I am reminded of Joseph's story again when he is falsely accused of a sexual assault by the wife of his Egyptian master:

"The Hebrew slave you brought to us burst in on me to make a fool of me. But when I screamed, he left his tunic beside me and ran away.' When his master heard his wife say, 'This is how your slave treated me,' he became furious. Joseph's master had him arrested and committed to the gaol where the king's prisoners were kept. (Genesis 39: 17 – 20)

Joseph/Yosef found himself in jail (the gaol). He lost his position at the Egyptian master's estate. I lost my position in the prayer group X. The pastor at their church expressed concern over my "high visibility" and involvement in ministry and he was worried at the possibility of lawsuits, money loss and me being a "danger" to others. So he told me to stop all involvement in his church and restrict myself to a "private devotion".

Soon after I was contacted by a spokesperson for the college that earlier had invited me to present my book publishing experiences to their writing class. He said I would not be welcome there after all. I soon received a correspondence stating I wouldn't be able to present at any other local colleges as well. A student I'd been tutoring there let me know that the same individuals from the prayer group were responsible for this as well.

At this time certain educational and media agencies in two cities helped their newspaper place a web page with a full screen size picture of me and an article requesting anyone else who I'd "victimized" in my past self defense classes to come forward. This page was published over two years after my case had been closed by the court; I hadn't even stepped foot in their county for close to that long. This prompted several Martial Art web sites to write negative internet articles about me as well. I was also listed in business directories as a criminal alongside company presidents, business owners and other community members who were listed only for their business accomplishments. These two cities, along with four other small towns, regularly published negative articles and opinions of my case from fall of 2006 to spring of 2008.

A friend of mine who lived in a small town close to one of the two cities called me, angrily saying that a couple of neighborhoods near hers were literally rejoicing at the negative media attention on me. An acquaintance living nearby called their satisfaction "pure evil". I thought of an Israeli woman I saw on TV who was saddened at how people in bordering countries dance in the streets when Jewish people die in terrorist acts. I thought of my own Jewish ancestry, distant though it is. I found myself asking, "What is it about people that drives them to dance and rejoice when someone with Jewish ancestry is murderously victimized or disgraced?"

I naturally was very angered, and expressed so to a few close friends and to the Lord especially. I thought of David in Psalm 41:

> **My enemies speak to me only of disaster, 'When will he die and his name disappear?' When people come to see me their talk is hollow, when they get out they spread the news with spite in their hearts. All who hate me whisper together about me and reckon I deserve the misery I suffer. 'A fatal sickness has a grip on him; now that he is down, he will never get up again.' (Psalm 41: 5 – 8)**

Well, after David expressed himself honestly to God, he always moved beyond his feelings to turn the situation over to God in praise and thanksgiving. Psalm 41 continues in this way:

> **I will know you are pleased with me if my enemy doesn't defeat me. You uphold me because of my innocence you establish me in your presence forever. Blessed be *ADONAI* the God of Isra'el from eternity past to eternity future. Amen. Amen. (Psalm 41: 11 – 13) CJB**

I began to follow the example set by the man after God's heart. I expressed myself honestly to God and though it went against "common sense" I actually thanked the Lord for the predicament I was in. I thanked Him for allowing it as part of his wonderful plan to draw me closer to Him. I thanked Him for allowing every insult, public label, accusation, threat and deception in my situation. I praised God for the good He was going to do for allowing monthly negative press on me for two years. I thanked Him for allowing the gossip and for allowing my ministry involvement at the first prayer group to end. I praised Him for the extra blessings He was going to bring from these things for the glory of His name. I even sang and danced as He strengthened me. "How silly and undignified!" someone may say. And yet, that is exactly what the man after God's own heart did.

> **Then David danced and spun around with abandon before *ADONAI*, wearing a linen ritual vest. (2 Samuel 6: 14) CJB**

As I thanked and praised the Lord, I found myself blessing those who attacked me, for Scripture says:

> **You have heard how it was said, You will love your neighbor and hate your enemy.' But I say this to you, love your enemies and pray for those who persecute you; so that you may be children of your Father in heaven, for he causes his sun rise on the bad as well as the good, and sends down rain to fall on the upright and the wicked alike. (Matthew 5: 43 – 45)**

I made a conscious decision to love my persecutors, to bless them and pray for them, wanting them to come to Christ as I had done. I prayed aggressively for their salvation, remembering what Scripture said about those who chose evil.

> **For it is not against human enemies that we have to struggle, but against the principalities and the ruling forces who are masters of the darkness in this world, the spirits of the evil in the heavens. (Ephesians 6: 12)**

I felt peace, joy, inner strength and a release from the ownership of these personal attacks. I let the Lord own these attacks. They were His. Although let me tell you, it was not easy at first. To respond in this way definitely was the sacrifice referred to in Psalm 50.

> **'Let thanksgiving be your sacrifice to God, fulfil the vows you make to the Most High; then if you call to me in time of trouble I will rescue you and you will honour me.' (Psalm 50: 14 – 15)**

However I saw changes begin occurring in me: The peace I enjoyed was becoming more permanent, the joy was lasting, and I was developing an inner strength that poured out into all areas of my life. This came from releasing the persecutors to God's care and refusing to let whatever motivated them take away my peace. If I let this negativity take my peace away, I would be permitting it to become an idol to me.

I chose to loose, or release the persecutors' actions away from me so the power of God would be loosed in the situation instead. This led to much good that would come later.

This is not to say that God's power is bound up or anything, but when we dwell on enemies' actions and seethe inwardly or get our inner peace disturbed regularly from such actions, we are owning the situation emotionally. We hang on to it, binding it to ourselves and thus refusing God's help. The Bible says:

> **In truth I tell you, whatever you bind on earth will be bound in heaven; whatever you loose on earth will be loosed in heaven. (Matthew 18: 18)**

As to the loss of ministry involvement and the persecution, I confessed over and over again that I didn't know what to do in my situation, but my eyes were on the Lord.

The Lord gave me the same words He gave King Jehoshaphat. He told me not to fear, that the battle would be His, not mine. I'll admit, there were times when I felt too concerned or frightened to trust Him in this. I'd begin thinking that I'd never be able to contribute positively to my community again. I'd respond to such a passing thought in this way: "Fearful, negative thought, I reject you in the name of Jesus. You are not God's will for me, based on 2 Timothy 1: 7. Go to the foot of the cross and be dealt with." I persisted in resisting the fear and concerns, choosing instead to submit to God's Holy Spirit, who gave me the strength to do so. (The Holy Spirit is a "Who", not an "it".) His Spirit also led me when to act in a few things, just as Jehoshaphat was led where to take his armies and lead them in praise.

Interestingly enough, the Lord began to call my attention to Psalm 18, which was a passage in the Bible I was totally unfamiliar with. I felt a strong pull in my heart and spirit to meditate on it and claim it as a gift from Him to me. These verses in the psalm encouraged me:

> **In my distress I called to *ADONAI*; I cried out to my God. Out of his temple he heard my voice; my cry reached his ears. (Psalm 18: 6) CJB**

There are times when the Lord has us take overt action, but we are to let Him guide us in that. In any case, we need to keep our focus on Him in praise and thanksgiving. In doing so we will find that He'll bless us greatly.

On two occasions, I was alone in the church sanctuary praising God when an earthquake struck both times. I remembered the following verses in the 18th Psalm:

> **I cried for help to my God; from his Temple he heard my voice, my cry came to his ears. Then the earth quaked and rocked, the mountains' foundations shuddered; they quaked at his blazing anger. (Psalm 18: 6 – 7)**

Soon after being excluded from involvement at the original prayer group, I was invited to be the Sunday Adult Bible School teacher at another nearby church. I was invited to be a visiting speaker at a couple of other prayer groups as well. Since I had some extra time on my hands, I even entered graduate school and earned a Masters degree in Christian Education. I am now a doctoral candidate in this same field! I have published this book with others on the way. The Lord truly rescued me from a permanent end to my ministry. I am truly in an "open place" as Psalm 18 says:

> They came against me on my day of disaster; but *ADONAI* was my support. He brought me out to an open place; he rescued me, because he took pleasure in me. (Psalm 18: 18 – 19) CJB

I am invited to preach at prayer groups and services, bragging about Jesus and being one of His soldiers, warring against the things that oppose Him. I've been anointed as a teacher in another church and have been honored by recognition of what the Lord has done for me. I am also honored for how fast the Lord is taking me in sharing about what His teachings say about many subjects and themes. So my ministry situation ended up being much better for me than it would have been had the persecution not taken place! Once again I am reminded of Joseph's (Yosef's) story. The Bible says the following about his time in the gaol, or prison:

> But *ADONAI* was with Yosef, showing him grace and giving him favor in the sight of the prison warden. The prison warden made Yosef supervisor of all the prisoners in the prison; so that whatever they did there, he was in charge of it. The prison warden paid no attention to anything Yosef did, because *ADONAI* was with him; and whatever he did, *ADONAI* prospered. (Genesis 39: 20 – 23) CJB

The Lord continued speaking to me through Psalm 18. The following verse in it spoke to me about the training I was undergoing as preparation to share the message of Christ:

> This God who girds me with strength, who makes my way free from blame, who makes me as swift as a deer and sets me firmly on the heights, who trains my hands for battle, my arms to bend a bow of bronze. (Psalm 18: 32 – 34)

In the meantime there has been much strife, unethical money practices, time - consuming business meetings and fighting in the original group from where I had been removed from ministry. They were verbally scolded in front of hundreds by a priest during one of their services. Disciplinary action was put on them over these things, eventually leading to a tight restriction in their activities from the church pastoral office. This Scripture in Psalm 18 spoke to me:

> You free me from the quarrels of my people. (Psalm 18: 43)

I mentioned earlier how negative articles were published online monthly from fall of 2006 to late spring of 2008. I believe they would have continued much longer had it not been for a very unusual occurrence stopping them for good.

Seven days after the last negative web page had been put up about my past legal problems (Early June of 2008), massive fires broke out in the exact property lines owned by the leaders in the media agencies mentioned earlier as well as leaders of the groups supplying them with my case information. The grass and fields next to where a dozen of them lived were engulfed in huge flames. The two cities and the four small towns mentioned before were the only areas struck by these flames. It was the time of the mysterious "dry lightning" which struck California around this time.

Smoke rose from his nostrils, from his mouth devouring fire (coals were kindled at it). (Psalm 18: 8)

I was coming back from the mall with my father a week and a half later when we saw lightning bolts fly across the sky above us in a horizontal direction, heading towards the same flame engulfed areas. The bolts shot over the mountain ranges separating my town from the six towns' suburbs where these persecutors lived and ran their business offices, their newspapers, internet, radio and other media. We followed the lightning, finding that it changed direction when it reached one of the two cities and began to strike the outskirts of it, two lightning bolts at a time, over and over.

A brown cloud with patches of fiery orange inside it hovered over the city and was referred to by a local radio station as being "like something out of Armageddon". A state of emergency lasting several weeks was called in the entire area because of the fires. A photographer friend of mine took a picture of this, as can be seen here. The darkness to the upper right is not smoke but a dark brownish grey cloud from which the lightning came.

(Photo courtesy of Memorable Moments Photography)

The cloud ended up hovering over the area for days. No more negative articles were ever written about my legal case again after this. The last article (along with a huge close up photograph of me) was in a business directory from one of the two cities, coming out about a week before the lightning, strange cloud and fires. No more negative articles followed. My heart was drawn to the following verses in Psalm 18:

> **He lowered heaven and came down with thick darkness under his feet. He rode on a keruv (winged angel); he flew, swooping down on the wings of the wind. He made darkness his hiding-place, his canopy thick clouds dark with water. From the brightness before him, there broke through his thick clouds hailstones and fiery coals. *ADONAI* also thundered in heaven, *Ha 'Elyon* sounded his voice – hailstones and fiery coals. He sent out arrows and scattered them, shot out lightning and routed them. (Psalm 18: 9 – 14) CJB**

One of the agencies sent correspondence to me in which they called me immoral and mentally ill, while vowing to send a nation-wide warning to all adult schools and colleges prohibiting me from ever teaching or working in them. Naturally that would exclude me from being a guest speaker as well. A week later a car mysteriously exploded in front of their building; the explosion burst all the windows in the top floor of the school, making its occupants duck, turn their backs away and "scurry for cover" as the newspapers put it. Soon the staff would be overwhelmed in dealing with a grand jury investigation over their office's ethics and behavior. Their attention was turned away from me. The following verse in Psalm 18 spoke to me:

> **You made those who rise against me sink under me. You made my enemies turn their backs to me. (Psalm 18: 39 – 40)**

Out of all the areas struck by the fires, the neighborhoods which had been "rejoicing" at all the negative press had the highest amount of evacuations, at over 1400. Fortunately and miraculously there were no injuries or deaths.

> **He reached down from on high, snatched me up, pulled me from the watery depths, rescued me from my mighty foe, from my enemies who were stronger than I. (Psalm 18: 16 – 17)**

What's in all this for You, Lord? I asked Him on more than one occasion. He answered that He wants me to tell others of the compassion He has for all of us and the willingness He has to use His power on His behalf. For His kids, love for persecutors is the only option open to them. In this also He has taught me and led me in how to share the great things He has done for me with others. I think not only of my Biblical training in this next passage from Psalm 18, but the restoring of my health as well:

> **Who trains my hands for battle, my arms to bend a bow of bronze. You give me your invincible shield, your right hand upholds me, you never cease to listen to me, You give me the strides of a giant, give me ankles that never weaken. (Psalm 18: 33 – 36)**

I wished no harm on these enemies; I chose to love and bless them in prayer. I believe what happened to them had a restorative purpose, a design to bring as many of them as were willing back to God. This was what I hoped and continue to hope for seeing as how many of them were involved in the occult, homosexuality and other things contrary to what God wishes of us.

Any previous attempts to speak to them about these things were met with sarcasm and verbal attacks.

In his works St. Augustine said the following about people who were enemies of God's word, using the symbol of "a two edged sword" to represent the Old Testament and New Testament:

"Strongly do I hate its enemies! Oh that you would slay them with a two edged sword, that they would no longer be its enemies! Thus do I love them, that they be slain to themselves, so that they might live for you." ("The Confessions of Saint Augustine; Book 12, Form and Matter; Chapter 14)

In the same way I directed all my efforts to loving the enemies in prayer that they would be slain to themselves so they would turn to God and choose to be His children. In this chapter I've simply wanted to glorify my Lord and point out my faith in knowing that more than a few of the persecutors mentioned have drawn closer to Him through these difficulties. There was no loss of life or even physical injury in these fires, lightning or smoke, and I in faith believe that more than a few hearts were changed for good. I give my God all the thanks and glory for allowing me to experience so much of Psalm 18. What a gift! It brings me to echo the words of King David:

He delivers me from my enemies. You lift me high above my enemies, you rescue me from violent men. "So I give thanks to you, ADONAI, among the nations; I sing praises to your name." (Psalm 18: 48 – 49) CJB

I have been able to give thanks to God among people from many nations through my personal testimony and through this book. I truly believe people would see more of God's deliverance from enemies in such powerful ways as I did simply by blessing, loving and praying for their enemies. Many people though, seethe, complain, insult and seek revenge against their enemies. They choose to hold on to the issue with their enemies and so they miss out on God's powerful intervention. They try to "save" what they perceive are their "rights" and end up losing the very thing they are trying to save.

Do you remember Chapter 4, where I pointed out how certain people in Jerusalem tried to "save" their religious establishment by rejecting and crucifying Christ? They ended up losing this forever as a result of their backward priorities. Scripture says:

Anyone who wants to save his life will lose it; but anyone who loses his life for my sake, will save it. (Luke 9: 24)

I encourage you to respond as the Lord taught me to: express yourself honestly before Him, then move past this to "lose your life" by praising Him and thanking Him for allowing the situation exactly as it is and thank Him in advance for the good He is going to bring in it. Praise Him and thank Him for the glory He is going to bring to Himself in the situation. Love, bless and pray for your enemies as well.

In any case, I would say my experience was somewhat of a Jehoshaphat battle, wouldn't you? God strengthened my faith to a degree I never thought possible through these excruciating trials. His loving grace, or undeserved favor carried me through them and He also led a lot of His wonderful people to pray for me.

As others and I praised Jesus for all the details and circumstances in these trials, His divine force poured forth, causing changes beyond what could be explained as an unfolding of natural events.

And all this is just the beginning. I am excited to see what God will continue to do over the years.

So what I did was to, in faith, follow the steps in King Jehoshaphat's prayer: Sharing the concern with God and confessing that I didn't know what to do, but my eyes were on Him, praising Him and thanking Him in it. If enemies are involved, loving them, blessing them and praying for them is key. The Lord will be your strength and your deliverer! The apostle Paul writes:

> **It is, then, about my weaknesses that I am happiest of all to boast, so that the power of Christ may rest upon me; and that is why I am glad of weaknesses, insults, constraints, persecutions and distress for Christ's sake. For it is when I am weak that I am strong. (2 Corinthians 12: 9 – 10)**

Psalm 91, the inspiration for this book, says:

> **'Since he clings to me I rescue him, I raise him on high, since he acknowledges my name. He calls to me and I answer him: in distress I am at his side, I rescue him and bring him honour. I shall satisfy him with long life, and grant him to see my salvation.' (Psalm 91: 14 – 16)**

Yes, friend. God loves to deliver His children from trouble when they are willing to run to Him in loving trust, as Jehoshaphat and I did. God truly is the same today as yesterday. He says:

> **Yeshua the Messiah is the same yesterday, today and forever. (Hebrews 13: 8) CJB**

Chapter 9

Protocols for Victory over Enemies

Praying that the schemes of our persecutors, pursuers, attackers, etc. fail is a proper thing for God's people to do. We can see all throughout the book of psalms, prayer after prayer asking God for determined enemies to fail, suffer disappointment and humiliation.

As children of the Lord, our first desire needs to be so that these things happen so such enemies seek repentance and forgiveness from God and become His children too. This is always what we pray for, but if this is not to be, then our prayers go to God to permanently end the determined enemy's schemes in the way He sees best, so the proper relationship between sin and its consequences may be restored, preserving His justice and holiness in the situation we are praying over. Let's look at important steps in praying for deliverance from dangerous enemies through Psalms 3, 41 and 143.

Love your enemies and pray for those who persecute you. We, as children of the heavenly Father are called to respond to His will as expressed by the ministry of Jesus, or Yeshua. Since He shows grace and care for all His creatures, we as Yeshua's disciples are to imitate God and love both neighbor and enemy. Scripture says:

> **But I say this to you, love your enemies and pray for those who persecute you; so that you may be children of your Father, for he causes his sun to rise on the bad as well as the good, and sends down rain to fall on the upright and the wicked alike. For if you love those who love you, what reward will you get? Do not even the tax collectors do as much? And if you save your greetings for your brothers, are you doing anything exceptional? Do not even**

the gentiles do as much? You must therefore be perfect, just as your heavenly Father is perfect. (Matthew 5: 44 – 48)

By being obedient to the Lord in responding compassionately towards enemies we are not permitting any barriers to be formed between us and the blessings, ministry, power and protection the Lord wishes for us. The Lord showered me with an abundance of these as I described in the last chapter. Had I been willing to hold and nurture a grudge and retaliate in some fashion I would have formed a barrier blocking all that the Lord wished for me. Also, if we are merciful, the Lord can be merciful to us.

Blessed are the merciful: they shall have mercy shown them. (Matthew 5: 7)

If praying and loving enemies is difficult for you, pray for the grace and strength to love and pray for those who have persecuted you. He will give you what you need for this.

Keep your eyes focused on the Lord in praise and thanksgiving. In these following verses, King David starts with praise to God, remembering the goodness He's done in the past, trusting in His steadfast character to continue doing the same. King Jehoshaphat did this also. (2 Chronicles 20: 6 – 9). In this way, the Lord is glorified and an idol is not made of the situation with the enemies.

How blessed are those who care for the poor!
When calamity comes, *ADONAI* will save them.
***ADONAI* will preserve them, keep them alive,**
And make them happy in the land.
You will not hand them over
to the whims of their enemies.
***ADONAI* sustains them on their sickbed;**
When they lie ill, you make them recover.
(Psalm 41: 1 – 3) CJB

I remember the days of old,
Reflecting on all your deeds,
Thinking about the work of your hands.
I spread out my hands to you,
I long for you like thirsty land.
(Psalm 143: 5 – 6) CJB

I relate well to this because I was pretty sick while going through the legal problems I talked about in the last chapter. Adonai did not hand me over to enemies' whims which were anything from lengthy imprisonment, life – long sickness, death, never being able to make a positive contribution to my community and who knows what else. I praise God for allowing this because I got to see His loving intervention and I learned to love and pray for the enemies too.

Let God make an honest assessment of your responsibility in the situation. One of the things I also had to do was take an honest look at myself and even more importantly, let the Lord show me what I needed to change in myself. At times we may have a problem with enemies because of our own poor choices. We are to allow God to give us His assessment of us and do what He asks us to do and remedy what we can. We repent of any wrongdoing and seek God's mercy, not because we deserve it, but because God is merciful.

Let your good Spirit guide me
on ground that is level.
For your name's sake, *ADONAI*, preserve my life;
in your righteousness, bring me out of distress.
(Psalm 143: 10b – 11) CJB

I said, "ADONAI, have pity on me!
Heal me, for I have sinned against you!"
(Psalm 41: 4) CJB

Psalm 143 has this plea for mercy as well:

Listen to my pleading; in your constancy save me, in your saving justice; do not put your servant on trial, for no one living can be found guiltless at your tribunal. (Psalm 143: 1b – 2)

Trust God at His Word; ignore the distractions of others. He wants us to focus on His words and trust in His willingness and His ability to transform us, restore us, provide for us and protect us. This is important because our opponents may tell us we won't get help from God because "we don't deserve it":

***ADONAI*, how many enemies I have!**
How countless are those attacking me;
How countless those who say of me,
"There is no salvation for him in God."
(Psalm 3: 1 – 2) CJB

Can you identify with this? I can. Many people said that of me when I was going through my legal trials years ago. You may not have thousands of enemies like David and I did. But how many enemies does it take to make your life miserable? One is enough, if he or she is determined enough. Maybe you're not being attacked by forces led by your own son as David was when he wrote Psalm 3. But you may be hated by members of your family, former friends or your spouse. It could be that these people are saying what they said to David, "After the way you've been, the Lord won't save someone like you." I found out right away that was a lie. The Lord says to us:

> **But you, *ADONAI*, are a shield for me;**
> **You are my glory, you lift my head high.**
> **With my voice I call out to *ADONAI*,**
> **And he answers me from his holy hill.**
> **(Psalm 3: 3 – 4)**

Yes, the Lord is faithful to help us when we cry out to Him in faith. He lifts up our head while others around us might be trying to get us to hang it down. He helps us realize we are wonderful works of His, we are worth transforming and have great value in His eyes!

Keep your eyes on the Lord and your enemies will shrink greatly. He will be faithful to help you. Maybe you are facing a battle of some sort. You may be somewhere where people are trying to beat you or everyone. The weapons can be bureaucracy, lying, rumors, gossip, stealing and even violence or something else.

A certain individual, let's call him Bob, once made small talk with me, asking me about books I'd written, my educational background, professional experience etc. He sounded friendly. I found out otherwise a couple of weeks later when he tried to convince a judge to place me in jail for four months using the words spoken in our conversation to do so. This he did before my very eyes!

The district attorney wished me to complete a week of work service for the misdemeanor I mentioned in the last chapter. "Bob" actually used the information I'd given him to show that because of my education, I had an evil criminal intent I skillfully concealed because of my educational experience and so I needed to be punished further. Thank the Lord he was not successful! This gave me all the more reason to depend on my God.

> **When they come to see me they speak insincerely,**
> **their hearts meanwhile gathering falsehoods;**
> **Then they go out and spread bad reports. (Psalm 41: 6) CJB**

Ask God to save you! Ask the Lord plainly and directly to deliver you, to save you from the onslaughts you face. Trust in Him to intervene for you! You read how He did this for me in the last chapter. You've read how He did this for people mentioned in other chapters and more are still to come. If you are going through some serious stress or danger, please meditate on these psalms and take the steps I encourage you to take in these chapters. It is in the middle of that exact danger that the Lord will appear to you and deliver you!

Notice too, when you meditate upon these psalms in your Bible, you'll see the word "Selah" by the sides of certain lines. The Holy Spirit is telling you to stop and let what you just read in those sections enter your heart. Dwell on it, feed on it, hide yourself in it. Let it heal you and increase your trust in God's power and willingness to use this power on your behalf.

> **ADONAI, rescue me from my enemies;**
> **I have hidden myself with you.**
> **Teach me to do your will,**
> **because you are my God.**
> **(Psalm 143: 9 – 10a) CJB**

Let the Lord lead you in any action He wants you to take. Now the Lord will take care of the whole situation. At times part of this may be to lead you to take legal action or another appropriate course. Personal revenge is not an option; all it will do is lead us to poor choices causing a chain of disasters, not to mention separating us from our God. We are to let the Lord guide us if we are to take action.

> Let dawn bring news of your faithful love, for I place my trust in you; show me the road I must travel for you to relieve my heart. (Psalm 143: 8)

> Never try to get revenge: leave that, my dear friends to the Retribution. As scripture says: Vengeance is mine – I will pay them back, the Lord promises. (Romans 12: 19)

When I began my week of work service the sheriff, concerned for my safety, took me and locked me in protective custody. I stayed in this compound next to the jail's "general population" for seven days. When I entered, I was given a rolled up mattress and I walked to a triple bunk bed. As I placed my mat on the top bed I stood on a chair and one of my feet touched the edge of the second bed. I heard a loud angry voice yell, "Get your –ing foot off my stuff."

I lowered my foot and prayed silently, taking care not even to appear to touch the man's things. Let's call the yelling man Mark.

On my sixth night, I felt the Spirit lead me to share the gospel with two other inmates there. I went to their room and shared the power of praising the Lord in everything.

"You mean I'm supposed to thank God and praise Him for letting me commit this crime so serious it made a SWAT team chase after me?" asked a young man. "Yes!" I answered him. "He allowed you to get in this situation you're in as part of His perfect plan to draw you to Him! Thank Him for allowing it and for the good He's bringing in it for you, your family and others."

I went on to share what's in much of the earlier chapters of this book with these young men. They began to accept Jesus into their hearts as their Savior, thanking Him and praising Him for allowing them to make the mistakes they had, using them to bring great blessings into their lives. They were overjoyed and began calling other people to come into their room for prayer. One of them was Mark. I prayed for him out loud, asking the Lord to bless him and use his circumstances for His glory and to draw Mark closer in a wonderful relationship with Him. Mark was silent as he kept his head lowered.

I was released on the morning of the seventh day. Mark was released at the same exact time I was. As I went to get my bedroll Mark interrupted me. "Let me carry it for you," he insisted. He carried all my things out of the unit as I went home, including my bedroll which was had angered him so on the first day!

> **And something more: If your enemy is hungry, give him something to eat; if thirsty, something to drink. By this, you will be heaping red – hot coals on his head. Do not be mastered by evil, but master evil with good. (Romans 12: 20 – 21)**

Thank the Lord for His saving grace and help as it continues to come and come in your situation. As you trust in the Lord to deliver you, you will see instance after instance where He acts and takes care of the enemy schemes. A friend once commented to me how amazing it was that so many individuals who expressed openly to me that they'd be around a long to make my life miserable aren't even around anymore two years later. Some have had changes of heart;

others have moved on or physically moved away, or been busy dealing with the effects of fires, lightning, floods, sickness, grand jury investigations and other things. Our God is good and He loves to take care of His children. Always.

Stay in communion with God and trust Him to bring good out of your situation. Interact with Him. Draw close to Him in an honest love. When you do this, you will be able to see beyond anyone's treachery and recognize God's purpose in all that's happening in your situation. It may take a while to see it, but as a believer in the Lord, your destiny is in His hands, regardless of what other people do. If you don't know all the story of Joseph in the 37th – 50th chapter of Genesis, I strongly encourage you to read it and know it well.

Joseph was sold into slavery by a bunch of jealous brothers and later falsely accused of attempted rape and imprisoned. In spite of these abuses, God was in control and used them to guide a curious series of events leading to Joseph becoming the second in command in the land of Egypt. As a result Joseph was not only able to help the Egyptian nation survive a seven year famine and but also save the life of the young nation of Israel. God's hand overruled the evil plans of others, giving him the grace to triumph and grow spiritually stronger because of the experiences. This is why Joseph didn't seek revenge on anyone but responded in love. It caused a great positive change in his brothers as well who sought his forgiveness years later.

At the time of this writing I have my master's degree in Christian Education and am a doctoral candidate in the same field. I work as a Bible teacher in my community and have published this book with others on the way. I am called occasionally to preach and lead prayers for others. The Lord is using me greatly in evangelizing my community and sharing His love with many.

I mentioned earlier the gossip and church ruling that was originally intended to permanently destroy my Christian service. These intentions were overruled by the Lord to bring me to where I am now, in a much greater Christian service than before. If they hadn't have happened, I would not have my Master's degree nor any books published! I would not be a doctoral candidate, nor would I be teaching or evangelizing as much as I am now.

The person who lives in close relationship to the Lord can be gracious towards those who try to do him harm because he knows he is always in God's hands. He has the Lord's full assurance that God can overrule all evil and bring blessing out of it. Joseph puts it well in these words to his brothers at the end of Genesis:

> **"You meant to do me harm, but God meant it for good – so that it would come about as it is today, with many people's lives being saved." (Genesis 50: 20) CJB**

Chapter 10

More Victories

*   *   *

We've covered some serious situations so far, showing God's deliverance in them as we are willing to let Him work in all things for good. This chapter will be a little unorthodox, simply telling of several real life day to day situations of different levels of seriousness, but all being situations in which praise and thanksgiving were used, resulting in extra blessings, good for others and glory for God. By seeing God centered prayer in action, prayer which minimizes the "problem", you can better apply it to your own life in all situations, great and small. No names are mentioned, and any personal details that would give people in my area any idea of who these testimonies are about have been changed slightly.

*   *   *

I was in a well known electronics store the other day, looking to buy a CD burner to make copies of language lessons for my business. I bought a middle priced Sony CD recorder and took it home. Following the instructions to the letter, I still could not make it record. The instrument lights wouldn't even work properly. I went back to the store and explained the problem to the support staff. They used the same steps I had for using the machine, but it worked just fine for them. They claimed the problem was due to me using the Memorex brand of audio disks. I needed to use the Sony brand of audio disks to have my CD recorder work best.

I praised and thanked God for there being such friendly support staff as well as for having the money to buy a second packet of blank audio disks, this one being the Sony brand. So I did and went home, carrying my CD recorder back with me. I tried the Sony brand of disks on my recorder, but again it wouldn't work. I thanked the Lord for a working car that enabled me to return to the store a second time. It was better than having no car!

I arrived at the store again and told the staff that the machine still wouldn't work for me. This time the support staff was not able to make it work either. When I asked if they had any more models of the recorder I had they answered that they didn't. They suggested I go to the front desk and request a refund.

As I waited in line for a refund I held the CD recorder in front of my chest, one hand on each hand. For some reason I can't explain, the recorder slipped out of my hand and fell to the hardwood floor, hitting it with a resounding crash which caught the attention of everyone there, the refund cashier and the other people in line. I picked up the banged up CD recorder, my face redder than a tomato in July.

"Thank you Jesus for a hot blushing face and for hands that weren't able to hang onto this CD burner," I prayed. "It's better than having no face and no hands at all. Praise You Jesus. Use this all for good and for your glory. Amen."

I knew I couldn't ask for a refund now. So I sheepishly walked out the electronic store's front door, my CD burner in hand. "Thank you Jesus for the one hundred fifty bucks I was able to use in buying this machine. I'm glad I had the money to spend, Lord. Bless this whole situation with this machine. Be glorified in it and use it for good."

I felt great! I found myself rejoicing instead of using words not suitable for print. Scripture says:

Always be joyful; pray consistently; and for all things give thanks; this is the will of God for you in Christ Jesus. (1 Thessalonians 5: 16 – 18)

Notice that this verse says we are to give thanks in "all circumstances", not just some. We give thanks for the "good" ones and the "bad" ones, loosely speaking.

I returned home and plugged the machine in, expecting the panel lights to be as mixed up as before. To my surprise they lit up all nice and orderly; all the lights on the CD burner's console were working. I put a couple of disks in and was able to record for the first time! I've recorded over two hundred disks since then. And my recorder now can use both Sony and Memorex disks.

Since then my language lessons have blessed many language learners and the telling of this true story has blessed hundreds. *Lord, it's great being your kid!*

*   *   *

It's a little humorous now but it wasn't at the time. Yesterday, we were swamped (no pun intended) by flooding all throughout the southern Santa Clara County area. It rained hard for a day and a half, and as Californian towns aren't prepared to deal with rain as our fellow countrymen in other states are, streets were closed everywhere and small lakes were showing up everywhere.

The city of Morgan Hill was hit pretty badly by these torrents of rain, and while driving through my favorite cowpoke city I decided to do an errand at a small shopping center downtown. I drove in the parking lot which was completely covered with brown water and seconds later I sunk into a dip with a huge splash and my car died out completely with a wet sputter. I'd underestimated how deep the water was in the parking lot. I tried starting the engine. Nothing.

I drive a 1996 Chevy Camaro, which is built pretty low to the ground to begin with, so I was already at a disadvantage in such heavily wet weather. Tall trucks and other large vehicles had the edge in such a storm.

I immediately had water all around my vehicle reaching as high as the middle of my doors. A man hollered in the distance urging me not to open my car door. The whole inside of my car would be full of the murky water if I did. He said there was no way I'd be able to get out of the parking lot's "lake" without a tow truck.

"If water starts to enter your car, exit the vehicle immediately!" he yelled. Water began to cover my car floor.

I called for help on my cell phone, praising and thanking God for the rain and for allowing me to get in the predicament I was in.

"Would you like me to call the police?" asked the operator at the tow truck and road service.

"No thanks. They can't help me and they have enough to do already," I answered. In the meantime tow trucks drove by carrying dead cars that had been defeated by the rain and could run no more, cars much taller than my own.

I tried starting my car again. I heard nothing but a sputter. Alleluia. The tow truck would be arriving in about twenty five minutes, according to the road service. Waves of brown water rose higher and higher, pounding against my door and lower edges of my window. My car shook. Water was also continuing to seep in on the passenger side door. It was about five inches high on my inside carpet and rising.

"Lord, your kid has a situation here. Thank you for allowing it. I could use your help. Bring blessing out of this and be honored in it as in everything," I prayed. A sudden impulse came to my insides, hitting me like a spiritual ton of bricks. I tried turning the engine over again and this time it started. Instead of trying to go forward as before, I went into reverse, tracing the path I'd used to enter the parking lot lake to begin with. I felt the little car roar through the waves of the "Brown Sea" defiantly and I honked furiously at some fellow trying to enter the lot himself in a pickup truck. He changed his plans and drove elsewhere as I exited the lot and backed into the street.

I drove off and my car sputtered and coughed before dying out a few blocks ahead. I let it rest while I called and cancelled the tow truck. I started the engine once more and the car ran without dying out again this time, gathering more and more strength with each passing mile. So much for the tow truck!

> **No disaster can overtake you, no plague come near your tent; he has given his angels orders about you to guard you wherever you go. (Psalm 91: 10 – 11)**

Thank you Lord for letting me share this testimony of your goodness with others. This truly has been a blessing.

Naturally, you might be thinking, "Ephrain, you're a little 'out there', don't you think? Maybe your studies about the Lord have driven you crazy. Of all things, praising the Lord for letting you drive into a lake." Well thanks for reminding me about when Paul spoke before King Agrippa and Governor Festus:

> **He had reached this point in his defence when Festus shouted out, 'Paul, you are out of your mind; all that learning of yours is driving you mad.' But Paul answered, 'Festus, your Excellency, I am not mad: I am speaking words of sober truth and good sense.' (Acts 26: 24 – 25)**

So dear reader, I too am "speaking words of sober truth and good sense." And thanks for reading so far, your Excellency.

*   *   *

Frank, a minister at our church shared with us last week of a time in which he was fired from a mechanic's job he had at an auto repair garage in Los Angeles. Things had gone for him rather smoothly for the first few weeks of his employment until his boss and co-workers found out he was a committed Christian. They were irritated at the Christian music he'd play on his small radio at his work station, which had less than a fourth of the loudness in the secular music coming from their own huge car trunk speakers.

The workers tried to avoid Frank like the plague but found out they really couldn't because of the small space in which they worked. The boss fired our minister without an explanation and when Frank asked him for one, none was given. Frank was told several times to come for his paycheck only to be told to go home and come back at another time. The week passed before the manager finally told him he wouldn't be paid for the last week of work. Not only that, the boss also refused to return very valuable tools Frank had purchased and left on the job site.

Frank politely protested the unfair treatment but when he was finally told to leave the garage for good he actually responded with "May the Lord bless you" to the boss. This was only met with cold sarcasm. Frank persisted in responding courteously and allowing the man to keep the tools, remembering the following scripture:

> **Whatever your work is, put your heart into it as done for the Lord and not for human beings, knowing that the Lord will repay you by making you his heirs. It is Christ the Lord that you are serving. (Colossians 3: 23 – 24)**

> **But I say this to you who are listening: Love your enemies, do good to those who hate you, bless those who curse you, pray for those who treat you badly. To anyone who slaps you on one cheek, present the other cheek as well; to anyone who takes your cloak from you, do not refuse your tunic. (Luke 6: 27 – 29)**

A couple of days later, Frank received a phone call from another employer, one with whom he hadn't even applied for work from. He accepted the position at nearly twice the salary of the former job. Soon after this, the previous job site he'd been in suffered a fire which forced the garage to permanently close. "The Lord ensures His children are never disgraced when they obey Him and remain true examples of Christian conduct in front of enemies," Frank shared with me. "He defends His children and never disappoints them." How true.

I live in California, a state which has been ravaged by many bizarre fires the last couple of years. Some say it's the Lord doing them, others say it's just a lot of random events. I would encourage people to look at these verses in scripture:

> **For all these hateful things were done by the people who lived in the country before you, and the country became unclean. If you make it unclean, will it not vomit you out as it vomited out the nations there before you? (Leviticus 18: 27 – 28)**

"Unclean" is not referring to pollution here. It is referring to actions motivated by intense hatred. When these actions take place by people continuously defiant against God and everything and everyone that is His, often times the land "vomits" out such offenders. This can take place through earthquakes, fires, dry lightning, and other "natural" disasters which are on the rise these days. We need not fear these things, though. Our eyes are to be stayed and focused on Yeshua Messiah, our Lord and Protector.

*   *   *

On a lighter note: a sister church in a nearby city shared with me the humorous story of one of their members, a single mother who had half a dozen children and despite struggling to provide for them daily, kept an attitude of praise and thanksgiving in everything, despite how it appeared to the natural senses.

This mother prayed to the Lord one day, asking for the means to take herself and her children out to McDonald's someday to enjoy some hamburgers and fries. Later that week, as she was in front of her home, a big brown hound came along, carrying a large white bag. The large dog dropped the bag on the porch and trotted away. The mother was shocked to find the bag to be a McDonald's bag containing enough hamburgers and fries to feed her whole family. As if that weren't enough, the food was still warm!

> **And when we eat and drink and find happiness in all our achievements, this is a gift from God. (Ecclesiastes 3: 13)**

*   *   *

On another occasion a couple from my prayer group invited me to a business seminar in San Jose. I had looked forward to it all week long, and was greatly interested in the products they were promoting. As I pulled up to their house, the husband expressed his regret that they wouldn't be able to go. A crisis had occurred at the home of a family from the church and they would have to go out to pray for them and encourage them.

Well I left, praising the Lord for something better He had in store for everyone. I went to the church and sat outside in the back reading some Scripture. My cell phone rang. A friend of mine from the east coast was on the line, very upset because he had completely lost the vision in his right eye. Apparently a blood vessel had burst and he'd felt the pain from this early in the day and asked his wife to take him to the hospital but she assured him it was nothing serious and according to him, they could see the doctor later.

The pain worsened and my friend went to the doctor hours later, when he was scolded by the doctor for having taken so long to be examined. The prognosis for recovering his sight was not good; he probably would remain blind in one eye and the possibility that the same thing would happen to the other eye was high.

My friend was very angry, blaming his wife for the delay in being examined. He said it would be her fault that he would be blind. He continued by complaining about her negativity, moodiness and lack of caring. I listened to him and let him express himself honestly. I then encouraged him to go to the Lord with his concerns.

I encouraged my friend to praise and thank God for allowing him to have the wife he did, using his marriage to learn patience and dependence on the Lord. I encouraged him to even thank God for allowing this blood vessel to burst in his eye, praising Him for the good He was going to accomplish in it. He responded by saying it seemed a little strange what I was saying but that I was probably right. So we hung up and several hours past.

I received a phone call from him saying that he'd been watching TV when the sight in his right eye began to return. He has recovered his vision completely, although he has a slight mark in a corner of the white of the eye. Praise God for all He does and for all the reminders He gives us about how He cares for us!

So God allowed me to miss out on my business meeting and allowed my friend to lose his sight for a little while so good could come out of it and He would be glorified. Had I gone to the meeting I would not have been able to spend the time with my friend I needed to. He got healed instead and I shared the story with 350 people a few days later and the Lord received thunderous applause. Alleluia!

*   *   *

A fellow Christian expressed a troubling concern to her pastor. Her daughter was a dancer at one of those semi – nude bars and had separated herself from the family, living a life that was taking her further and further down a very dangerous path. The pastor began with a prayer of thanks to the Lord for allowing the daughter to be doing exactly what she was doing. The mother was shocked, saying, "It's surely the devil behind all this and the one to thank for my daughter rejecting all that's good and decent in this world!"

The pastor responded by saying that God allows people to fall into mistakes in this world as part of His loving plan to get people to realize how much they need Him. This can be seen in Genesis 3: 15 in which the Lord says to Adam in response to his rebellion: "Cursed be the ground for your sake". The Lord, who does everything for good, allows problems and mistakes to occur for our sake, so we may turn to Him. If everything went smoothly all the time, we would think we had no need of Him at all. In addition, God commands us to love Him, giving thanks in everything (1 Thessalonians 5: 17 and Ephesians 5: 20), so He may use the situation for good (Romans 8: 28) that we may honor Him (Psalm 50: 13) in His saving grace.

The mother agreed with the pastor and together they prayed, praising and thanking God for each day He'd allowed her daughter to work where she did, to drink what she did, and be with the kind of crowd she was with, trusting that He would use all these things to draw her to Him as part of His perfect plan for her. They thanked Him in advance for the good He was doing. The mother went home joyful and enjoying Christ's peace which is beyond human understanding. Scripture says:

> **Always be joyful, then, in the Lord; I repeat, be joyful. Let your good sense be obvious to everybody. The Lord is near. Never worry about anything; but tell God all your desires of every kind in prayer and petition shot through with gratitude, and the peace of God which is beyond our understanding will guard your hearts in Christ Jesus. (Philippians 4: 5 – 7)**

Only a few days later, a Christian man was out for a walk when he suddenly felt a strong prompting from the Holy Spirit to enter this bar and tell a girl named Janine that Jesus loved her. He went inside and found the mother's daughter, named Janine, and gave her the message. Janine had heard many things from the men in the club before but never that. She asked the man to wait and she went and got dressed.

She asked the Christian man what made him say what he did and he told her he was walking by and the Lord told him her name and what to say to her. In obedience he gave her the message. She then began to express how lost she was and how she was making a complete disaster of her life. The two praised the Lord together and she accepted Christ right then and there, as her Lord and Savior. She walked out of the club, never to return.

*   *   *

A couple of weeks ago I received a phone call from a very distraught mother. Her adult son and father of three was arrested 16 months ago and had been in jail all that time while a very long trial went under way very slowly. He'd been accused of 20 felony crimes against a young female and was facing at least 45 years in state prison. I had prayed long and hard for this son and all the members of my friend's family. On this day two weeks ago, this friend called from the courthouse to tell me the trial was over and the members of the jury were meeting to determine this young man's fate. The district attorney appeared confident of a serious conviction and even the judge appeared this way.

Our phone conversation was brief and I tried to encourage my friend as best as I could. After we hung up, I immediately began to plead before Adonai on behalf of this young man. I asked the Lord to be Shophet (sho PHAIT), which in Hebrew means "Judge". I asked Him to also be El Roi (EL raw EE), the "God who sees". I praised Him for those aspects of His holy character, expressing that I knew He is a wiser, more compassionate judge than any man, and He also knew the exact truth in this court case better than anyone for He sees more clearly than any man as well. I also asked Adonai to give this young man a portion of the mercy He gave me a few years ago in my own legal problems back then.

Three hours later I received another phone call from the incarcerated man's mother. He had been released! All charges were dropped because the jury had declared him "Not Guilty"! The miraculous had occurred. The Lord had triumphed. Adonai Tzva'ot (The Lord of Hosts/Armies) was victorious again.

*   *   *

This next incident occurs in the Bible but I'll relate it to you because it shows helps point out a few important points that need to be made. It takes place in the book of 2 Kings, chapter 6, verses 8 – 14. In it the evil king of Aram wants to find Elisha, a prophet of God, and kill him. Why? Because Elisha was hearing God reveal where the Aramaeans were planning to attack Israel and Elisha would let the Israeli king know so he could avoid these ambushes or prepare himself enough to win every time.

In verse 11 the king of Aram asks who the spy in their kingdom was but in the next verse one of his servants reveals that Elisha the prophet was revealing Aram's plans to Israel. The king responded in this way:

> 'Go and find out where he is,' the king said, 'so that I can send people to capture him.' Word was brought to him, 'He is now in Dothan.' So he sent horses and chariots there, and a large force; and these, arriving during the night, surrounded the town. (2 Kings 6: 13 – 14)

The evil king wasn't taking any chances. He was treating Elisha as a very serious threat. When Elisha's servant woke up the next morning and saw the huge army waiting for them, he was terrified and told his master. Elisha responded in a very unusual way.

> 'Oh my lord,' his servant said, 'what are we to do?' 'Do not be afraid,' he replied, 'for there are more on our side than on theirs.' (2 Kings 6: 15 – 16)

How was that possible? Was the prophet's math worse than mine? No, the prophet realized that there was much more going on in the situation than one could know by using the five senses. We read this next:

> Elisha prayed, "*ADONAI*, I ask you to open his eyes, so that he can see." Then *ADONAI* opened the young man's eyes, and he saw: there before him, all around Elisha, the mountain was covered with horses and fiery chariots. (2 Kings 6: 20) CJB

I have shared many examples of God's incredible intervention with you already. In them you saw that as others and I kept our focus on God and the wonderful things He was working at doing (starting from the invisible), He came through with wonderful victories for us, making the good (invisible at the time) visible to us! Let's continue with the book of 2 Kings. Elisha prays for the Lord to strike the enemy army with blindness:

> When they came down to him, Elisha prayed to *ADONAI*, "Please strike these people blind"; and he struck them blind, as Elisha had asked. Next, Elisha told them, "You've lost your way, and this isn't even the right city. Follow me, and I'll take you to the man you're looking for." Then he led them to Shomron. (2 Kings 6: 18 – 19) CJB

This blindness was probably not a physical blindness, since they could see enough to follow Elisha. It was a kind of foggy mental condition where they'd be open to suggestion and led by the prophet to Samaria (Shomron in Hebrew) which at the time was the capital of Israel! When Elisha prayed again so that they may see, the Aramaean army found itself surrounded and captured by Israel. These overly proud soldiers were outwitted and defeated by just one man! They must have been hoping for a speedy death. However, people of God do not play the game of life by the usual rules:

> When the king of Israel saw them, he said to Elisha, 'Shall I kill them, father?' 'Do not kill them,' he replied. 'Do you kill your own prisoners with sword and bow?' (2 Kings 6: 21 – 22a)

This event ends on a note I find a little humorous. Elijah was God's man and he chose to humble his enemies with unusual kindness. The clever prophet gave the king the following order:

> 'Offer them food and water, so that they can eat and drink, and then let them go back to their master.' So the king provided a great feast for them; and when they had eaten and drunk, he sent them off and they went back to their master. Aramaean raiding parties never invaded the territory of Israel again. (2 Kings 6: 22b – 23)

So Elisha and the Israelites sent away their enemies with full stomachs and never heard from them again!

There is an invisible world in which every situation we are in can serve as a catalyst in which to glorify God and receive incredible blessings unless we choose to focus on the problem and devilish influence more than Him, and thus block God's intervention and blessings. There is hidden evil. That is true. But the goodness and power of God are far more powerful than it; He is the One in whom we are to focus and confide in. He lives in us and is greater than the evil in the world. The Bible says:

> Children, you are from God and have overcome them, because he who is in you is greater than he who is in the world. (1 John 4: 4)

> Do you not realize that your body is the temple of the Holy Spirit, who is in you and whom you received from God? (1 Corinthians 6: 19)

> No, in all these things we are superconquerors, through the one who has loved us. (Romans 8: 37) CJB

So let us keep ourselves focused on our Lord Yeshua that we may constantly remain in His perfect peace and victory.

Author's Note:

Jesus is Lord over everything, even thoughts and imaginings. We would do well to know this because of the effect they can have on us. A friend of mine once shared a true story of a beloved young Christian man who became a close friend of her family. Barely in his early twenties, the young Christian died in a tragic head on collision with another car. When my friend asked me a couple of questions on why such things happened, I asked her a few questions in response. From these I found out that the young man remarked to her on a few occasions, a fear of dying in a head on car collision. He had visions of this, thoughts of this and fears of this. It ended up happening. What he envisioned repeatedly occurred for real. It reminds me of what Job said, after all his children had died tragically.

> **"My sighing serves in place of my food, and my groans pour out in a torrent; for the thing I feared has overwhelmed me, what I dreaded has happened to me." (Job 3: 25) CJB**

We can often bring to happen what we put our mind and energy to, whether good or bad. Most of us have heard a coach or other leader say to us, "If you believe you'll fail, you will". We have a choice on whether to accept or reject dreams, visions, thoughts and memories. If any of these things exalt themselves above what God has spoken as His will for us, then these things must be rejected aggressively. In the above case, the fear of this death by car collision was not from God. How do I know? I know because God does not desire us to focus on terrors in this world. He says the following in these scriptures:

> **God did not give us a spirit of timidity, but the Spirit of power and love and self-control. (2 Timothy 1: 7)**

> **Finally, brothers, let your minds be filled with everything that is true, everything that is honourable, everything that is upright and**

pure, everything that we love and admire – with whatever is good and praiseworthy. (Philippians 4: 8)

He wants us to focus on His words and trust in His willingness and His ability to protect us. The Lord says to us:

My child, do not forget my teaching, let your heart keep my principles, since they will increase your length of days, your years of life and your well-being. (Proverbs 3: 1 – 2)

And:

Don't be afraid of sudden terror or destruction caused by the wicked, when it comes; for you can rely on *ADONAI*; he will keep your foot from being caught in a trap. (Proverbs 3: 25 – 26) CJB

So terror – producing visions and thoughts such as what this young man had are not from God. Rather they are from something that challenges what God says to us as truth in His word. We must reject them with confidence. Scripture says:

It is ideas we demolish, every presumptuous notion that is set up against the knowledge of God, and we bring every thought into captivity and obedience to Christ. (2 Corinthians 10: 5)

Anytime you get a scary or negative imagining, thought, recurring memory or whatever, you must say something to the effect of this:

"Thought/memory/negative imaging or dream, I reject you in the name of Jesus. You have no place or effect on me. In the name of Jesus my Savior, go to the foot of the cross to be dealt with. Praise You Jesus. Amen!"

That's it! The thought has to go to the Lord! Jesus is Lord even over those negative frightful thoughts! They are, as the Scripture says, "presumptuous". It means we can say, "Just who do you think you are? You're not in charge here! Beat it and go to the foot of the cross in Jesus' name!" Spend time thanking God for all the wonderful privileges He gives us in Christ Jesus, Yeshua Messiah. Alleluia!

"A person whose desire rests on you you preserve in perfect peace, because he trusts in you." (Isaiah 26: 3) CJB

Chapter 11

Victory over Temptation

Temptation is an enticement to commit evil or sin. Everyone is tempted, even Jesus, when He walked the earth as a human being. Temptation in itself is not evil; our response to it is evil if we choose to give in to the temptation instead of rejecting it.

Acting on a temptation can cause great damage. It can destroy marriages, relationships, careers, health and opportunities while bringing about danger and harmful consequences of many kinds. It also forms barriers that will keep us from experiencing blessings and victories like the ones we've seen in the previous chapters. Scripture says:

> *ADONAI's* **arm is not too short to save, nor is his ear too dull to hear. Rather, it is your own crimes that separate you from your God; your sins have hidden his face from you, so that he doesn't hear. (Isaiah 59: 1 – 2) CJB**

Since only the Lord can give us true and lasting victories, it is best for us to be right with Him at all times. We deal with sin in as much a preventative way as possible, not even allowing an opening for it to enter. The Bible teaches us both how to resist temptation and how a person falls into temptation in chapter 39 of the book of Genesis, which is the story of Joseph and Potiphar's wife. A few verses into the chapter we read the following:

> **Now Joseph was handsome in form and appearance. And it came to pass after these things that his master's wife cast longing eyes on Joseph, and she said, "Lie with me." (Genesis 39: 6 – 7)**

Temptation often is subtle, starting with something small, like a long glance at something or someone. Potiphar's wife gave Joseph a long glance. Notice in the middle of this verse the words, "and it came to pass after these things that his master's wife cast longing eyes on Joseph." Potiphar's wife let a desire for Joseph develop over a period of time. It started in her eyes and then spread to fantasies in her mind.

The eyes are often referred to as the "gateway to the soul." Potiphar's wife was tempted by what she saw in Joseph. Over time, she let it create desire in her mind, and it spread to her heart, making her lose all self control, modesty or righteousness of any kind.

The subtlety in the temptation now became open in her actions, which were to tell Joseph to lie with her. How could she do such a thing so aggressively with no shame of any kind? She could because she had allowed the desire to commit adultery grow and grow in her mind. She clearly fed this lust at the level of her imagination.

When we feed lust or desire in our imagination, we are always taking the risk of doing what we are imagining doing. Temptation, when fed in our imagination willingly, can become strong, uncontrollable urges that can easily break forward and become our action. All that is left is the opportunity to act on these urges. Scripture says:

> **Everyone is put to the test by being attracted and seduced by that person's own wrong desire. Then the desire conceives and gives birth to sin, and when sin reaches full growth, it gives birth to death. (James 1: 14 – 15)**

When the urges become our action, we sin against God, bringing separation between Him and us. The relationship and communion we had with the Lord becomes damaged and this separation can lead even to spiritual death.

Writers in the field of copywriting advertising know that the greater job you do in making a reader imagine himself using the sales product you are writing about, the greater chance you have of convincing him to purchase it.

For instance: an overweight man and woman see a powerful advertisement about a fast weight loss/body sculpting product. The advertisement cleverly gets them to imagine how different and how better their lives will be by purchasing this product.

The advertisement gets the couple to picture themselves, in great detail, how it would feel to have the beautiful bodies shown in the advertisement.

They imagine receiving the compliments from others, the admiring stares at the beach or wherever they go, as the ad implies they will.

The advertisement makes the couple imagine themselves fitting into the clothes they wore in high school as well as moving with the confidence they had back then. They see themselves making more money and becoming extremely attractive to the other sex. Pretty soon, they buy this weight loss/body sculpting product.

There's no mistake about it. Something appealing is seen in the eyes. From there, if the person allows it, it spreads to his mind where it can grow in his imagination. Following this, the desire spreads to the heart, where all that's left is for the occasion to occur where the person has the opportunity to act on it; then he or she does.

We see in the case of Joseph and Potiphar's wife, that fantasizing over the temptation was also maintained, or allowed to continue. We read in the same chapter of Genesis:

> **Although she spoke to Joseph day after day, he would not agree to sleep with her or be with her. (Genesis 39: 10)**

Did she give up when Joseph refused to give in to her? No; she continued being driven to sustain this lustful desire more and more. It actually got to the point where she attacked him:

> **But one day when Joseph came into the house to do his work, and none of the men of the household happened to be indoors, she caught hold of him by his tunic and said, 'Sleep with me.' But he left the tunic in her hand, took to his heels and got out. (Genesis 39: 11 – 12)**

The woman was so caught in sin's grip that her actions became even more open, planned and strategic. It wouldn't surprise me if she had been responsible for no servants being around. Did she order them to attend to duties elsewhere? Every occasion now became an opportunity for her to plan and possibly act on her lust. She was now totally enslaved by the temptation.

We can see the pattern of falling into temptation from Potiphar's wife's example. First it started with a subtle notice of a temptation; in this case it was a physical attraction to Joseph.

Next, she let this subtle temptation grow in her imagination, spread to her heart and lead to open action.

After this, Potiphar's wife sustained the temptation. She let it continue living in her.

Finally, the temptation consumed her so much she actually became strategic with it. She started to plan how to enjoy it either by action or letting it live in her lustful imagination.

This pattern is what we need to avoid. If we let a subtle notice of a temptation take root in our mind by thinking about it and letting our imagination run wild with it, we will soon find the temptation living in our heart and are in danger of acting on it if the opportunity arises. We also take the risk of desiring to keep it living in us. We become enslaved to it and every occasion becomes some kind of opportunity to act on it physically or in our imagination. We then risk death, spiritually, and possibly physically.

So what can we do to avoid this? Joseph gives us an excellent example of how to respond to temptation and experience victory over it.

First, Joseph had already made up his mind to reject sin. In this case the sin took the form of sexual offers; he was decisive about it. In Joseph's case, he had his response to the temptation of adultery already settled in his mind beforehand. There was a degree of preparation beforehand seen in his response; he didn't hesitate, he directly said "no."

Joseph knew he was in Egypt, far from home. The Egyptian women were known for their looseness and extra marital affairs. Joseph's resistance to this was strong and decisive. Do you remember verse eight? It simply says, "But he refused."

Joseph directly said no. He didn't beat around the bush with statements like, "Oh I don't think it would be a good idea" or "Well, I wouldn't want to hurt you or your husband."

Joseph, a stranger forced to live in Egypt, had already decided in his mind how to respond to these Egyptian women. It was a big NO in response to whatever temptation they might throw his way. The resistance to any temptation for us is not to be made in the heat of the moment, as some kind of last second reaction. The best and only way to plan for it is in the quiet time of prayer, well before hand.

Next, Joseph had principles for his refusal. He didn't hesitate in saying to others what these principles were. He said "no" firmly and gave his reasons why. It wasn't an "I don't think I'm going to do this" or an "I don't want to do this," but instead an "I am not going to do this." He then gave his principles for his refusal.

'Look,' he said to his master's wife, 'with me here, my master does not concern himself with what happens in the house, having entrusted all his possessions to me. He himself wields no more authority in this house than I do. He has exempted nothing from me except

yourself, because you are his wife. How could I do anything so wicked, and sin against God?'(Genesis 39: 8 – 9)

Joseph's refusal of temptation was very principled. He said it would be wrong. He must never intrude upon the privileges of someone's marriage. He was well aware of what God's Word said of adultery:

You shall not commit adultery. (Exodus 20: 14)

And:

You shall not set your heart on your neighbour's house. You shall not set your heart on your neighbour's spouse, or servant, man or woman, or ox, or donkey, or any of your neighbor's possessions. (Exodus 20: 17)

And Joseph had no shame in speaking of the fact that there is no more powerful force than the fear of God.

This fear of God is the fear of damaging the relationship with our Heavenly Father and the fear of damaging the lives of our neighbors and family along with it. Scripture says:

The fear of *ADONAI* is the beginning of knowledge, but fools despise wisdom and discipline. (Proverbs 1: 7) CJB

Joseph's refusal of temptation also was unyielding. As we read in the first half of Genesis 39: 10, he refused Potiphar's wife day by day. How can we have the strength to be unyielding? Only the Holy Spirit can give us this strength.

When we walk close to God daily, and allow His Holy Spirit to dwell in us, His Spirit will prompt us regularly on how to walk in His will and grow in our love of Him. The Holy Spirit's will for each of us is to love God's Word and meditate on it daily as the Spirit leads us. Scripture says:

How can a young man keep his way spotless? By keeping your words. With all my heart I seek you, do not let me stray from your commandments. In my heart I treasure your promises, to avoid sinning against you. (Psalm 119: 9 – 11)

Have the book of this Law always on your lips; meditate on it day and night, so that you may carefully keep everything that is written

in it. Then your undertakings will prosper, then you will have success. (Joshua 1: 8)

Love God and His Word and He will give you the strength to be unyielding. He says:

'Not by force and not by power, but by my Spirit,' says *ADONAI Tzva'ot*. (Zechariah 4: 6b) CJB

Keep my steps firm in your promise; that no evil may triumph over me. Rescue me from human oppression, and I will observe your precepts. Let your face shine on your servant, teach me your will. (Psalm 119: 133 – 135)

Now Joseph was a practical man. He didn't know that he could continue to be successful. That is true for us as well. We should never put ourselves in a situation where we will be at risk. To say things like this shows a character flaw: "I have nothing to worry about by staying alone with my girlfriend at her place so late all the time. I'm strong enough to resist any temptation to sleep with her." Scripture says:

Everyone, no matter how firmly he thinks he is standing, must be careful he does not fall. (1 Corinthians 10: 12)

And through the grace that I have been given, I say this to every one of you: never pride yourself on being better than you really are, but think of yourself dispassionately, recognizing that God has given to each one his measure of faith. (Romans 12: 3)

King David seemed invincible for the first half of his life. He had conquered numerous enemies, captured Jerusalem and became King. But one evening he committed adultery with a married woman and conspired to kill her husband when he found out she was pregnant by him. These terrible sins caused inner violence in his household for his remaining years, a violence that would claim the lives of several of his sons. What took place to bring on this sin? It started with King David being somewhere he wasn't supposed to be. Scripture says:

At the turn of the year, at the time when kings go campaigning, David sent Joab and with him his guards and all Israel. They massacred the Ammonites and laid siege to Rabbah-of-the-Ammonites. David, however, remained in Jerusalem. (2 Samuel 11: 1)

So when all kings were supposed to be out to battle, David was idle in Jerusalem, instead of working for the Lord by commanding Israel's troops against those who wanted to destroy God's people. I would be willing to bet that David's prayer time was not as good as it was in his earlier years. He hadn't prepared himself beforehand how to respond to sexual temptation, but rather was like Potiphar's wife. While wasting his time "strolling" he saw something, or rather someone he quickly saw as a sexual object. We read:

> **It happened towards evening when David had got up from resting and was strolling on the palace roof, that from the roof he saw a woman bathing; the woman was very beautiful. David made enquiries about this woman and was told, 'Why, that is Bathseba daughter of Eliam and wife of Uriah the Hittite.' (2 Samuel 11: 3 – 4)**

Well this set off a chain of events that damaged David's household for the rest of his life. We need to follow Joseph's example of refusing to be where we shouldn't. In his case Joseph refused to be in the situation where temptation could continue trying to entice him. Let's look at Genesis 39: 10 again, noting Joseph's actions this time.

> **Although she spoke to Joseph day after day, he would not agree to sleep with her or be with her. (Genesis 39: 10)**

Joseph refused to even be with Potiphar's wife. We should follow Joseph's example by not putting ourselves at risk of being enticed. Sin cannot force itself on you. God will always provide us with a way out. God's way out for Joseph was to be somewhere else, away from Potiphar's wife. Scripture says:

> **No temptation has seized you beyond what people normally experience, and God can be trusted not to allow you to be tempted beyond what you can bear. On the contrary, along with the temptation he will also provide a way out, so that you will be able to endure. (1 Corinthians 10: 13) CJB**

Joseph was intense in his response. Scripture tells how Joseph responded when Potiphar's wife grabbed him by his clothes:

> **But he left the tunic in her hand, took to his heels and got out. (Genesis 39: 11 – 12)**

So too should we reject temptation, so much that we stay far from it, even if it means we have to run away or "take to our heels". God's Word says:

> **So flee the passions of youth; and, along with those who call on the Lord from a pure heart, pursue righteousness, faithfulness, love and peace. (2 Timothy 2:22) CJB**

> **Run from sexual immorality! Every other sin a person commits is outside the body, but the fornicator sins against his own body. (1 Corinthians 6: 18) CJB**

In my much younger years I once foolishly went to the Mexican border town of Mexicali to meet the sister in law of a coworker. My coworker told me that she (his sister in law) was a friendly, attractive professional Catholic single with good family values. She seemed friendly and humorous on the phone, and after checking on her, found out she had a rather successful real estate business in Mexico. "That's good," I thought. "If I meet her I know I won't be going out with some wild yahoo." So without consulting the Lord (big mistake), I drove down south to meet her. Logically speaking, she seemed like a good person to meet. Scripture says this though:

> **Where are the philosophers? Where are the experts And where are the debaters of this age? Do you not see how God has shown up human wisdom as folly? (1 Corinthians 1: 20)**

Well a few hours after this young lady and I met, I was disturbed to hear her speak positively of the occult, and as she did so she became very physically friendly with me. She was obviously "Catholic" in name only. I immediately tore myself away from her clutches, leapt out of her vehicle (which fortunately was not moving) and ran away, fleeing in Joseph fashion, not resting easy until I crossed the border to the US side a mile away where I breathed a sigh of relief. I was so happy to be safely back on my soil that I could have kissed the ground had it not been so dusty. I hadn't even left behind my coat! By the Lord's grace He had given me the values to reject a temptation decisively and He protected me enough to be able to flee the temptation though I had gone where I shouldn't have gone to begin with. It was a valuable lesson learned.

To summarize briefly, we can effectively resist temptation by following Joseph's example. First, we must be decisive by knowing how we will respond to temptation beforehand.

Next, we must have principles which we develop from what God's Word says is right or wrong. Following this we must be unyielding in our rejection of evil, relying God's strength, not ours.

Then we are to be practical and not foolishly put ourselves at risk of being enticed to sin against God and others. We don't allow ourselves to be where we shouldn't. Finally, we are to be intense in our rejection of a sinful act, even if it comes across as appearing ruthless in our response. Run away if you have to! We must decide to love God more that whatever it is that tempts us.

Prayer for help regarding temptation

Heavenly Father, great are You and great is your love for me. Thank You for sending Jesus to die for my sins on that cross. Help me remember, oh Lord Jesus, that You did this for me, that your suffering, which was done on my behalf, was indescribable. How can I go back to old sins knowing what You went through out of love for me? How can I merrily do evil knowing that it was that same evil that caused your death? No. I choose to reject giving in to sin. Keep me far from being tempted more than what I can bear and limit as much as possible the things that may tempt me. Transform me more and more through your Holy Spirit who lives in me so that I may become more and more like your Son Jesus. Help me always be honest before You, that I may always be prepared to receive your blessings and best plans for me. I pray all these things in Jesus' name. Amen.

Chapter 12

With Love like this. . .

We've just completed the important chapter on guarding ourselves against temptation. We will soon study what to do when we fail. Before we continue with the extremely important chapter, "Confession and repentance – Honesty before God", there are a few things we should know which can help put things in perspective.

Right before He was crucified to die for our sins, Jesus was scourged by a professional team of four Roman soldiers led by a fifth one, called an exactor mortis. They were highly trained and skilled in crucifixion procedures and torture. The exactor mortis' goal was to weaken the victim and break his will as much as possible without killing him. If he did, he would have to substitute himself for the victim. So these Roman soldiers were extremely motivated and expertly trained in torturing the victim so he was left with just enough strength to walk to his place of execution.

The Roman team used a whip that consisted of three leather thongs attached to a wooden handle. Each thong had a single dumbbell shaped piece of bone or lead attached to the end of it. This would mean that each time a soldier whipped the accused (in this case Jesus), he would receive nine deep wounds. These wounds pierced all layers of skin and muscle, penetrating the internal organs and bones.

The victim would receive one wound from each leather thong (three total), and he would receive two wounds each from the piece of metal/bone attached to each of the three thongs (six total). At least nine wounds came with each lash.

Some scholars say that because Jesus was Jewish, He could only receive 40 lashes minus 1, or 39. There are problems with this theory because the Romans would not have followed Jewish law in whipping. The Romans would have followed their own methods of administering torture. This means Jesus would have received between 60 and 120 lashes according to Roman methods. By doing the math, we can know that *Jesus received between 540 to 1080 lashes.* (60 x 9 = 540 and 120 x 9 = 1080 lashes)

Roman soldiers would have whipped Jesus in a synchronized fashion. There would be no 8 second intervals between lashes as seen in the movies. Jesus would have been tied to a whipping post with a soldier on each side of Him. They would take turns; one would whip Jesus and as that soldier's whip left Christ's body, the whip from the other soldier would immediately whip him again. This would mean that *Jesus received between 540 to 1080 deep lash wounds in less than three minutes.* Words cannot describe the brutality of this, nor the evil to which humans can sink. And Jesus went through this inhuman, brutal pain so He could confront the ugliest in us and destroy the separation our sin formed between us and the Father.

The crown of thorns placed on Jesus was significant. It represented the curse of sin placed on the earth in Genesis 3:

> To Adam he said, "Because you listened to what your wife said and ate from the tree about which I gave you the order, 'You are not to eat from it,' the ground is cursed on your account; you will work hard to eat from it as long as you live. It will produce thorns and thistles for you, and you will eat field plants." (Genesis 3: 17 – 18) CJB

The thorns were anywhere from two and a half to three inches long. As Jesus was struck by the soldiers, these thorns would have imbedded themselves in His head deeply.

> And they stripped him and put a scarlet cloak round him, and having twisted some thorns into a crown they put this on his head and placed a reed in his right hand. To make fun of him they knelt to him saying, 'Hail, king of the Jews!' And they spat on him and took the reed and struck him on the head with it. And when they had finished making fun of him, they took off the cloak and dressed him in his own clothes and led him away to crucifixion. (Matthew 27: 28 – 31)

Seriously weakened from the lashes and beatings, Jesus next carried the crossbeam known as a petibulum, which weighed between 50 and 100 pounds all the way to His crucifixion site about a half mile away. This beam would have been tied to His outstretched arms so it couldn't fall off or be thrown off.

Words can't describe the horrible effects crucifixion has on the human body. The crucified one was thrown to the ground with his arms still tied to the petibulum when he reached the place of crucifixion. Jesus would have fallen on His wounds, opening them up more and contaminating them with dirt and splinters.

The "nails" used to crucify Jesus were tapered iron spikes between five to seven inches long with a square shaft (not round) 3/8's of an inch across. He was lifted with the petibulum nailed to His wrists and attached to a bigger beam that was already in the ground pointing up. The piercing of the wrist with those spikes tore into nerves and ligaments, causing fiery pain rivaling that of a continuous electric shock going from the wrist all the way to the chest. It was common for the hands to become paralyzed in a clawing like position.

One of Jesus' feet was placed on the other and a third spike nailed through both feet and the upright beam. His feet would not have been on a foot rest as some statues and art portray, but were directly nailed to the beam. So Jesus' full body weight would have rested on his arms and nailed feet, causing these spike wounds to tear even more. His weight would have gone forward and downwards, causing His arms to come out of their sockets. We read the following prophecy in Psalm 22:

> **My strength is trickling away, my bones are all disjointed, my heart has turned to wax, melting inside me. My mouth is dry as earthenware, my tongue sticks to my jaw. You lay me in the dust of death. (Psalm 22: 14)**

An inability to breathe in such a weak position usually caused the crucified victim's death. Muscle cramps contributed to this problem. Flexing the elbows, adjusting the shoulders and pushing from the damaged feet were all the victim could do to continue breathing for a while longer. The length of survival on the cross was from three to four hours to three to four days, depending on how severe the beatings and lashes he received before the crucifixion. Every time Jesus attempted to breathe while on the cross, His lash wounds would have pressed into the wooden beams He'd been nailed to as well, causing even more agony. Blood loss from these wounds would have continued while He was on the cross.

Insects and birds of prey would often begin to feed on the victims on the cross while they were still alive.

When Jesus was on the cross He was offered a drink, a mild analgesic which would make it easier to go through the pain. Jesus refused it because He didn't want anything to numb His mind or alleviate the suffering He was undergoing for your sins, my sins and those from the rest of humanity.

During the six hours Jesus was on the cross, many prophecies were fulfilled. One of them was this verse, uttered by King David a thousand years before:

> **I can count every one of my bones, while they look on and gloat; they divide my garments among them and cast lots for my clothing. (Psalm 22: 17 – 18)**

The callous hearted soldiers who kept watch on Jesus while He was on the cross a thousand years later did just that. The gospel of Matthew says the following:

> **When they had finished crucifying him they shared out his clothing by casting lots, and then sat down and stayed there keeping guard over him. (Matthew 27: 35 – 36)**

This prophecy from Psalm 22 came true as well:

> **But I am a worm, not a man, scorned by everyone, despised by the people. All who see me jeer at me; they sneer and shake their heads: "He committed himself to *ADONAI*, so let him rescue him! Let him set him free if he takes such delight in him!" (Psalm 22: 6 – 8) CJB**

This indeed happened in Jesus' crucifixion a thousand years later. The crowd ridiculed Him and challenged Him. We read the following in the gospel of Matthew:

> **The passers-by jeered at him; they shook their heads and said, "So you would destroy the Temple and in three days rebuild it! Then save yourself if you are God's son and come down from the cross!' The chief priests with the scribes and elders mocked him in the same way, with the words, 'He saved others; he cannot save himself. He is the king of Israel; let him down from the cross now, and we**

will believe in him. He has put his trust in God; now let God rescue him if he wants him.' (Matthew 27: 39 – 43)

Without knowing it, these mockers fulfilled a prophecy God said would happen; they also unwittingly uttered a spiritual truth. Jesus couldn't save Himself because He had no need or reason to be saved. He was the perfect, sinless Son of God. His crucifixion was to save humanity, not Himself. We are all sinners.

We all, like sheep, went astray; we turned, each one, to his own way; yet *ADONAI* laid on him the guilt of all of us. (Isaiah 53: 6) CJB

God using Jesus as our atonement for sins is central to His work for our salvation. Sinners in rebellion toward God need a representative to offer sacrifice on their behalf if they are to be reconciled to a holy God. We see the intensity of God's desire for us to be reconciled to Him through all Jesus went through for us. Because Jesus was sinless, He alone was able to offer His life as a sacrifice for us without needing any atonement for Himself. He was the perfect, spotless Lamb of God willing and able to go through the indescribable for you and me so that we could be right with God and have the best in our lives. With love like this expressed for us on that cross, how can we go anywhere else or turn to anything or anyone else? And as the next chapter points out, how can we refuse to be honest before a Lord who loves us so?

Thank You Lord for humbling yourself so and becoming one of us. Thank You for all You went through on my behalf so I could be reconciled to God. You truly are perfectly good, loving and merciful. You are truly worthy to be praised. O Messiah, your love for all of us is more than any of us could possibly imagine. Help me humbly appreciate your great sacrifice and your desire to draw me into your loving presence. Thank You for dying for me, Lord Jesus. Thank You for wanting my salvation so much. I will love You and praise You Lord all the days of my life. Amen.

Chapter 13

Confession and Repentance – Complete Honesty before God

How can anyone in their right mind refuse the love of a God who went through so much to save them? When we accept Christ, He heals us, restores us and transforms us into the best human beings we could be. We've read about many great blessings already and there's more to come.

Now everything we've covered so far, and all that is to follow is nothing more than a wonderful plate of food to look at from behind a thick glass window unless we are honest before God. We can't enjoy "the wonderful plate" fully if we aren't honest with Him. Is there a sin you need to confess and repent from? Is there something you are supposed to do but haven't? Is there any disobedience going on? If so, be honest before God, openly confess it before Him and turn away from it, or repent.

There is also a turning toward the Lord involved in true repentance. This means to obediently do what the Lord is calling you to do to regarding this sin. Otherwise the guilt from unrepentance will cause you health problems, spiritual and/or physical danger, loss of prosperity, loss of guidance, the missing of God's intervention in problems and an infinite amount of blessings lost from not being right with God. I'm going to mention the following Scripture again as my way of encouraging you to be brutally honest with yourself and God regarding all actions of yours:

> ADONAI's arm is not too short to save, nor is his ear too dull to hear. Rather, it is your own crimes that separate you from your

God; your sins have hidden his face from you, so that he doesn't hear. (Isaiah 59: 1 – 2) CJB

Iniquity is guilt over doing something wrong, but it is a guilt that is not acknowledged before God and others. It is a guilt that is buried and comes out in ways like physical sickness, emotional illness, disorder in more and more areas of your life, death before your time and other things that are less than God's best for you.

In 2 Samuel 11, King David committed adultery with Bathsheba, the wife of Uriah, a dedicated soldier in Israel's army. A pregnancy resulted from this and David tried to get rid of Bathsheba by manipulating the situation so it would seem that Uriah had gotten her pregnant. When that didn't work, David tried hiding the pregnancy by conspiring with one of his commanders to set things up so Uriah (Uriyah in Hebrew) would die in battle.

David and his commander succeeded in Uriah's murder and David tried to move on for about a year as if nothing happened. We sadly read what the Lord felt about this right from the start.

When the wife of Uriyah heard that Uriyah her husband was dead, she mourned her husband. When the mourning was over, David sent and took her home to his palace, and she became his wife and bore him a son. But *ADONAI* saw what David had done as evil. (2 Samuel 11: 27) CJB

David couldn't move on as if nothing happened, though. David's season of unrepentance brought him great guilt, emotional anguish, arthritis – type problems, and separation from the wonderful God who passionately drove him and blessed him with incredible life victories in the past. David wrote about this unrepentant time in Psalm 32:

How blessed are those whose offense is forgiven, those whose sin is covered! How blessed those to whom *ADONAI* imputes no guilt, in whose spirit is no deceit! When I kept silent, my bones wasted away because of my groaning all day long; day and night your hand was heavy on me; the sap in me dried up as in a summer drought. (Psalm 32: 2 – 4) CJB

I know what it's like to have this sin sickness. I too was sapped of my strength and had many lung and joint problems some years ago. I was in a type of mental fog so I wasn't doing much of anything meaningful to the cause of Christ. I made myself deaf to God's correcting voice and so I suffered with poor choices in my work, relationships, finances, health and more. I thank the Lord for His grace in leading me to repent of my sinful attitude and behaviors. I am still healing and being restored from the effects of these mistakes, and by God's goodness He is even using those for good in my life.

God's will is always that you confess and repent of sin right away; it is always in your best interests to do so. Delaying only cuts you off from Him and leaves you open to more problems. If you delay, you have to harden your heart so you can resist the gentle correction of His Holy Spirit, and you have to make yourself deaf to His voice. There is no other way. You HAVE to harden your heart and make yourself deaf to Him. That's the way to resist His Holy Spirit. You put yourself at spiritual, physical, mental, emotional, etc. risk in this, and can cause natural consequences to occur that will affect you and others indefinitely.

When God sent the prophet Nathan to rebuke David for what he did, the prophet told David he would not die for his sin, but other consequences would occur. Scripture says that the Lord spoke to David in this way through Nathan (Natan in Hebrew):

> **'Now therefore, the sword will never leave your house – because you have shown contempt for me and taken the wife of Uriyah the Hitti as your own wife.' Here is what *ADONAI* says, 'I will generate evil against you out of your own household.' (2 Samuel 12: 10 – 11a) CJB**

> **David said to Natan "I have sinned against *ADONAI*." Natan said to David, "*ADONAI* also has taken away your sin. You will not die. However, because by this act you have so greatly blasphemed *ADONAI*, the child born to you must die." (2 Samuel 12: 13 – 14) CJB**

David ended up repenting. We read the following in Psalm 32:

> **When I acknowledged my sin to you, when I stopped concealing my guilt, and said, "I will confess my offenses to *ADONAI*"; then you, you forgave the guilt of my sin. (Psalm 32: 5) CJB**

David pleaded with God for the life of the child. The 12th chapter of 2 Samuel tells us:

> ***ADONAI* struck the child that Uriyah's wife had borne to David, and it became very ill. David prayed to God on behalf of the child; David fasted, then came and lay all night on the ground. The court**

officials got up and stood next to him trying to get him off the
ground, but he refused, and he wouldn't eat food with them. (2
Samuel 2: 15 – 17) CJB

David fasted, prayed, wept and lay on the ground for seven days, after
which the baby died. I am sure the Lord heard his cries and felt his pain; yet
the Lord will not compromise His stand against evil nor cancel the lesson
He needs to teach. He could not give David what he asked for. He needed to
teach him, and those future generations who would study this tragic account,
a valuable life lesson.

David could not continue to think of himself as invincible, as one who
had gotten as far as he had on his own. He needed to give all the glory and
focus to God, and the discipline coming from his sinful actions needed to
come. Natural consequences of these sins would follow as well; a couple of
David's sons would die violent deaths; one occurred as a result of a rape of one
of David's daughters, and the other from causing a rebellion in the kingdom
and trying to overthrow King David himself.

The Lord used David's fall to bring him back to where he needed to
be, following God's perfect will. And we today are blessed by having the
wonderful Psalm 51, David's prayer of repentance, which starts in this way:

Have mercy on me, O God, in your faithful love, in your great
tenderness wipe away my offences; wash me clean from my guilt,
purify me from my sin. For I am well aware of my offences, my sin
is constantly in mind. (Psalm 51: 1 – 3)

God is incredibly gracious and merciful. We not only experience His
peace, forgiveness and loving presence in our lives from being completely
honest and willing to confess and repent before him, we also find ourselves
being in a position once again to receive His unexpected blessings. Let's see
what happened with David sometime later:

David comforted his wife Bat-Sheva, came to her and went to bed
with her; she gave birth to a son and named him Shlomo. *ADONAI*
loved him and sent through Natan the prophet to have him named
Y'didyah [loved by God], for *ADONAI's* sake. (2 Samuel 12: 24 –
25) CJB

The Lord also said the following about David's son, Solomon (Shlomo in
Hebrew) some time later:

I shall be his father and he will be my son, and I shall not withdraw my favour from him, as I withdrew it from your predecessor. (1 Chronicles 17: 13)

The union between David and Bathsheba ("Bat-Sheva" in Hebrew) had been wrong; that is true. Their motives had been wrong, and David tried to conveniently get rid of Bathsheba before committing the murder. Despite all this evil and all the consequences brought about by it, the Lord allowed the couple to be drawn together by the tragedy. He removed the curse of their marriage and brought a wonderful child from their marriage. Solomon was given the additional name "Jedidiah" ("Y'didyah" in Hebrew) meaning, "Loved by God." Many generations later, from David's family line, Jesus Christ would be born. God's grace, allowed to flow through confession and repentance resulted in great goodness. This is all the more reason for us to confess honestly before God and turn away from wrongdoing.

Let's not say to ourselves, "Well let me improve myself a little. Then I'll come to the Lord." This is a lie. The Lord is the only one who can truly change us to the best we can be, and He wants us to come to us exactly as we are when He calls us, so He can do so. Scripture says:

Each one of you, brothers, is to stay before God in the state in which you were called. (1 Corinthians 7: 24)

So for anyone who is in Christ, there is a new creation: the old order is gone and a new being is there to see. It is all God's work; he reconciled us to himself through Christ and he gave us the ministry of reconciliation. I mean, God was in Christ reconciling the world to himself, not holding anyone's faults against them, but entrusting to us the message of reconciliation. (2 Corinthians 5: 17 – 19)

Only Christ has the power to change us, to reconcile us with God. We cannot. And the work He begins in us He is always faithful to finish:

I am quite confident that the One who began a good work in you will go on completing it until the Day of Jesus Christ comes. (Philippians 1: 6)

I encourage you to practice letting the Lord examine your conscience every day. Let Him tell you if you've sinned in your thoughts, your words or your actions. The end of Psalm 139 is excellent to use:

God, examine me and know my heart, test me and know my concerns. Make sure I am not on my way to ruin, and guide me on the road of eternity. (Psalm 139: 23 – 24)

Fearlessly ask the Lord to do this for you. Don't be a coward about this! Try it and you will see that it was easier than you thought it would be after you do. A certain religious order teaches people to ask the Lord to point out one sin or mistake and one positive thing they've done each day. Talk about a bunch of boring, quasi spiritual wimps! This is nothing more than an attempt to keep the Lord from speaking honestly to them. As we've seen in the Scriptures, why would the Lord confide much in people who are so dishonest and carry an obsession in always feeling comfortable? Such people are neither hot nor cold, spiritually speaking. As a result, they cannot do many great things for God, if any. God has this to say about such people:

I know about your activities: how you are neither cold nor hot. I wish you were one or the other, but since you are neither hot nor cold, but only lukewarm, I will spit you out of my mouth. (Revelation 3: 15 – 16)

Who wants to be spit out by the Lord? Not me! Why lose great blessings, purpose and protection from the Lord in exchange for living like a coward? Now I've been told by those close to me that the Lord manifests Himself in my life in amazing ways. These people have seen many incredible "Psalm 18" incidents in my life, along with great ministry to the Lord, wisdom in daily affairs, and other things like good health, an orderly life, lots of fun, good friends and a wonderful family. I have a rewarding business and an excellent education, along with a discernment that allows me to make good choices in easy times and difficult ones.

When I make mistakes, I've found the best course of action is to confess any and all wrongdoing and repent of the sin involved. The blessings I've mentioned have come as a result of simply being honest with God and He has chosen to bless me greatly.

When I was living a sinful life and being dishonest with God, all I had was a score of health problems, chaotic relationships, an out of control work schedule, legal problems and all sorts of dangers, for starters. I've seen similar things with others who say they are Christians yet are "living together" with their girlfriend, stealing regularly on the job, practicing witchcraft or other sins. They choose to be slaves of "comfort". So they think. The results of this comfort they pursue always catch up to them real quick. It did with me and it will with them. It amazes me how dishonest, unrepentant people wonder why they have depression, boredom, serious legal and financial problems, lousy health or disastrous relationships while members of their family are dying, going to prison or falling into all kinds of addictions.

> **And in spite of all this you say, "I am innocent, let his anger turn from me!" Now I pass sentence on you for saying, "I have not sinned." (Jeremiah 2: 34 – 35)**

I'm not saying that all problems a person has are a result of sin. Problems often come from the fallen state of the world we live in. Still, more problems come from dishonesty with God and an unrepentant heart than people care to admit.

The Lord is merciful, wise and compassionate. When He points out a sin you need to repent of, even though His words may be difficult to hear, you always feel great when you repent. You'll feel alive! You will be renewed! His words are always meant to restore your relationship with Him, not condemn you and shove your face in the dirt. Peace, joy, enthusiasm, healing and energy (to name a few) are normal byproducts of being turning away (repenting) from sinful behavior to get right with God.

> **They refused to obey, forgetful of the wonders which you had worked for them; they grew obstinate and made up their minds to return to their slavery in Egypt. But because you are a forgiving God, gracious and compassionate, patient and rich in faithful love, you did not abandon them! (Nehemiah 9: 17)**

Let me give you a little insight on how our heavenly Father is towards us when we repent. It is a stunning portrait of Him, and one that is, for the most part, lost these days. It can be found in the parable of the prodigal son. Jesus begins to tell the parable like so:

> **Then he said, 'There was a man who had two sons. The younger one said to his father, "Father, let me have the share of the estate that will come to me." So the father divided the property between them. A few days later, the younger son got together everything he had and left for a distant country where he squandered his money on a life of debauchery. When he had spent it all, that country experienced a severe famine, and now he began to feel the pinch; so he hired himself out to one of the local inhabitants who put him on his farm to feed the pigs. And he would willingly have filled himself with the husks the pigs were eating but no one would let him have them. (Luke 15: 11 – 16)**

One thing that is important to note in the parable is that despite the younger son's rebellion and foolishness, the father left an impression with the son so he knew he'd be welcome back if he chose to return. He didn't say something like, "If you leave don't think you can ever come back." This is a valuable lesson for fathers: leave things such that your wandering son/daughter always knows they are welcome back into your arms. We see this father portrayed as having done this in the next few verses.

> **Then he came to his senses and said, "How many of my father's hired men have all the food they want and more, and here am I dying of hunger! I will leave this place and go to my father and say: Father, I have sinned against heaven and against you; I no longer deserve to be called your son; treat me as one of your hired men." (Luke 15: 17 – 19)**

Ann Spangler, on pages 321 – 322 of her excellent devotional book titled, "Praying the Names of God", points out the following: "In Jesus' time the Jewish community had a way of punishing sons who lost the family inheritance, squandering it among Gentiles. Angry villagers would gather together to conduct what was known as a qetatsah ceremony, a ritual that consisted of filling a large pot with burned nuts and burned corn and then breaking it in front of the guilty party."

The qetatsah concluded with the villagers smashing the pot to pieces while shouting that the guilty son (whom they would mention by name) was cut off from his people and any further relationship was as permanently destroyed as the pot. He then had to leave forever. In this prodigal son parable however, the father didn't give the villagers enough time to organize this qetatsah. Here is what the father did at seeing his prodigal son return:

> **So he left the place and went back to his father. While he was still a long way off, his father saw him and was moved with pity. He ran to the boy, clasped him in his arms and kissed him. (Luke 15: 20)**

Since the father ran to his son, beating the other villagers to him, he was able to prevent the qetatsah. His behavior was also such that it took the village's negative attention off his son. He actually ran and welcomed his son with an embrace and kiss! Now the father would have been a distinguished landowner and traditional Middle Eastern father; he'd be quite dignified. He'd also have been wearing long robes designed to always hide the legs. For someone like this to run, reveal his legs and act this way would be considered undignified and humiliating behavior in public. But his strategy was masterful because instead of the public having their attention on the prodigal son, saying something like, "Will you look at that son? Isn't he a disgrace?" their attention instead would have been completely on the father. At seeing the father act with such unrestrained compassion and running with exposed legs, the villagers would instead say "Will you look at that father? Isn't he a disgrace?"

This is how the Lord is with us. He doesn't give us what we deserve when we repent. He joyfully restores our relationship with us, builds us up, blesses us and is willing to take the shame for us if need be. Scripture says:

> **We too, then should throw off everything that weighs us down and the sin that clings closely, and with perseverance keep running in the race which lies ahead of us. Let us keep our eyes fixed on Jesus who leads us in our faith and brings it to perfection: for the sake of the joy which lay ahead of him, he endured the cross, disregarding the shame of it, and has taken his seat at the right of God's throne. (Hebrews 12: 1 – 2)**

He brings us to lift our heads when we repent, not hang them in shame. The Word of God says:

> **But you, *ADONAI*, are a shield for me; you are my glory, you lift my head high. (Psalm 3: 3) CJB**

Pray the ending of Psalm 139. Ask the Lord to let you know if you've sinned in your thoughts, words or actions. Then wait and let Him respond. If He points out a sin in any of these areas, confess it to Him and say you are sorry. Reject the sin and repent, which means you turn away from it, choosing to do it no more. Turn to the Lord and what He wishes you to do. If His Spirit leads you to seek someone's forgiveness, be humble and courageous and seek it. If His Spirit leads you to make some kind of amends to someone, do so. Be obedient and you will be at peace with God, well prepared to receive the many blessings, protection and privileges found in His Word.

> **He reserves his advice for the honest, a shield to those whose ways are sound; he stands guard over the paths of equity, he keeps watch over the way of those faithful to him. (Proverbs 2: 7 – 8)**

> **If we acknowledge our sins, he is trustworthy and upright, so that he will forgive us our sins and will cleanse us from all evil. If we say, 'We have never sinned, we make him a liar, and his word has no place in us.' (1 John 1: 9 – 10)**

By letting the Lord correct you, you can be right with Him and be confident knowing you can reach for the "food" of His blessings and promises to you. There is no thick glass window in the way!

Taste and see that *ADONAI* is good! How blessed are those who take refuge in him! (Psalm 34: 8) CJB

Chapter 14

God's Holy Spirit, Our Comforter and Counselor

"Come to me, all you who labour and are overburdened and I will give you rest. Shoulder my yoke and learn from me, for I am gentle and humble in heart, and you will find rest for your souls. Yes, my yoke is easy and my burden light." (Matthew 11: 28 – 30)

As children of Jesus, we are given the help of His Holy Spirit, who manifests Himself to us in many ways. Two of the ways the Holy Spirit comes to us are as Comforter and Counselor.

OUR COMFORTER

Are you grieving from a loss of some kind? Have you been hurt or mistreated? Do you suffer from anguish, disappointments or troubling problems, questions and decisions? If you have experienced any of these, know that the Lord has promised His children a wonderful Comforter, the Holy Spirit. God's Holy Spirit desires to help us through all of these troubles. The Bible says:

Blessed be the God and Father of our Lord Jesus Christ, the merciful Father and the God who gives every possible encouragement; he supports us in every hardship, so that we are able to come to the support of others, in every hardship of theirs because of the

encouragement that we ourselves receive from God. (2 Corinthians 1: 3 – 4) CJB

Please note the words "in every hardship". Our loving Father is willing to help us with them all, large or small. Some Christians only like going to the Lord when they have big problems, but think of all the practice they miss in developing a trusting relationship with the Holy Spirit from turning to God in even the small things. And for God, every "problem" is a "small thing."

Consider a believer who, every day, turns to the Holy Spirit to receive help for everything from managing a busy work or social schedule, the missing of a friend, losing weight and confusing driving directions, to planning a vacation and treatment of a sport injury.

With such experience in trusting and listening to the Holy Spirit in all situations, such a believer is much more experienced and ready to receive the Spirit's help during a severe crisis than someone who only turns to the Holy Spirit every few months or even years, whenever an emergency happens to come around.

So whether your concern, problem or trouble is large or small, all you need to do is ask the Lord's Holy Spirit to comfort you. The Spirit will come and often times send you the help you need as well.

But God, who encourages all those who are distressed, encouraged us through the arrival of Titus; . . . (2 Corinthians 7: 7)

If it's healing and comfort you need, the Lord will send His Spirit to help you when you request it. Just wait for His Spirit to come and work on healing your heart and emotions. At times a hurt or issue may be buried so deep one has no idea it exists, let alone know how to pray about it. The Spirit can pray through us in groans and see clearly what it is we need. The Comforter helps us in all this. Scripture says:

And as well as this, the Spirit too comes to help us in our weakness, for, when we do not know how to pray properly, then the Spirit personally makes our petitions for us in groans that cannot be put into words, and he who can see into all hearts knows what the Spirit means because the prayers that the Spirit makes for God's holy people are always in accordance with the mind of God. (Romans 8: 26 – 27)

His Spirit will come as He has promised. The following scripture verses testify how Jesus' Holy Spirit wants to comfort and heal us:

The Spirit of *Adonai ELOHIM* is upon me, because *ADONAI* has anointed me to announce good news to the poor. He has sent me to heal the brokenhearted; to proclaim freedom to the captives, to let out into light those bound in the dark; to proclaim the year of the favor of *ADONAI* and the day of vengeance of our God; to comfort all who mourn, yes provide for those in Tziyon who mourn, giving them garlands instead of ashes, the oil of gladness instead of mourning, a cloak of praise instead of a heavy spirit, so that they will be called oaks of righteousness planted by *ADONAI*, in which he takes pride. (Isaiah 61: 1 – 3) CJB

As a mother comforts a child, so I shall comfort you. (Isaiah 66: 13)

What encouraging news for us! Our broken hearts can be healed, our depression (heavy spirit) can be replaced with a joyful desire to praise God (the cloak of praise), and we can experience great consolation and comfort from whatever brings us great sadness and inner turmoil. Psalm 51 says:

Sacrifice gives you no pleasure, burnt offering you do not desire. Sacrifice to God is a broken spirit, a broken, contrite heart you never scorn. (Psalm 51: 16 – 17)

God is a friend of the broken hearted; He identifies very closely with them because of what His Son, the Lord Jesus went through. For the most part, the religious leaders among His people rejected Him. One of His friends betrayed Him and contributed to His arrest.

Jesus was falsely accused of many wrongdoings, and His blessings and good works were misunderstood and interpreted as being evil. He was tried unjustly and subjected to insults, beatings, whippings, and given an excruciatingly painful execution on a cross. As if that weren't bad enough, He also endured a temporary separation from the Father as He carried the sins of the world.

Jesus can identify with any pain you may have. Give it to Him, let Him be Lord over it; ask His Spirit to comfort and heal you. Psalm 116 is one of many psalms that give us insight into God's loving nature and desire to comfort us in all of our troubles. He'd love to take on your problem and heal you. Psalm 116 says:

I love that *ADONAI* heard my voice when I prayed; because he turned his ear to me, I will call on him as long as I live. The cords of death were all around me, Sh' ol's constrictions held me fast; I was finding only distress and anguish. But I called on the name of

ADONAI: "Please, *ADONAI*! Save me!" *ADONAI* is merciful and righteous; yes, our God is compassionate. *ADONAI* preserves the thoughtless; when I was brought low, he saved me. My soul, return to your rest! For *ADONAI* has been generous to you. (Psalm 116: 1 – 7) CJB

"Sh'ol" or "Sheol" as read in English is a dull, shadowy place believed to be inhabited by souls of the dead (2 Samuel 22: 6; Ecclesiastes 9: 10). God is present in this place; it is well known to Him:

Sh'ol and Abaddon lie open to *ADONAI*; so how much more people's hearts! (Proverbs 15: 11) CJB

Even in death God's people remain in His care and comfort, so we need not fear death or anything that would try to stand between us and His care for us.

For I am certain of this: neither death nor life, nor angels, nor principalities, nothing already in existence and nothing still to come, nor any power, nor the heights nor the depths, nor any created thing whatever, will be able to come between us and the love of God, known to us in Christ Jesus our Lord. (Romans 8: 38 – 39)

The Lord sure goes out of His way to assure us of His care. He sent us His Son Jesus, and as we've read in this chapter, we have also His Holy Spirit living in us. He gives us encouragement also in His Word. Paul, in his letter to the Romans, has this to say about Scripture such as the one above:

And all these things which were written so long ago were written so that we, learning perseverance and the encouragement which the scriptures give, should have hope. (Romans 15: 4)

To help you, you can pray in this way:

Lord Jesus, thank You for loving me and offering me the wonderful comfort of your Holy Spirit. I praise you for your goodness and compassion. My Savior, I give you this concern (name it) - _____.
Thank you for using this concern to bless me and draw us closer together. Send me your Holy Spirit to comfort me and heal me. Send me the help I need in the way you know I best need it. Thank You for hearing me from heaven and giving me the

help I need. Come Holy Spirit and live in me. In faith I receive your comfort and
healing presence in Jesus' name. Thank you, Jesus. Thank you, Lord. Amen.

Wait upon the Lord, and His Spirit will come to you. He will also send
you the help you need. Reading and reflecting on Psalm 116 or any other
psalm that touches your heart can help as well. Express yourself honestly
to the Lord and remember that praise and thanksgiving in all of this is
important, since it keeps our focus on Him, as we've already studied. Believe
in the healing power of God's Holy Spirit, and He will provide the comfort
you need. He is faithful to always do this for His children who ask Him.

Notice that the above prayer mentions the concern, but its focus is on
God. It magnifies God instead of the problem. By praying this way we turn
the concern into an act of worship. It is an act of trust and faith on our part.
This pleases the Lord. You will see more prayers like this later. Study this
book carefully so that you may pray in this way naturally.

OUR COUNSELOR

In addition to providing us great healing and comforting, the Holy Spirit
is available to us as our Counselor or Helper (Paraclete). If we have a decision
to make, or seek direction, we can ask the Lord's Holy Spirit to counsel us.
Jesus says:

> **But the Paraclete, the Holy Spirit, whom the Father will send in my**
> **name, will teach you everything and remind you of all I have said**
> **to you. (John 14: 26)**
>
> *(Author's note: New Testament manuscripts were originally written in*
> *Greek. "Paraclete" is a Greek word meaning "advocate", "counselor" or*
> *"protector". Nice, huh?)*

We have this promise that the Lord will send us His Spirit to teach us
whatever it is we need to learn about in any aspect of our lives (all things).
The Holy Spirit also reminds us of words Jesus said to us in Scripture that
will help us.

The Holy Spirit's counsel is there for us whenever we need it if we will
only ask for it and trust in God to deliver it. The Holy Spirit is gentle. He
will not force himself on you, but will come when invited. He needs you to
ask Him in. Jesus says:

"If you then, evil as you are, know how to give your children what is good, how much more will the heavenly Father give the Holy Spirit to those who ask him!" (Luke 11:13)

So ask the Holy Spirit to counsel you in the need you have. In faith, wait for Him and He will respond to you. He will give you your answer and you can confirm that it is the Spirit and not a counterfeit by doing the following:

* Check to make sure the counsel is consistent with the Word of God. It must not contradict anything God has said in his Word, for He never deviates from what He tells us in the Bible. For example, if the "counsel" tells you to lie, commit adultery, cheat, or hurt someone, then it is not from the Spirit. It is either from the devil, a sinful nature, or the world's way of dealing with things.

* Ensure that the counsel does not contradict the voice of God's Church. The Church gives us wisdom concerning modern issues not seen so easily in Scripture, such as abortion, birth control, cloning, stem cell research, etc. The counsel received must follow the guidance of the Church in this otherwise it must be rejected.

* Plead the precious blood of Jesus to flow in you and cover you. As we will discuss in more detail in Chapter 17, we must take care not to interpret the "blood of Jesus" as a kind of magical formula or substance to believe in that will get us out of troublesome situations. The term "the blood of Jesus" refers to Christ's faithfulness to God in willingly shedding His blood by undergoing a horrible, undeserving painful sacrificial death on our behalf. The Lord's death on the cross and resurrection defeated the power of the devil. In the First Letter of John we read:

> **'This was the purpose of the appearing of the Son of God, to undo the work of the devil.'** (1 John 3: 8b)

Demonic spirits are terrified of the Lord Jesus and the sacrifice He made on the cross. Claim Jesus' faithfulness to God in defeating the devil on the cross by pleading the blood of Jesus. Demonic forces trying to confuse you when you are awaiting counsel will flee instead. Scripture says:

> **Give in to God, then; resist the devil and he will flee from you.** (James 4: 7)

'Salvation and power and empire forever have been won by our God, and all authority for his Christ, now that the accuser, who accused our brothers day and night before our God, has been brought down. They have triumphed over him by the blood of the Lamb and by the word to which they bore witness, because even in the face of death they did not cling to life.' (Revelation 12: 10 – 11)

Satan is the accuser, the one who constantly reminds Christians of their past sins to try to get them to forget or disbelieve Christ's complete victory on the cross.   Or he can lie to us by convincing us that we are completely blameless or deserving people who have the right to do such and such. This too we must avoid. We are to reject our self righteousness, sure. But we are to listen to God's assessment of us, not Satan's. We are also to accept God's means of forgiveness through Yeshua, depending completely on His mercy. In chapter 5 of Revelation, Jesus is referred to as the Lamb who was slain for the sins of the world.

The blood of Jesus (meaning Jesus' obedience to the Father in His willing sacrifice to shed His blood for us by dying on the cross), defeats Satan and his evil demonic horde. We can claim His blood as protection from spirits of deception, pride, etc. We will spend time reading about the power of the blood of Jesus in Chapter 18.

*   Confirm the counsel with your inner spirit. The counsel you received should bring you peace in your conscience and a greater closeness to Christ. Paul writes:

This is the truth and I am speaking in Christ, without pretence, as my conscience testifies for me in the Holy Spirit. (Romans 9: 1)

*   It can be good to wait two or three days to make sure we aren't mixing up the counsel with an emotional high. Emotions don't carry us very long and are not consistent. Recently I was phoned by a leader in charge of a prayer group I'd participated in before. She sounded sad and said she missed my presence and that of my family. I felt overwhelmed with her sadness and instinctively I wanted to commit myself to coming again even though the Lord had moved me to go elsewhere. I resisted the temptation, making myself wait for three days before deciding anything. Within that time the feelings subsided and I realized the instinct to return to the previous prayer group was not from the Spirit. The Spirit is always consistent and unchanging. If the counsel you received still brings you peace in your inner spirit after two or three days and the other conditions are met, you can proceed with following the counsel in faith.

Wait upon the Holy Spirit's counsel and you will always receive God's best plan for you. Let me tell you a little bit of how the Lord moved me from the first prayer group mentioned above. I enjoyed the group very much; I had many friends there and was encouraged often. At the same time, I felt like I wasn't challenged in the way I needed, nor was I growing in the way I believed I needed. I visited another group in south San Jose and felt spiritually drawn to it. "Should I stay where I was or should I come here?" I asked myself. Using the steps outlined above, I asked the Holy Spirit to guide me in what to about the prayer fellowship. As I waited for the Spirit to speak to me, I soon felt a strong need to read chapters 31 and 37 of the book of Genesis.

As I read through Genesis 31 I felt the words in the third verse of that chapter speak to me: 'Go back to the land of your ancestors, where you were born, and I shall be with you'. The south San Jose church I'd visited was in an old neighborhood I worked at long ago. I began my walk with the Lord when I lived and worked there years back. I felt a strong drawing to be a part of that community and the verse in Genesis 31 confirmed this.

There was another confirming verse that spoke even more powerfully to me although that was to come some weeks after I joined the south San Jose church prayer group. Genesis 37 spoke to me in the eight verse in which Joseph's brothers complain about a dream he had in which he was honored over them. They complained, saying "Are you to pass us? Do you want to lord it over us?"

I began attending a Bible ministry training Wednesday nights at this south San Jose church, joining a small group of dedicated classmates who had already been in the program two months. I was faithful to complete all the assignments for the classes I'd missed but I was a very new member. Two days after my third week of attendance, a priest from Mexico came and gave a Eucharistic celebration (We'll cover this in Chapter 23) and a strong preaching message to a congregation of over 600 people at this San Jose church. Towards the end of the celebration he asked a small group of people (the Bible ministry training class) to come forward and receive a special blessing and gift. Many people came forward but the priest firmly ordered them to sit down. It was only the group from the Bible ministry training program (eleven members plus me) who was asked to come forward.

I felt uncomfortable about being included with the rest of the group seeing as how I was so new, but the teacher insisted I accompany the eleven, so I knelt with the rest before the altar. The priest began to pray over the twelve of us and he placed a cross over our necks. While this began, one of the other eleven, a young woman who I'd never seen before leaned over and complained to me. She protested me being there. Using words similar to those of Joseph's brothers in Genesis 37, she complained that I didn't belong with the rest of the eleven being called. Who was I to pass up the rest of the congregation and be included with them? Was I going to being lording over people?

I responded firmly by saying that the teacher was in authority and she wished me to be included with the other eleven class members so there I stayed. Moments later, the woman leaned over again and complained to me again. I responded the same way. She finally left me alone. The text the Holy Spirit led me to in Genesis 37 weeks back came true, forming a powerful confirmation of hearing the Lord's voice. It was interesting how Joseph had eleven brothers as well. He was one of twelve, as I had been one of twelve that evening. I knew then I was in the community God wished me to be a part of.

This is how the Lord wants to speak to all of us! He will counsel you and make known to you exactly what He wants you to do. Be honest before Him, praise Him and thank Him in everything, and meditate upon His word regularly. Ask Him whatever you wish and He will respond!

Yes, let our Heavenly Father counsel you; don't get impatient and make the mistake of counseling Him or acting impulsively and asking Him to bless your choice after you've begun to run with it. Psalm 106 lets us know what happened to the Israelites who became impatient and refused to listen to the Lord's counsel:

> **But they soon forgot his achievements, they did not even wait for his plans; they were overwhelmed with greed in the wastelands, in the solitary wastes they challenged God. He gave them all they asked for, but struck them with a deep wasting sickness; (Psalm 106: 13 – 15)**

> **Many times [God] rescued them, but they kept making plans to rebel. Thus they were brought low by their wrongdoing. (Psalm 106: 43) CJB**

The rebellious Israelites suffered death, plagues, oppression from enemies and much more for rejecting God's counsel to them. We do well to listen patiently to our Heavenly Father's counsel. He loves us more than we can imagine, and He always wants the very best for us.

We were created to need God and become one with Him. Only by living in dependence on God and His counsel can we ever be truly fulfilled.

Chapter 15

God's Holy Spirit, Our Strength and Advocate

The Holy Spirit also desires to be our Strength in time of weakness or need and our Defender or Advocate when anything comes against us.

OUR STRENGTH

> "For who is God but *ADONAI*, and who is a Rock but our God? God is my strength and protection; he makes my way go straight. He makes me swift and sure – footed as a deer and enables me to stand on my high places. (2 Samuel 22: 32 – 34) CJB
>
> There is nothing I cannot do in the One who strengthens me. (Philippians 4: 13)

The Holy Spirit of God is a source of strength when you need Him. Whenever you feel weak, fearful or discouraged, whenever you feel drained, exhausted or wanting to give up, just stop and ask for the strength of God's Holy Spirit. Wait confidently in God's presence and the Heavenly Father's strength will come to you.

I once attended a Catholic mass with a gentleman I was sponsoring for entrance into the Christian community. I sat in the pew next to him waiting for the priest to call us up for the welcoming ceremony into the church. At the time I was doing all I could to keep from running out of the church from the pain of the symptoms of food poisoning. My head and stomach were in agony and I wasn't sure I could make it through the 90-minute service.

I knew it was the Lord's will for me to be this man's sponsor and support him in this rite. The praise and worship I gave the Lord in this service gave me spiritual joy and peace, so I knew in faith I was doing what I was supposed to do.

It became obvious to me that I couldn't make it through this mass on my own strength, so there in the pew, I quietly made my prayer to the Lord:

"Heavenly Father, You are awesome, ever powerful, and loving towards all of us. Thank you for the many times you've helped me in the past. I know you want me here. There's just a small problem, and it's not really any problem as far as you are concerned. I need the strength and healing of your Holy Spirit because I recognize all too well the symptoms of food poisoning. I give this concern to you and thank You for taking care of it in Jesus name. Thank you that I can come to you with this. Great is your love for us, and great are you and worthy to be praised. Amen."

Within a few minutes after praying this, I felt strength come to me. The pain and symptoms of food poisoning disappeared. I was able to concentrate on giving the support I needed to the gentleman I was sponsoring. The Lord came through, as I knew He would.

Notice that this prayer had no complaining, whining or blaming God for anything. In fact the prayer magnified God in a form of worship because of the adoration and thanksgiving to Him throughout it. Of course I can't take the credit for this; the Lord has shown it to me in His grace, answering the prayers of faithful patient people loving me.

Magnifying the Father is the way Jesus prayed. I encourage you to prayerfully study, practice and ask for the Lord's help in guiding you to pray more as Jesus prayed. He'll give it to you.

It was the strength of the Holy Spirit that empowered Jesus' disciples, turning them from cowards into fearless preachers of the gospel. His strength is available to us today. The Bible says:

In the evening that same day, the first day of the week, when the talmidim were gathered together behind locked doors out of fear of the Judeans, Yeshua came, stood in the middle and said, "*Shalom aleikhem!*" (John 20: 19) CJB

"Shalom" is a greeting which means "peace, welfare, health and success" while establishing a foundation on which a relationship or discussion can be built. "Aleikhem" is plural for "you". "*Shalom aleikhem*" were the Lord's first words to them during this dangerous time. And it was a very dangerous time indeed. The disciples were terrified. They thought their Lord had died for good on that cross; they were also hiding from some powerful, murderous Judean people, those who were hostile towards the Lord Yeshua's ministry. And Peter, one of the Lord's closest friends, denied he even knew the Yeshua/ Jesus when questioned about Him by a servant girl.

Jesus was aware of their fears and concerns. So He said to them "*Shalom aleikhem*", a greeting from God to bring peace, well being, success and strength to His scared and weakened children. It was an invitation, an exhortation to encounter such blessings by building a foundation based on God's own Son, Yeshua the Messiah. *Shalom aleikhem.*

> **Therefore, everyone who listens to these words of mine and acts on them will be like a sensible man who built his house on a rock. Rain came down, floods rose, gales blew and hurled themselves against that house, and it did not fall: it was founded on rock. (Matthew 7: 24 – 25)**

In Luke 24: 36 – 42 the Lord comforted His disciples further by proving to them He indeed had risen. He showed them the wounds on His hands and feet and He ate a piece of grilled fish in their presence. Verse 41 says their joy was so great they were dumbfounded. Yeshua then opened up their understanding of the scriptures and made confirmed a promise He had made to them before, on the night of His arrest.

> **And now I am sending upon you what the Father has promised. Stay in the city, then, until you are clothed with power from on high. (Luke 24: 49)**

Shortly thereafter, the Holy Spirit came and entered these men, turning them into fearless leaders of the Christian faith who would transform the world forever. We read in the book of Acts that Peter and another disciple named John were questioned about healing a crippled beggar:

> **Then Peter, filled with the Holy Spirit, addressed them, "Rulers of the people and elders! If you are questioning us today about an act of kindness to a cripple and asking us how he was healed, you must know, all of you, and the whole people of Israel, that it is by the**

name of Jesus Christ the Nazarene, whom you crucified, and God raised from the dead, by this name and by no other that this man stands before you cured. This is the stone, which you, the builders, rejected but which has become the cornerstone. Only in him is there salvation; for of all the names in the world given to men, this is the only one by which we can be saved." They were astonished at the fearlessness shown by Peter and John, considering that they were uneducated laymen, and they recognized them as associates of Jesus. (Acts: 4: 9 – 13)

The Lord promises to hear our prayers and not merely give us strength, but instead to BE our strength. How? When we keep our focus on God and receiving his Holy Spirit, instead of worrying about the problem or challenge around us, we can rest assured that the Lord's peace will come to us and shield us. He'll take over this problem and guide us in any action we may need to take. His strength will live in us! *Shalom aleikhem.*

A few months ago, the Lord guide me towards some work training a group in anti terrorism and self defense. A large man charged at me during this session (It was all in fun) and I stopped his charge by jabbing my fingertips into his chest while he was in mid step. He fell backwards, completely immobilized.

At this point my return to teaching classes like this was recent because of my injury and years had passed since attempting any finger striking movements against ruffians of all sizes. Although I'd stopped my "attacker" cold, I felt pain in my right middle finger afterwards. The part of the finger above the last joint just hung loosely. I could not straighten it or more it in any way. It just hung like a dead piece of skin. It had no feeling at all.

I had my finger examined by a therapist at a clinic the next day. He said there was nothing anyone could do. The nerves were torn and only surgery could provide a slim chance of recovery. "My son had the same thing happened years ago," he said, shaking his head sadly. "The end of his pinky still just hangs down. I'm sorry."

Naturally I was upset and told the Lord the man's words that evening.

The Lord didn't say anything. He just laughed! His laugh wasn't at my predicament; rather it was at the therapist's "diagnosis". Well that was encouraging. So in faith, I exercised the finger over the next few weeks, praising the Lord as I did. My finger is now perfectly straight and normal again. Now I too can give a "Ha ha!" at what I was told at the clinic. As Scripture says:

> **Believe me, God neither spurns anyone of integrity, nor lends his aid to the evil. Once again laughter may fill your mouth and cries of joy break from your lips. (Job 8: 21)**

This is how our relationship with God should be! If we are right with Him, we'll be able to ask Him anything, large or small (for me, having a dead finger was big deal) and know that He will respond. The Bible says:

> **Blessed be *ADONAI*, for he heard my voice as I prayed for mercy. *ADONAI* is my strength and shield; in him my heart trusted, and I have been helped. Therefore my heart is filled with joy, and I will sing praises to him. *ADONAI* is strength for [his people], a stronghold of salvation to his anointed. Save your people! Bless your heritage! Shepherd them and carry them forever! (Psalm 28: 6 – 9) CJB**

As we see, this passage starts out with worshiping the Lord by blessing Him and expressing trust in Him. By doing so, our focus goes to God and His ability and willingness to meet our need, instead of focusing over the stress of the concern. The psalm continues with God's promise of divine intervention and safety. It ends with a reminder of the promise that God will "shepherd" or guide us. We are assured that His Spirit will let us know if there is any action we need to take.

Words like "my strength and shield," "the strength for his people" and "carry them forever" remind us how God's strength takes over and lives in His people. We can confidently expect to "be helped" and with this, experience gladness in our heart that comes not from what may happen around us, but rather from God's strength within us. We'll then find ourselves in God's "secret place" for us.

OUR ADVOCATE

The Lord is our defender, our Lawyer of lawyers. He contends with those who contend against us, whether it is in the workplace, a courtroom, some public opinion news or anything and anyplace else. A police officer once pulled me over on a dark road. I was on my way to an evening Christmas party at church and the officer believed he had seen me weaving over the yellow line. The road did have a crooked line and a z shaped curve at one point, and perhaps I didn't follow the curve well. I don't know. In any case he flashed those red and blue lights and pulled me over.

My wallet slipped out of my grasp and fell under my seat as the officer approached the car. As I rolled down the window he began to yell at me, "How many drinks have you had!? How many drinks have you had!?" in a military, alpha male tone of voice. "None", I answered, looking at him calmly in the face.

The officer ordered me to hand him my license and I answered by saying it was under my seat. He didn't seem to hear me and yelled once again "Show me your license!"

"It fell under my seat," I explained. He yelled at me to get out of the car. I began to do so and as I got out I saw my wallet on the on the floor between the seat and the door. It was very visible. I reached for it, praying the following in my mind:

Every evil spirit here trying to cause trouble, I order you in the name of Jesus to go to the foot of the cross and be dealt with by the Lord.

Now there are Christians who believe we need to say things like this out loud because demons can't read our thoughts. But mental prayers like this are calling on God's power to hear our thoughts and respond to them. These prayers are not relying on demons being able to hear. Besides, the prayer worked in my situation and other Christians praying likewise have said the same.

The change in the officer's manner was immediate after I prayed. He calmed down so much he seemed like a completely different person. At the time I was nearing the end of those legal challenges mentioned in an earlier chapter. The officer went to his car and did a background check on me. He came back very friendly and mentioned nothing other than that he'd been concerned I'd be the first person he arrested for "driving under the influence" during the Christmas season. He wished me well and let me go without even a ticket. The Lord truly defended me in what could have been a volatile situation. He fought against what was fighting with me. We read in the book of Isaiah:

> **"I myself shall fight those who fight you and I myself shall save your children." (Isaiah 49: 25)**

Later in the same book we can also read:

> **It is I who created the craftsman who blows on the coals and forges weapons suited to their purpose; I also created the destroyer to work havoc. No weapon made will prevail against you. In court you will refute every accusation. The servants of *ADONAI* inherit**

all this; the reward for their righteousness is from me. (Isaiah 54: 16 – 17) CJB

If we look at Jesus' example, He was insulted, beaten, spat on, lied about, falsely accused of many things and there was one thing that Herod, Pontius Pilate and his other accusers noticed about Him: His silence. Scripture says:

> Pilate put to him this question, 'Are you the king of the Jews?" He replied, "It is you who say it.' And the chief priests brought many accusations against him. Pilate questioned him again, 'Have you no reply at all? See how many accusations they are bringing against you!' But, to Pilate's surprise, Jesus made no further reply. (Mark 15: 2 – 5)

We also read the prophecy about Jesus in the book of Isaiah:

> Ill-treated and afflicted, he never opened his mouth, like a lamb led to the slaughter-house, like a sheep dumb before its shearers he never opened his mouth. (Isaiah 53: 7)

The apostle Peter gives us insight into why Jesus was silent in the face of all this attack:

> He was insulted and did not retaliate with insults; when he was suffering he made no threats but put his trust in the upright judge. (1 Peter 2: 23)

God acted uprightly regarding this. His power allowed Jesus to rise from the dead three days later and show His disciples that they too would rise from the dead by trusting in Him. Jesus' teachings went on to spread rapidly throughout the whole world, and thousands were healed and saved. The lives of Jesus' persecutors fell apart soon after. We can read about this in the book of Acts:

> A day was fixed, and Herod, wearing his robes of state and seated on a throne, began to make a speech to them. The people acclaimed him with, "It is a god speaking, not a man!" and at that moment the angel of the Lord struck him down, because he had not given the glory to God. He was eaten away by worms and died. The word of God continued to spread and to gain followers. (Acts 12: 21 – 24)

According to Jewish philosopher Philo of Alexandria, Pontius Pilate was removed from office due to many complaints about him to the Roman government offices in Syria. He was recalled to Rome where he was never seen again.

Jesus' enemies, the legalistic religious leaders and their followers would soon fade into oblivion after the Romans destroyed Jerusalem in 70 AD, while Christianity would continue to spread like wild fire and transform thousands of lives. Even now, Jesus continues to touch, heal and save lives in every corner of the world to this very day.

If you suffer condemning attacks, gossip, judgments, slander or any other kind of weapon against you, ask the Holy Spirit of God to come to your defense as Advocate. Trust in the scriptural promises we've read and praise and thank God for the good He's going to perform in your situation.

You can pray like this:

Heavenly Father, I praise You and thank You for your great love for me and on those who call on your Holy Name. I come to You in worship, thanking You that I can give You this _____.
(Name your concern.)

I thank You for allowing every word that has been said against me, knowing that You promise in Isaiah 49: 25 to contend with those who contend with me. Send your Holy Spirit to come and defend me! Come and live in me, Holy Spirit! You set me free from the pride of man.

Lord, I worship and adore You, knowing that You take things like any injustice and turn them into good, as your word says in Romans 8: 28. Take all the details and circumstances of what has been said against me and use them for the glory of your Wonderful Name. Your Holy Spirit is my Defender, my Advocate.

Holy Spirit of God, thank You for defending me from those who rise up against me as You did for Jesus, the Son of God. Use everything that has been said and done against me as blessings to draw me closer to the Lord. Use them for my good, and the good of everyone else you wish, so others may see that You live!

I bless those who rise up against me. Use their actions as part of your perfect plan to draw these people closer to You for their good and your glory. May they quickly know your displeasure at their choices so they may repent. And should they harden their hearts even more against You, I will continue to bless them and pray that You be glorified in all this as You restore justice and goodness to this situation.

I bless and do not curse, for I don't wish to give anyone or anything any power over me nor do I wish to disobey You. You are the all powerful God, El Shaddai who will contend with those who contend with me. You are the maker of all, and I know that no weapon formed against me shall prosper. Great is your holy name Lord Jesus! Amen.

Of course if a sudden occurrence doesn't give you the time for a long prayer like this, short ones like the one I used while with the officer work well too. The Lord is our strength and our shield! Rest peacefully, knowing that the Holy Spirit will come and be your Defense. He will intervene for you in your circumstance, and if needed, He will also give you the words to use at the right moment if He wishes you to speak. You need not worry about having to defend yourself. Jesus says:

> 'When they take you before synagogues and magistrates and authorities, do not worry about how to defend yourselves or what to say, because when the time comes, the Holy Spirit will teach you what you should say.' (Luke 12: 11 – 13)

We have this wonderful promise as well:

> Safe in your presence you hide them, far from human plotting, shielding them in your tent, far from contentious tongues. (Psalm 31: 20)

Yes, we can find ourselves in God's secret place for us again. The apostle Paul also writes that the Lord will defend us even when no one else will:

> The first time I had to present my defense, no one came into court to support me. Every one of them deserted me – may they not be held accountable for it. But the Lord stood by me and gave me power, so that through me the message might be fully proclaimed for all the gentiles to hear; and so I was saved from the lion's mouth. The Lord will rescue me from all evil attempts on me, and bring me safely to his heavenly kingdom. To him be glory forever and ever. Amen. (2 Timothy 4: 16 – 18)

Just remember to keep your focus on the Lord, not the trial you face. Keep an attitude of praise and thanksgiving, as you'll see throughout the prayers in this book and the scriptures listed. God will deliver! He always does.

Author's Note

When the Lord Yeshua was fasting in the desert, the devil tried to convince Him to break His fast by using His power to change stones into loaves of bread. Yeshua/Jesus responded in this way:

> **But he replied, 'Scripture says: Human beings live not on bread alone but on every word that comes from the mouth of God.' (Matthew 4: 4)**

Yeshua defeated the devil and his temptations by using the Word of God. To know God, you must know what He says. Knowing and living His Word, the Bible, is crucial to your well being, like air, food and water. When you treasure His word, it shows you are willing to listen to Him and learn what He wishes from you. When His Word is firmly in your mind, body, soul and spirit, He can use you and mold you the way He desires. You will also be equipped to deal with the battles you will encounter on this earth.

Ask for the Lord's Holy Spirit to teach you and touch your heart as you read. You will find that you will begin to delight in His Word and will experience great joy, peace, healing and wisdom through the love you see He has for you.

You don't have to get into a rigid routine of having to read a chapter of some Bible book a day, or an entire book weekly, etc. If God's Spirit speaks to you in a verse or passage, keep your spirit open to pause and meditate on it. If one of His promises leaps out at you, claim it! Make it yours. Memorize it by meditating, reflecting or resting on it. Recall it throughout the day and night. God's will for you is that you meditate on His Word day and night. The Lord says:

> **How can a young man keep his way spotless? By keeping your words. In my heart I treasure your promises to avoid sinning against you. (Psalm 119: 9, 11)**

Have the book of this Law always on your lips; meditate on it day and night, so that you may carefully keep everything that is written in it. Then your undertakings will prosper, then you will have success. (Joshua 1: 8)

Can you recall important passages in God's Word and find them or quote them as His Son Jesus did when He defeated the devil in the desert? When you can, you will be better equipped to face the world.

"So take heart! I have overcome the world!" Jesus says. "The victory is mine! Through me, by knowing, loving, and following my Word, it is my desire that my disciples live in victory too!" (1 John 5: 3 – 5)

Points to Remember as You Read

If you are new to reading the Bible, the books of John and Acts are good books to start with. They are easy to read, full of Jesus' teachings, and detail much of the Christian Church history. Ask the Lord to send His Holy Spirit to guide you in your reading. If you sense the Holy Spirit is leading you to spend a little more time thinking, praying, or meditating on a passage, then do so. Let God teach you in this way. Jesus says:

"But the Paraclete, the Holy Spirit, whom the Father will send in My name will teach you everything and remind you of all I have said to you." (John 14: 26)

The book of Psalms is excellent for praising and adoring God, and you will most certainly find psalms that will speak to your heart. They are not only wonderful ways of worshiping God, they also encourage us to be honest in how we express ourselves to the Lord.

The psalms have many different emotions throughout them all so you're sure to find more than a few psalms that will become your friends. Many of them were written by King David, one who God said was "a man after my own heart." You can read the story of David in the books of 1 Samuel, 2 Samuel and 1 Chronicles.

The book of Proverbs will serve you well if you are in search of God's wisdom for daily life. You'll find a lot of godly wisdom by reading a few verses of this book every day. Ask Him to give you wisdom as you read the verses in Proverbs and have faith that He will give it to you generously. The Lord says:

If any of you lacks wisdom, let him ask of God, who gives to all liberally without reproach, and it will be given to him.   (James 1: 5)

Solomon is an example of someone whom God gave wisdom to liberally. When he asked the Lord for wisdom this is how God responded.

"Here and now I do what you ask. I give you a heart wise and shrewd as no one has had before and no one will have after you." (1 Kings 3: 12)

Solomon, David's son wrote the book of Proverbs in which we can all find much helpful advice for wise living. And look at what King David wrote in Psalm 119:

How I love your Law! I ponder it all day long. You make me wiser than my enemies by your commandment which is mine forever. I am wiser than all my teachers because I ponder your instructions. I have more understanding than the aged because I keep your precepts. (Psalm 119: 97 – 100)

All this is true! As I've written about already, being people who love God's Word and meditate upon it all the time has allowed us to be victorious over difficult decisions, stress, crisis, sickness, family problems, physical dangers, dangerous enemies, loneliness, lack of purpose, death and much more!

By this time now you've seen dozens and dozens of beautiful promises to us in God's Word and testimonies of these promises coming true in this life time. There's a love more intense than we can possibly imagine in each one of them. How can one read these and not begin to love every word the Lord has spoken to us? We should live for them and meditate on them day and night!

Scriptures

He humbled you, allowing you to become hungry, and then fed you with *man*, which neither you nor your ancestors had ever known, to make you understand that a person does not live on food alone but on everything that comes from the mouth of *ADONAI*. (Deuteronomy 8: 3) CJB

(Author's note: "Man" means "bread" in Hebrew)

Have the book of this Law always on your lips; meditate on it day and night, so that you may carefully keep everything that is written in it. Then your undertakings will prosper, then you will have success. (Joshua 1: 8)

How can a young man keep his way spotless? By keeping your words. With all my heart I seek you, do not let me stray from your commandments. In my heart I treasure your promises, to avoid sinning against you. (Psalm 119: 9 – 11)

The word of God is something alive and active: it cuts more incisively than any two – edged sword: it can seek out the place where soul is divided from spirit, or joints from marrow; it can pass judgment on secret emotions and thoughts. (Hebrews 4:12)

All scripture is inspired by God and useful for refuting error, for guiding people's lives and teaching them to be upright. (2 Timothy 3:16)

For *ADONAI* gives wisdom; from his mouth comes knowledge and understanding. (Proverbs 2: 6) CJB

Chapter 16

Fasting in Prayer

When we have been honest before the Lord and we ask the Lord for the permission, blessing and strength to fast in prayer, we can be confident of receiving these things. Fasting can open the door for us to enter into the resources in God's power. It gets us to move past our "flesh" nature in our prayer and lets our spirit dominate us instead. Our spirit is what we should want to approach the throne of God in prayer, not our flesh.

The "flesh" refers to the inherent human desire to do evil or wish to please one's self at the cost of being displeasing to God. A more modern term would be "self indulgence". Wanting worldly comforts instead of God, desiring things such as emotional fulfillment through an object or person, ego, greed, constant complaining, impatience, disobedience, fear, lust, etc. are examples of how our "flesh" or self indulgent nature can manifest itself. God's Word says:

> When self – indulgence is at work the results are obvious: sexual vice, impurity and sensuality, the worship of false gods and sorcery; antagonisms and rivalry, jealousy, bad temper and quarrels, disagreements, factions and malice, drunkenness, orgies and all such things. And about these, I tell you now as I have told you in the past, that people who behave in these ways will not inherit the kingdom of God. (Galatians 5: 19 – 21)

If we are honest and humble before the Lord and seeking to draw closer to Him in fasting, we can discipline ourselves against self indulgence or the flesh.

I punish my body and bring it under control, to avoid any risk that, having acted as herald for others, I myself may be disqualified. (1 Corinthians 9: 27)

Fasting, when done in honesty, humility and love for God, can thus increase the effectiveness of our prayers. Kevin P. Joyce, Ph.D., on page 13 in his booklet "Liberation from the Seven Deadly Sins (Plus One)" says the following about fasting: "Controlling the desire for food and drink was very important to the desert monks. Why? If I can eat and drink moderately then I can more be moderate with other more complex thoughts, such as thoughts related to sexual desires, the craving for possessions, and angry impulses. By pulling one leg of the table, the other three legs come along at the same time. For example, fasting is recommended as an antidote for lust. I can use the food thought as a training tool. If I am compulsive in my ways of eating and drinking, the thought of food or drink consumes my mind. This is reversed by fasting."

The practice of fasting is widespread throughout the Bible. In the book of Esther, Chapter 4: 15 – 17, we see that Esther asked her friends to fast and pray with her during a crisis; she had to win the king's favor to protect her Jewish people from destruction. In the book of Nehemiah, chapter 1: 1 – 11, we can read that Nehemiah fasted in repentance for the nation of Israel.

In 1 Kings Chapter 21: 27 –28, the evil King Ahab humbled himself by putting on sackcloth and fasting in order to request God's judgment be lifted. When the Lord saw how he had repented, the judgment was not carried out in King Ahab's lifetime.

In Matthew Chapter 4: 1 – 2, and Luke Chapter 4: 1 – 2, we see that Jesus fasted for prolonged periods before beginning His earthly ministry.

In Acts 9: 1 – 18, we read that Paul fasted for 3 days before receiving the Holy Spirit and beginning his ministry. Jesus Christ, when speaking about fasting to His disciples said,

"When you are fasting, do not put on a gloomy look as the hypocrites do: they go about looking unsightly to let people know they are fasting. In truth I tell you, they have had their reward. But when you fast, put scent on your head and wash your face, so that no one will know you are fasting except your Father who sees all that is done in secret; and your Father who sees all that is done in secret will reward you." (Matthew 6: 16 – 18)

Please notice that Jesus said *"When* you fast", not *"If* you fast." He assumed His followers would fast in the future and He gave them specific directions for doing so.

Fasting can take a powerful role in your prayer activities and spiritual walk. Just be sure that you are determined to minister to the Lord when you fast. Remember, it's all about Him. Ask for Him to lead you in your fast and examine your motives for fasting. Be specific in your prayer petitions and humble yourself. The Lord says:

> **Humility towards one another must be the garment you all wear**
> **constantly, because God opposes the proud but accords his favour**
> **to the humble. Bow down, then, before the power of God now, so**
> **that he may raise you up in due time. (1 Peter 5: 5 – 6)**

As we read the Lord Jesus' words to us in the gospel of Matthew, we saw that Jesus expected fasting to be a regular part of our lives as Christians. He Himself fasted in the wilderness and He also told us that fasting would be rewarded by God. This can happen of course only if we are not letting sin separate us from God. Certain people of Israel once thought they would be right with God simply by performing fasting as if it were a magical ritual. They didn't hear from God after fasting and they had no idea why. The reason was because their sin and disobedience had separated them from God so He would not listen to their cry. The prophet Isaiah said the following to them:

> **Your guilty deeds have made a gulf between you and your God.**
> **Your sins have made him hide his face from you so as not to hear**
> **you. (Isaiah 59: 2)**

God was concerned with their motives as well as their behavior. Their fasting would be useless until they dealt with their sin. Remember Psalm 139: 23 – 24. Use it! Let the Lord examine your heart and see if there is any way in you that is displeasing to Him. Confess any wrongdoing and repent or turn away from it. Isaiah's rebuke to the unrepentant of Israel shows that fasting alone, when done only as a ritual doesn't make anyone right with God.

The Lord is also pleased when people humble themselves before Him. Bible heroes such as Moses, Samuel, Daniel, Nehemiah and others prayed for their nation with fasting, mourning, wearing sackcloth, confessing sins, weeping and other humbling actions. Not only is fasting used with confession of sin, it is also used when we face circumstances beyond our control. These Bible heroes sought God's favor through fasting and these other humbling actions and they received it.

Let's talk a little bit more about circumstances beyond our control, those which may even seem like impossible ones. Are you at risk because of a stand you have to take between right and wrong? Is there a physical or spiritual enemy (or both) coming against you? We've spent some time on that already. Are you or someone you care about threatened by danger, serious disease, financial disaster, a crumbling marriage, rebellious children or other problems?

What are you going to do? Try to "figure out" how everything works in your situation? That's what some people encouraged me to do when I had my legal problems. "Run over to the law school at such and such university," they said. "Find so and so to help you. Write and call so and so as well" they said. "Come on! What are you waiting for? Get moving!"

That's how the world thinks. Had I done that I'd be a nervous wreck with only more legal problems and a separation between my Lord that would have been fatal. I would have given more of my time, energy and spiritual focus to the problem than to Him. The "problem" would have become my "false god" or "idol", and thus I'd be setting myself up for disaster.

Children, be on your guard against false gods. (1 John 5: 20)

I thank Him that whenever I considered what the world counseled me to do, I would get a lack of peace right away. The Lord gave me a strong, guarding radar that prevented me from trying to "figure out" things. He also blessed me with the faith to humble myself through honest prayer, confession and repentance; I praised, thanked and glorified the Lord in the situation and sought His face, waiting to hear from Him and walking in obedience. That is the true formula for winning. I'll say it again.

For the Christian, the true formula for winning is in humbling one's self through honest prayer, confession and repentance, always praising, thanking and glorifying the Lord in the situation, seeking His face, waiting to hear from Him and walking in obedience.

In the book of Joel, we see that Judah was left in devastation after a locust plague. The prophet Joel challenged them to respond with these steps:

Priests, put on sackcloth and lament! You ministers of the altar, wail! Come here, lie in sackcloth all night long, you ministers of God! For the Temple of your God has been deprived of cereal offering and libation. Order a fast, proclaim a solemn assembly. (Joel 1: 13 – 14)

A "solemn assembly" was a group of persons coming together before God who realized that their crisis was as great as was their sin, and both of these things were all of their responsibility, not those of a private individual.

Because the Lord our God is holy, He cannot ignore sin. That must be addressed. A fast is useless without sin being recognized in the life of the individual or individuals; the sin must be recognized, confessed, repented of, and rejected or it will be judged.

And you? Will you choose to draw near to the Lord's heart by fasting, ensuring that there is no sin between you and the Lord. Will you fast and pray, seeking God's mercy and compassion for your family, your church, your ministry, your neighborhood, community or nation? Please consider seriously what great things could happen if you chose to do so.

There are seven types of fasts mentioned in the Bible:

I.   The 3 Day Fast – involves giving up all food and drink for three days. Its purpose is for God's help during a crisis. As mentioned earlier, this is the type of fast Esther used to pray for the survival of her people. Read Esther, chapter 4: 15 – 17.

II. The 21 Day Partial Fast – involves giving up choice foods like bread, starchy food, meat, and wine. You limit your meals to vegetables, fruits, and fish. The purpose of the 21- day fast is to seek God's revelation for you in prayer. Read chapter 10 in the book of Daniel to see how fasting and prayer allowed Daniel to gain insight into a message he had received concerning a great war.

III. The 1 Day Fast – involves humbling yourself in prayer and going 24 hours without food. This type of fast is used for reexamining yourself spiritually, and consecrating yourself or a situation to the Lord. King David is believed to have written about having done this for others in Psalm 35. He wrote:

> But I, when they were ill, had worn sackcloth, and mortified myself with fasting, praying ever anew in my heart, as if for a friend or brother; I had wandered restless, as if mourning a mother, so bowed had I been in sorrow. (Psalm 35: 13 – 14)

IV. Another 1 Day Fast – involves going 24 hours again without food. The purpose of fasting in this way would be for deliverance from some trial or concern. Fasting in this way is mentioned in Ezra 8: 23. Ezra proclaimed a one day fast for the community as a way of humbling themselves and asking God for a safe journey for their families. Ezra felt ashamed to ask the king for protection because of a comment he said to him earlier. The community fasted and petitioned God and He answered them.

V. No Duration Fast – is to go without food for no set duration as part of a petition for God for a judgment to be lifted. This is detailed in the book of 1 Kings 21: 27 – 28. In this biblical account, the prophet Elijah tells Ahab, an evil king, that God was going to bring disaster upon the king, his family, and country. When Ahab heard this, he tore his clothes, fasted, and went around meekly. When the Lord noticed how he had humbled himself, he decided to bring this disaster down upon the days of Ahab's son, instead of the king.

VI. Another 3 Day Fast – is used for healing. The book of 1 Samuel 30:1 – 12 tells of the time David and his men arrived to the city of Ziklag, to find it burned down by the Amalekites who also took their sons and daughters in this raid. David's men became very bitter at seeing this and began talking of stoning him. David became greatly distressed and went without food or water for 3 days. He found strength in the Lord, who told him to overtake the raiding party. David did so (1 Samuel: 30:13 – 20), and was successful in the rescue.

VII. 40 Day Fast – is the last of the seven types of fasts. It is used for dominion. In Luke 4: 1 – 2, we read that Jesus used this fast when He defeated the devil in the desert. In this type of fast, it is important that the Lord has spoken for you to do this. This kind of fast can only be completed with the supernatural strength from the Lord.

Remember this valuable advice concerning fasting beyond one day:

1. Check with your doctor.
2. Come to fast longer periods slowly.
3. On the 21-day partial fast, follow the same advice as fasts that are longer than a day.
4. For anything longer than 21 days, make sure that God has really spoken to you to do this.

In coming out of fasts there should be a gradual return to normal eating to give your body chance to get used to regular meals again.

1. Day one – have juice only.
2. Day two – add fruit because it's easy to digest.
3. Day three – add soup to the juice and fruit.
4. Day four – add salads to the rest.
5. Day five – add breads
6. Day six – add fish or chicken
7. Day seven – resume normal eating habits.

I encourage you to prayerfully make fasting a part of your spiritual walk with God. You will find your faith strengthened and your spirit will dominate over your body. Above all, fasting can allow you to enter into a much greater intimacy with the Lord. Throw your will away! Seek His! Starve your body and feed your soul in prayer and God's Word. Starve that will, smash it, trample it; don't even let it breathe! Seek God's will in patient silence, having no barriers between you and Him. Let Him greatly bless you with the strength, direction and clear speaking He gives to you!

Father in heaven, holy are You and worthy of all my love and praise. Teach me please how to make fasting a part of my walk with You. May I be honest before You and obedient in all You ask me to do, so I may please You and You may bless me greatly. May I toss my will away like ashes in the wind. I seek yours and long to humble myself before You that You may lift me up in your good time. Strengthen me and give me the desire and love for You to fast. Speak to me, direct me, show me the wonderful things You want me to do for You, so that You may be glorified. In Jesus' holy name I pray. Amen

Barukh ata Eloheinu, ki tov ata
(Blessed are You, our God for You are good.)

Chapter 17

The Armor of God

Finally, grow strong in the Lord, with the strength of his power. Put on the full armour of God so as to be able to resist the devil's tactics. For it is not against human enemies that we have to struggle, but against the principalities and the ruling forces who are masters of the darkness in this world, the spirits of evil in the heavens. That is why you must take up all God's armour, or you will not be able to put up any resistance on the evil day, or stand your ground even though you exert yourselves to the full. (Ephesians 6: 10 – 13)

What is the armor that the Apostle Paul writes about with such an urgent tone? It is a special spiritual protection given to us by our Heavenly Father. Do you really need it? Absolutely. Your life depends on it. When you draw closer to God or begin a ministry that leads others to Him, you can be assured of being targeted for attack by Satan, the enemy of God.

Whenever you expose one of the devil's schemes against humanity or do anything that will strike a blow against the devil, his territory, or his evil forces, you can be assured of being placed on his hit list. Being on Satan's attack list is good; it shows you are walking with the Lord. Only those who, by choice, are on Satan's side or those who are so spiritually dead they aren't even a concern of the devil are left alone by this vicious enemy for a while.

Attacks on us by the devilish underworld can assume many forms: depression, guilt, pride, confusion, fear, greed, insecurity, illness, irritating inconveniences, paranormal assault, nightmares, temptations, and many others.

Years ago I went through some great challenges in a business I'd started. Turning to the Lord in the midst of these troubles I soon experienced His peace and guidance. The Lord used my business concerns as a means of drawing me to Himself and I was blessed with a great prayer life. Early morning time with His Holy Spirit led me to pray for the neighborhood around my business as well as the community around me, which had experienced multiple murders within the last few months.

I felt God leading me to write this book and it gave me great joy to know that the Lord desired to use my writing to bring help and healing to the community around me. I found myself wondering how God was going to change the circumstances of my hectic work schedule to allow this.

One dark morning, I awoke to feel an evil presence hovering over me in the bed, a presence filled with hatred so cold it was overwhelming. The next thing I knew, I felt the pressure of what seemed to be two invisible hands grasp the lapels of my shirt and shove me downwards with a power much like the maddening descent of an out-of-control roller coaster. Only this was no fun ride; it felt like a life and death struggle as the bed seemed to drop, amid forceful jerks, into some bottomless hole.

I began to panic and tried to use the name of Jesus to rebuke what obviously was a demonic attack, but as I tried to speak, I felt a third hand shove into my windpipe. The other two hands still gripped me. I was locked, completely helpless.

Finally, agonizing moments later, the pressure released, and I was free. I lay in bed, terrified, unsure whether what I'd experienced was real or just some twisted nightmare.

The hip injury I mentioned earlier in this book was recent at this point in my life; it was only a few weeks old. The pain of it became worse after the night's incident. I prayed for the Lord to heal me but healing didn't happen back then. Between this pain, (which was making it hard to work), the incident of the other night, and the stress of the business, I felt abandoned by the Lord.

The result of all this was I backed off on my prayer life and put all plans of this book away. I became content to continue sinking all of my energies into my work and business. My prayer life became sporadic and mediocre at best until the legal problems I mentioned in Chapter 8 caused me to lose my job and business eight months later.

Unemployed, in debt, and targeted by many enemies, I went running to my Heavenly Father again. He took me in His loving arms without hesitation and began working miraculous healing in me over the consequences of my many bad choices. The process was not easy; it was extremely painful to say the least.

Many mornings I would suffer from attacks of depression, guilt and fear. Other mornings it would be condemnation and grief. The anguish at times seemed like more than I could bear. In His grace, though, God led me out of these through prayer, praise, and the fellowship of Christians in my community. He also touched me by leading me to learn about using His protection, the armor described in Ephesians 6: 10 – 18.

I know now that the attack I experienced was no dream. Two other Christian authors, Chip Ingram, who wrote "The Invisible War," and Mary Baxter, author of "A Divine Revelation of Spiritual Warfare," have described experiencing attacks very similar to the one I did. (I highly recommend both of these books.)

Mr. Ingram states in his book that this form of attack I described earlier also occurred among several members of his church.

What also convinced me that my attack was no dream is that it occurred in my life several more times. Unlike the first time though, I wasn't afraid in any of those instances. The Lord's power is much greater, and through His love and grace, He allowed me to aggressively go after the source of these attacks in the name of Jesus and come out victorious.

The Lord revealed to me that He protected my spirit and I could call on the name of Jesus silently, with my spirit to win over any demonic attack. I did this once when I felt the gripping hands at my shirt and throat again. Calling on Jesus' name allowed me to shrug off the attack like a bunch of dry leaves. Praise God!

The armor of God will protect you against spiritual attack and give you the strength to stand up against attacks of the enemy, whatever form they may take. Jesus says:

> **The seventy – two came back rejoicing. 'Lord,' they said, 'even the devils submit to us when we use your name.' He said to them, 'I watched Satan fall like lightning from heaven. Look, I have given you power to tread down serpents and scorpions and the whole strength of the enemy; nothing shall ever hurt you. Yet do not rejoice that the spirits submit to you; rejoice instead that your names are written in heaven.' (Luke 10: 17 – 20)**

So we do have authority to overcome anything that comes at us from Satan but it is more important to keep our focus on Jesus and being one of His children now and in heaven.

In Paul's letter to the Ephesians, chapter six, he compares the armor of God to the equipment used by the Roman soldiers of his time. They were the fiercest fighting unit of his day, and held an empire feared throughout the world for four centuries.

The armor of God is available to all of Christ's children and should be put on daily. Here is how:

The Belt of Truth

So stand your ground, with truth a belt round your waist . . .
(Ephesians 6: 14a)

The Belt of Truth – is the first piece of armor we put on. It is crucial because it holds the rest of the armor in place. For the Roman soldier, it held his cloak in such a way to permit movement so he could protect himself. For the Christian, the belt of truth is coming before God in complete honesty and humility.

We ask the Lord to search our heart and conscience, to see if there is a sin to confess, an offense we need to resolve, a direction from God to obey, or anything else that could separate us from Him if ignored.

I've said it before, but I can't stress enough how helpful it is to include these verses in our daily prayer time:

God, examine me and know my heart, test me and know my concerns. Make sure that I am not on my way to ruin, and guide me on the road of eternity. (Psalm 139: 23 – 24)

After this, simply wait for the Spirit of God to reveal in your conscience whether there is something you need to act on. If there is, be obedient and do it right away. Otherwise you will have this blockage in your walk with God, which keeps you from experiencing God's very best in your life. It will also leave you vulnerable to the enemy since not having truth in your relationship with God separates you from Him. It forms a kink in your armor.

Disobedience also cuts you off from God's divine help. If you ask for God's guidance in something else later, how can you expect His total help if you didn't do the last thing He asked you to do? Also, to disobey the Holy Spirit, you have to harden yourself in order to ignore its soft, still voice. You will become deaf when it comes to hearing from God in the future.

Being honest in approaching God allows His strength and holiness to flow in you. David wrote how an unconfessed sin separated him from God and brought on all sorts of problems in his life:

> **I said not a word, but my bones wasted away from groaning all the day; day and night your hand lay heavy upon me; my heart grew parched as stubble in summer drought. (Psalm 32: 3 – 5)**

Honesty in our approaching of God also allows the Heavenly Father's power and protection to flow through us. This brings us to the next piece of armor:

The Breastplate of Uprightness

> **. . . and uprightness a breastplate. . . (Ephesians 6: 14b)**

The Breastplate of Uprightness – is like a spiritual bullet – proof vest. It protects our hearts, lungs, and other internal organs from feelings of condemnation, guilt, indifference, coldness, and other emotions. We have to be extremely careful in guarding our emotions because the devil can use them against us. Out of control emotions are also bad for our spiritual, mental and physical health!

We put on this spiritual breastplate by clothing ourselves with the only real righteousness there is – the righteousness of Jesus Christ. He alone is pure and holy. If our belt of truth has led us to confess and repent from a sin or apologize to someone about something, we do it immediately! Scripture says:

> **If we acknowledge our sins, he is trustworthy and upright, so that he will forgive our sins and will cleanse us from all evil. (1 John 1: 9)**

Then the Messiah's righteousness will cover us, so we can be righteous in God's sight because He sees what His Son Yeshua has done in us. The Lord Yeshua is our "Kapparah", our "atonement or expiation" from sin. The word "Kapparah" corresponds to the Hebrew "kapar" which is a root meaning of "cover" or "wipe clean". Our heavenly Father does these two things when He accepts Yeshua's atonement for our sin that we confess and repent from: He covers the sin from His sight and/or washes or wipes it away.

By acting on what the belt of truth has revealed to us, we stay in synch with God and can avoid the enemy's attacks in trying to make us feel unworthy, condemned, or unforgiven. It also keeps us from hardening our hearts to the point where we don't hear God or even feel our conscience anymore.

If our belt of truth leads us to some request from God we need to act on, we do so in obedience, and so we stay in God's will for us. Our relationship with Christ remains strong and we remain clothed in His righteousness.

So act upon what God's Spirit directs you to do when you put on the belt of truth. When you follow the Spirit's direction through action, you are placing on the breastplate of righteousness. These two pieces of armor need to work together.

Feet Fitted with the Eagerness to Share the Gospel of Peace

. . . wearing for shoes on your feet the eagerness to share the gospel of peace, ... (Ephesians 6: 15)

Feet Fitted with the Eagerness of the Gospel of Peace – is being eager and prepared to share the gospel of Jesus! Read and know God's good news (gospel), know the important fundamentals of the Christian faith. Know where you stand as one of His children.

Know that God loves us so much that He sent His Son Jesus Christ to us to die for our sins. Know that we are sinners in need of being saved by Christ. We need to be saved from the attacks on us by the world, the devil, and our own sinful nature. Jesus offers healing, forgiveness, and freedom from all these things, as well as eternal life with Him in heaven. These verses remind us of where we (and those we are going to share the gospel with) stand as children of God.

This is the testimony: God has given us eternal life, and this life is in his Son. Whoever has the Son has life. Whoever has not the Son has not life. (1 John 5: 11 – 12)

Thus, condemnation will never come to those who are in Christ Jesus, because the law of the Spirit which gives life in Christ Jesus has set you free from the law of sin and death. (Romans 8: 1- 2)

The footwear used by the Roman legions was meant to allow stability in movement for the Roman soldier. He had to have sure footing, and able to advance and conquer new territory. In the same way, we are to have strong footing or a strong foundation in our knowledge of God's Word. In addition to this, we are to conquer new territory for God, which means winning hearts over for Jesus. The gospel of Matthew says:

> **As he was walking by the Lake of Galilee he saw two brothers, Simon, who was called Peter, and his brother Andrew; they were making a cast into the lake with their net, for they were fishermen. And he said to them, 'Come after me and I will make you fishers of people.' And at once they left their nets and followed him. (Matthew 4: 18 – 20)**

The "eagerness" referred to means we are to have an enthusiastic readiness to share the gospel with whomever the Spirit leads us to share it with. Are you always ready to share what the Lord has done for you as I've done with you in this book? In the gospel of Mark, a man whom Jesus healed of demon possession asked the Lord if He could accompany Him. We can read the following verses:

> **Jesus would not let him but said to him, 'Go home to your people and tell them all that the Lord in his mercy has done for you.' So the man went off and proceeded to proclaim in the Decapolis all that Jesus had done for him. And everyone was amazed. (Mark 5: 19 – 20)**

"Decapolis" meant "the ten cities". The man who Jesus healed told people in ten cities about it! We need to do likewise. In addition to what the Lord has done for us, we have much to share in God's Word:

In Chapter two we learned that God's Word promises us peace, protection, eternal life, wisdom, healing, forgiveness, confidence and much more.

In chapters 14 and 15 we discussed how the Holy Spirit ministers to our needs as comforter, counselor, strength and advocate. Chapters three, four, eight and nine contained God's promises of victory and joy to us when we maintain an attitude of praise and thanksgiving in all circumstances.

Do you know these promises well enough to share them with others? (There are many more!) When you do know the promises in God's Word, you can be used by the Lord more to lovingly win hearts and conquer new territory for Jesus. This will keep Satan on the run as you allow the Spirit to guide you in helping God's kingdom on earth grow.

As you've probably heard, the best defense is often a good offense. I encourage you to take the promises and supporting scriptures listed in those chapters and keep them in your heart so you can share them in love with others as the Spirit leads you.

The Shield of Faith

. . . and always carrying the shield of faith so that you can use it quench the burning arrows of the Evil One. (Ephesians 6: 16)

The Shield of Faith – is used by the believer when he or she is bombarded by doubt, uncertainty, or distrust in God's care and unconditional love. Our shield of faith is an unwavering trust in the loving character of God. To have this, we in faith take God at His Word, not by our feelings.

Our feelings can be affected by the food we eat, our sleep, the weather, the amount of activity in our lives, and numerous other things. They are not a reliable indicator of God's loving presence in our lives.

God however does not change, lie, or fail to keep His promises. So we must choose to believe what He says to us in His Word. We know from the Bible that He is perfectly good in character, He loves us, and He always wants the best for us. We must choose to believe this, and not what our senses perceive to be happening based on things around us. Here are some scriptures that reveal the character of God:

> **Can a woman forget her baby at the breast, feel no pity for the child she has borne? Even if these were to forget, I shall not forget you. Look, I have engraved you on the palms of my hands, your ramparts are ever before me. (Isaiah 49:15 – 16)**

> **But the mercy of *ADONAI* on those who fear him is from eternity past to eternity future, and his righteousness extends to his children's children, provided they keep his covenant and remember to follow his precepts. (Psalm 103: 17 – 18) CJB**

> **For *ADONAI*, God, is a sun and a shield; *ADONAI* bestows favor and honor; he will not withhold anything good from those whose lives are pure. *ADONAI-Tzva' ot*, how happy is anyone who trusts in you! (Psalm 84: 11 – 12) CJB**

> **Unload all your burden on to him, since he is concerned about you. (1 Peter 5: 7)**

> **Since he did not spare his own Son, but gave him up for the sake of all of us, then can we not expect that with him he will freely give us all his gifts? (Romans 8: 32)**

Yeshua also says:

> **The sheep that belong to me listen to my voice; I know them and they follow me. I give them eternal life; they will never be lost and no one will ever steal them from my hand. The Father, for what he has given me, is greater than anyone, and no one can steal anything from the Father's hand. The Father and I are one. (John 10: 27 – 30)**

By reading and meditating on these scriptures, we can build up our faith by trusting in God's character and His Word, not our feelings. This faithful trust is our impenetrable shield. God's Word says:

> **God is no human being that he should lie, no child of Adam to change his mind. Is it his to say and not to do, is it his to speak and not fulfill? (Numbers 23: 19)**

We can also trust that God has our best in mind at all times. His plans and timing for us are always perfect. Have faith in this and experience His peace.

> **'For I know what plans I have in mind for you,' says *ADONAI.* 'plans for well-being, not for bad things; so that you can have hope and a future. When you call to me and pray to me, I will listen to you. When you seek me, you will find me, provided you seek for me whole-heartedly; and I will let you find me,' says *ADONAI.* (Jeremiah 29: 11 – 14) CJB**

> **We are well aware that God works with those who love him, those who have been called in accordance with his purpose, and turns everything to their good. (Romans 8: 28)**

> **I waited patiently for *ADONAI,* till he turned toward me and heard my cry. He brought me up from the roaring pit, up from the muddy ooze, and set my feet on a rock, making my footing firm. He put a new song in my mouth, a song of praise to our God. Many will look on in awe and put their trust in *ADONAI.* (Psalm 40: 1 – 3) CJB**

So we take up our shield of faith when we trust in God's character and His Word, which both tell of His immeasurable love for us, and His desire for the very best for us, in His perfect timing and plan. We don't let our feelings, the world's voice, or the voice of Satan cause us to doubt these things.

The Helmet of Salvation

And then you must take salvation as your helmet . . . (Ephesians 6: 17a)

The Helmet of Salvation – protects our minds in the spiritual battles we are sure to encounter in our Christian walk. The Lord promises to guard our minds if we stay close to Him, trust Him, and give praise and thanks in everything.

> **Never worry about anything; but tell God all your desires of every kind in prayer and petition shot through with gratitude, and the peace of God which is beyond our understanding will guard your hearts and your thoughts in Christ Jesus. (Philippians 4: 6 – 7)**

> **God did not give us a spirit of timidity, but the Spirit of power and of love and self control. (2 Timothy 1: 7)**

Some Bible translations translate the Greek for "self control" as being "sound mind". The Lord promises us this soundness, this control over our thoughts through the power of His Spirit living in us. His Spirit brings us life and peace:

> **And human nature has nothing to look forward to but death, while the Spirit looks forward to life and peace, because the outlook of disordered human nature is opposed to God, since it does not submit to God's Law, and indeed it cannot, and those who live by their natural inclinations can never be pleasing to God. (Romans 8: 6)**

> **"A person whose desire rests on you, you preserve in perfect peace, because he trusts in you." (Isaiah 26: 3) CJB**

So whenever you start getting anxious, fearful, negative, or depressed, you have the right as a child of God to tell those things to leave in the name of Jesus:

"Spirit of fear, spirit of negativity, spirit of depression, get away from me in the name of Jesus. I am a child of the King of kings and you have no right or place over me. Leave me and don't come back!"

Ask the Lord to renew you by filling you with His Holy Spirit of power, love and soundness of mind. He'll do it.

"Holy Spirit of my Savior Jesus come to me and fill me. Flow through me and send me your love, power and soundness of mind. Thank You, Jesus. Amen.

Remember God's Word, which promises to give you a sound mind, one that is steadfast and guarded in Jesus.

In previous chapters, we learned the importance of going to God with all our concerns, no matter how small or large. We pray in praise and thanksgiving, and by doing so, we direct our energies to Him, instead of to the problem. We practice worship in this way, and worship always pleases God. What He will do then is give us His peace and will deliver us from whatever circumstance is troubling us, either by changing us, changing the circumstance or both.

The Sword of the Spirit

. . . and the sword of the Spirit, that is, the word of God. (Ephesians 6: 17b)

The Sword of the Spirit – is the Word of God, according to Saint Paul, the author of the letter to the Ephesians. It is our tool, our offensive weapon against deception. We counter lies with the truth in God's Word, and the truth in God's Word wins every time.

Is the devil planting thoughts of guilt for an already confessed sin? Don't fall for them. Attack with the Word. Claim this promise:

If we acknowledge our sins, he is trustworthy and upright, so that he will forgive our sins and will cleanse us from all evil. (1 John 1: 9)

Is the devil trying to overwhelm you with fear about a circumstance in your life? Tell that spirit of fear to leave in the name of Jesus. These promises are for you to claim too:

> Even were I to walk in a ravine as dark as death I should fear no danger, for you are at my side. Your staff and your crook are there to sooth me. (Psalm 23: 4)

> Do not be afraid, for I am with you; do not be alarmed, for I am your God. I give you strength, truly I help you, truly I hold you in firm with my saving right hand. (Isaiah 41: 10)

Do you doubt that you are "good enough" to be used powerfully by God? Know what God says about that:

> No, God chose those who by human standards are fools to shame the wise; he chose those who by human standards are weak, to shame the strong, those who by human standards are common and contemptible – indeed those who count for nothing – to reduce to nothing all those that do count for something, so that no human being might feel boastful before God. (1 Corinthians 1: 27 – 29)

In the Bible we see that God used "unschooled, ordinary men" (Acts 4: 13), a con artist (Luke 19: 1 – 10), a murderer (2 Samuel 11 – 12), an adulterous woman (John 4), a prostitute (Luke 7: 36 – 49) and many other people who fell short of being "perfect." So take heart! If you love God and follow Him, He will use you greatly! It's all about Him and what He wants to do in you!

If you have been reading this book carefully, you already have quite an arsenal of scripture to use against the attacks of the enemy. You will develop this Sword of the Spirit especially by reading your Bible daily, asking God's Holy Spirit to teach you and speak to you through the Word. Spend time meditating on any scripture passages that the Lord speaks to you in.

If you want to be equipped with the full armor of God so as to be protected from any attack of the enemy, you are going to have to be a man or woman of the Word. There's no other way. It's crucial for you, much as sleep, water, food and shelter are. (Actually, more so!) You need to know the Bible in such a way that you can recall key passages, chapters and verses. In Luke chapter four, Jesus used scripture from the book of Deuteronomy to defeat the devil who attacked Him with various temptations and lies.

Please remember that we are to use the Sword of the Spirit in humility and under the guidance of God. It is His authority that makes the Word powerful, not ours. We are not masters of demons, the world, or ourselves. We are servants of Jesus, the Master of all. Praise God!

Chapter 18

Pleading the Name and Blood of the Lord Jesus

How great is the Name of our Lord Jesus! In Acts 4: 11 – 12 we read that there is no other name through which people are saved and brought into the kingdom of God. Throughout history, near and far, people have experienced the incredible love of God in His Name. Jesus saves people from fears, troubles, disease, pain, death and so much more that if we were to continue listing them, all the books in the whole world could not contain what could be written. (John 21: 25) Through Jesus people experience comfort, protection, purpose, guidance, saving grace, and on and on we could go in another list that could not be contained. His is the Name above all names:

> **He is the reflection of God's glory and bears the impress of God's own being, sustaining all things by his powerful command; and now that he has purged sins away, he has taken his seat at the right hand of the divine Majesty on high. So he is now as far above the angels as the title which he has inherited is higher than their own name. (Hebrews 1: 3 – 4)**

When we talk about the "Name" of Jesus we are, biblically speaking, referring to His character, His attributes, in fact everything that is true about Him. We are obediently submitting to His Lordship and His will in using His Name. We don't use the word "Jesus" or "Yeshua" as if the vocal sounds they make were a supernatural formula or something magical and separate from His Lordship as do occult practitioners. Nor do we use His Name to justify forcing others to our own will as religious bullies have done in the past. The evil they do shows they are not the Lord's. Scripture says:

> **Beware of false prophets who come to you disguised as sheep but underneath are ravenous wolves. You will be able to tell them by their fruits. (Matthew 7: 15 – 16)**

The following chapter, "The Fruits of the Holy Spirit" will deal with alerting ourselves to the characteristics found in those rejecting Christ's authority as well as honestly examining ourselves to make sure we are not becoming the problem.

> **However, God's solid foundation – stone stands firm, and this is the seal on it: 'The Lord knows who are his own' and 'All who call on the name of the Lord must avoid evil.' (2 Timothy 2: 19)**

Demons are terrified of Christ's Lordship, and thus fear His Name. They also run in fear from the blood of the Lamb, which is the blood that Jesus shed in His sacrifice for us on the cross. Once again, we must take care not to interpret the "blood of Jesus" as a kind of magical formula or substance to believe in that will get us out of troublesome situations. The term "the blood of Jesus" refers to Christ's faithfulness to God in willingly shedding His blood by undergoing a horrible, undeserving painful sacrificial death on our behalf. The Lord's death on the cross and resurrection defeated the power of the devil. A few days before He went to the cross for us, Jesus said:

> **'Now sentence is being passed on this world; now the prince of this world is to be driven out. And when I am lifted from the earth, I shall draw all people to myself.' (John 12: 31 – 32)**

Knowing this would happen, Jesus had earlier predicted Satan's fall.

> **'I watched Satan fall from heaven.' (Luke 10: 18)**

We can read more of this in verses 9 – 11 of the 12th chapter of the book of Revelation.

> **The great dragon, the primeval serpent, known as the devil or Satan, who had led all the world astray, was hurled down to the earth and his angels were hurled down with him. Then I heard a voice shout from heaven, 'Salvation and power and empire for ever have been won by our God, and all authority for his Christ, now**

that the accuser, who accused our brothers day and night before
our God, has been brought down. They have triumphed over him
by the blood of the Lamb and by the word to which they bore
witness, because even in the face of death they did not cling to life.'
(Revelation 12: 9 – 11)

The Blood of Jesus

Pleading the blood of Jesus is a special authority granted by God to His
children. It gives us the authority to use what Christ has done on the cross
for God's intervention over a person or situation. Pleading the blood of Jesus
over ourselves brings God's protection upon us and gives us bold access to
God's power and care. Whenever I get into my car for the first time every
day I always pray the following for me and my family:

*I plead the precious blood of Jesus over our health, safety, vehicles and travel
today as we go from place to place or as we stay put. Thank you, Jesus that it is
so. Amen.*

If Satan ever tries to attack you or remind you of past sins that God has
already forgiven you for, you can plead the blood of Jesus over you in this
situation too. Say, "Precious blood of Jesus, cover me and flow through me."
The devil's attack will be stopped and he will flee. "For the battle is the
Lord's." (1 Samuel 17: 47)

Pleading the blood of Jesus in a situation like this also reminds you (and
the devil) that God has already forgiven the sins you've confessed to Him
and He has forgotten them too. Once again, we are not talking about a
magical substance in pleading the blood of the Lord; we are claiming Jesus'
saving sacrifice on the cross reminding ourselves that past sin we've repented
from and these evil powers no longer have control over those who continue
trusting in Him.

When you pray for others as God leads you, you can plead the blood of
Jesus over them. This brings on the power of the new covenant we have with
God, one which the Lord initiated through His work so we could have bold
access to His heavenly throne through Jesus. Read what verses 19 and 20 of
the 10th chapter of the book of Hebrews say:

We have then, brothers, complete confidence through the blood of
Jesus in entering the sanctuary, by a new way which he has opened

for us, a living opening through the curtain, that is to say, his flesh. (Hebrews 10: 19 – 20)

When Jesus died, the curtain of the Temple in Jerusalem was torn from top to bottom:

But Jesus, again crying out in a loud voice, yielded up his spirit. And suddenly, the veil of the Sanctuary was torn in two from top to bottom, the earth quaked, the rocks were split. . . (Matthew 27: 50 – 51)

This curtain separated the outer court from the inner court. By His death, the Lord opened a new way into the presence of God. We can now approach God directly through Jesus. There is no more curtain between us and the Lord. It has been torn from top to bottom (from God's high hand) and is irreparable.

The Name of Jesus

We are God's children, those who believe in Jesus and receive Him as Lord and Savior. We can draw ourselves boldly to God's throne because we are servants of the King of kings, Lord Jesus and are given great authority in His Name. Jesus says:

'These are the signs that will be associated with believers: in my name they will cast out devils; they will have the gift of tongues; they will pick up snakes in their hands and be unharmed should they drink deadly poison; they will lay their hands on the sick, who will recover.' (Mark 16: 17 – 18)

For a period of two years, the Lord led me to Mexico to share my faith with different Christian youth projects throughout the country. This was during the worst time possible, humanly speaking. The terrorist attacks of 9/11 had occurred some months before and once when I went to the San Francisco airport I counted only five travelers in the whole airport! Not only that, I had absolutely no ID until a couple of days before when I received my passport. Talk about cutting it close! Well I was going on these trips under the Lord Jesus' authority so everything worked out well.

When I had been in Mexico before to visit relatives, I often got stomach problems from what I ate or drank there. These problems got so bad once that I was bedridden for two days and hospitalized for one day because of food poisoning.

In the Name of Jesus, I claimed the promise of the above verse from the gospel of Mark when I went on my faith sharing trips, especially the part of "when they drink deadly poison, it will not hurt them at all."

I soon found I was safe from any more stomach problems in Mexico. I ate everything I was given by the Mexican community there and I even drank their water with them, something I was warned against doing by people in the U.S.

Once, after visiting a prisoner, I even drank water from a sink in a Mexican jail and I was fine. It was the Lord's will for me to be on these trips so I had His promise of being safe from anything poisonous as I worked for Him.

The Lord also kept me safe while I was a passenger in Mexican vehicles which practically flew like out of control missiles over sidewalks, hills, traffic lights and other cars, narrowly missing them by inches and going into screeching tailspins as the drivers chuckled in good fun.

In Chapter 23 we will read about the new tongues that the Lord gives us in His name to help us pray to Him continually and powerfully. In Chapter 17 we read about being victorious over spiritual and demonic attacks in Jesus' name. More on these will be found in the chapters ahead. In Chapter 21 we'll also study about the healing power of Jesus name, although we've talked about it in a couple of chapters already, such as in Chapter 4.

I've never picked up a deadly snake with my hands before but I was stung by 16 bees last year. While out on a nature walk one of my friends stepped on their hive, angering the little guys who lashed out at the first person they saw behind her, which was me. The experience was painful and a little on the horrific side but after I scrambled to safety and calmed down a bit, I praised the Lord for permitting every stinger. I was quite energized for a couple of weeks afterwards by all that bee venom. If I could control the dose, I'd let myself get stung that many times again! Well since I've seen or experienced all of the other signs in Mark 16: 17 – 18, picking up snakes must be true as well.

It is important for us to know that these signs occur when we are doing God's work. We don't try to make them happen in and of ourselves, nor are we to deliberately put our lives in danger to test God. If we do, we are submitting to a spirit of pride, error or some other such thing, and our relationship with Jesus is not really where it should be. Remember Jesus' battle with the devil in the desert:

> The devil then took him to the holy city and set him on the parapet
> of the Temple. 'If you are the Son of God,' he said, 'throw yourself
> down; for scripture says: *He has given his angels orders about you,*
> *and they will carry you in their arms in case you trip over a stone.*
> Jesus said to him, 'Scripture also says: *Do not put the Lord your*
> *God to the test.* (Matthew 4: 5 – 7)

Since much of this book is based on Psalm 91, you may notice that Satan
quoted from that psalm to encourage Jesus to wow the crowds with a flashy
feat. He intentionally left out a piece. That's how the devil works: a little bit
of truth here mixed with a little deception there. I will quote the Psalm 91
verses correctly, underlining the piece the devil left out:

> He has given his angels orders about you <u>to guard you wherever you</u>
> <u>go.</u> They will carry you in their arms in case you trip over a stone.
> (Psalm 91: 11 – 12)

The first ten verses of Psalm 91 encourage us to focus unwaveringly on
our Heavenly Father and His ability and will to intervene for us. We walk
daily with this focus upon Him and as a result enjoy His protection for He
will order His angels to guard us as we walk where the Lord leads us. To draw
people to us through actions motivated by pride cause our downfall.

The Bible says the following about pride:

> Pride comes first; disgrace soon follows, with the humble is wisdom
> found. (Proverbs 11: 2)

> The human heart is haughty until destruction comes, before there
> can be glory there must be humility. (Proverbs 18: 12)

> God opposes the proud, but he accords his favour to the humble.
> (James 4: 6)

In addition to staying humble in the Lord, we must remember that the
Name of Jesus is too powerful and holy to simply be some part of a magic
formula. His Name can't be mixed in with Buddha, Confucius, spirits, the
Tao, or anything else. He is Lord of everyone and everything. Scripture says
the following about Jesus:

> For in him were created all things in heaven and on earth: everything
> invisible, thrones, ruling forces, sovereignties, powers – all things

were created through him and for him. He exists before all things and in him all things hold together. (Colossians 1: 16 – 17)

His Name is to be used for His glory by His children who have submitted to His authority over them as Lord and Savior of their lives.

For superstitious people who like using whatever they can to accomplish something, they should learn what happened to the sons of Sceva in Acts 19:

But some itinerant Jewish exorcists too tried pronouncing the name of the Lord Jesus over people who were possessed by evil spirits; they used to say, 'I adjure you by the Jesus whose spokesman is Paul.' Among those who did this were seven sons of Sceva, a Jewish chief priest. The evil spirit replied, 'Jesus I recognize, and Paul I know, but who are you?' and the man with the evil spirit hurled himself at them and overpowered first one and then another, and handled them so violently that they fled from that house stripped of clothing and badly mauled. Everybody in Ephesus, both Jews and Greeks, heard about this episode; everyone was filled with awe, and the name of the Lord Jesus came to be held in great honour. (Acts19: 13 – 17)

We know by the words these sons of Sceva used that they had no relationship with Jesus nor had they submitted to His authority over their lives. If they had they wouldn't be calling Him "the Jesus whose spokesman is Paul." They were also battling demons on their own strength without God's leading, guidance, or strength. They ended up taking quite a beating. It was fortunate for them they weren't killed.

So as one of God's children under the Lord's authority, recognize that you yourself have great authority to plead the Name and blood of Jesus over yourself, your thoughts, any attack of the enemy, any situation, family member, etc. It is a special privilege given by the Lord to His children.

Give in to God, then; resist the devil, and he will run away from you. The nearer you go to God, the nearer God will come to you. Clean your hands, you sinners, and clear your minds, you waverers. Appreciate your wretchedness, and weep for it in misery. Your laughter must be turned to grief, your happiness to gloom. Humble yourselves before the Lord and he will lift you up. (James 4: 7 – 10)

Chapter 19

The Fruits of the Holy Spirit

On the other hand the fruit of the Spirit is love, joy, peace, patience, kindness, goodness, gentleness and self control; no law can touch such things as these. (Galatians 5: 22 – 23)

In the chapters following this one, we'll spend some time on the spiritual gifts mentioned in Scripture. These gifts glorify the Lord, build up believers in the church greatly, and serve as a good witness to unbelievers, drawing them to Christ. The gifts can result in incredible works of God's power to free His people from all sorts of problems and difficulties and be signs to glorify His name and bring others to Him.

In this chapter however, we will discuss the fruits of the Holy Spirit. These serve as our "diagnostic tool" letting us know if we are in synch with God as we use our gifts or as we respond to what is around us. Knowing these fruits, and allowing ourselves to be transformed by God into the likeness of Christ helps us make good choices and be victorious over the circumstances instead of losing under them.

He decided beforehand who were the ones destined to be moulded to the pattern of his Son, so that he should be the eldest of many brothers. (Romans 8: 29)

And all of us, with our unveiled faces like mirrors reflecting the glory of the Lord, are being transformed into the image that we reflect in brighter and brighter glory; this is the working of the Lord who is the Spirit. (2 Corinthians 3: 18)

After we become the Lord's children, what next follows is that we be increasingly made more and more like him. We can see this by how the fruits of the Spirit show forth in our lives.

Love appears first in this list of fruits because it is the greatest quality since it most clearly reflects the character of God. Joy is a close second because in rejoicing in God's salvation and in His will to use us each for the divine purpose He has for us, we show that our affections are rightly placed in His will and purpose. Peace, the third fruit is the product of God having reconciled us sinners to Himself so we are no longer His enemies, which results in confidence for us, and freedom in approaching Him for anything at anytime.

Patience, the next fruit, shows that the Christian is following God's plan and timetable rather than His own, and has abandoned his own idea about how the world should work. Kindness means showing compassion, empathy and generosity to others, which are also attributes of the Lord. Goodness is working for the benefit of others and the glory of the Lord, not for one's own self, which sometimes happens as we shall soon read about.

Faithfulness is another characteristic of God. He always consistently does what He says He will do, as we should also do. Gentleness is a quality Jesus had; He was always approachable, enabling people to rest in Him and to encourage and strengthen others through Him. Self control is the discipline the Holy Spirit gives us to resist the temptation to commit evil by submitting to the fallen, evil human nature. "No law can touch such as these" says the verse in Galatians 5: 23, for those who live out these fruits of the Holy Spirit are automatically obeying the Lord's laws, more so than those who follow religious ceremonies or who display the evidences of being self indulgent, as we will soon see.

We see that our transformation into Christ's likeness is the Lord's priority for us when we become believers and such an emphasis can be seen in God's actions towards us. God's Word also says:

I am quite confident that the One who began a good work in you will go on completing it until the Day of Jesus Christ comes. (Philippians 1: 6)

As mentioned earlier, the fruits of the Spirit listed in Galatians 5: 22 - 23 can be our "diagnostic tool" to see if we are walking with Christ in our actions and allowing ourselves to be obediently molded into His image. We are to seek the giver first, not the gifts! This will ensure that our talents/gifts are being used properly, while also helping us discern whether a gift is even from Him rather than being a satanic counterfeit.

In my 30 years in the Martial Arts, I've seen everything from people knocking down others without touching them (even through doors), releasing poison through their hands, healing injuries through "counsel" from spiritual beings, performing superhuman type feats of strength and agility, knowing how many human presences are in a room before entering it, etc. In my younger years I myself used to enjoy going on late night walks through some of the worst neighborhoods in Mexico City as a kind of "spiritual radar" training exercise. I became pretty skilled at this, always returning to my hotel room safely.

Neither I nor the other individuals displaying these abilities back then ever gave the Lord the glory, but rather attributed them to our own studies or disciplines and even to spiritual, invisible beings. These were evidences of a desire to be in touch with the spiritual realm through means invented by people or unknown spiritual forces who do not lead to Christ. Scripture says the following about such forces:

> My dear friends, not every spirit is to be trusted, but test the spirits to see whether they are from God, for many false prophets are at large in the world. This is the proof of the spirit of God: any spirit which acknowledges Jesus Christ, come in human nature, is from God, and no spirit which fails to acknowledge Jesus is from God; it is the spirit of Antichrist, whose coming you have heard of; he is already at large in the world. (1 John 4: 1 – 3)

Some of us "miracle working" Martial Art/New Age practitioners back then would even claim we had God as our ultimate object, but would reject the Biblically – revealed way in which He should be worshiped. We'd reject making Christ as Lord of our lives refusing to praise Him and thank Him in everything, while following the Bible only when it was convenient. Yes, we'd be mini gods of own, centers of our own tiny misguided universes. "Gifts" such as these I'd described were either from Satan or the human spirit or a combination of the two.

In any case, these "gifts" lead people to believe they have no need of the Lord; it leads them to see themselves as being self sufficient. When people reject the Lord, they eventually turn in on themselves, and so relationships between human beings are destroyed as well. This was true among me and the other Martial Art/New Age practitioners I've mentioned. Our lives would always be characterized by selfish ambition, monetary greed, disunity, jealousy, fits of rage, envy, sexual immorality, constant breakups in our organizations and families, and other signs of lives apart from God.

Over the years each of these "miracle" working Martial Art people met with one tragic end or another, ending a life full of disorder, health problems and broken relationships. I know. I went through this myself; only through the Lord's mercy and discipline was I saved from permanent disaster when I repented and gave up this kind of life, choosing instead to follow the Lord.

Scripture gives us signs of the self indulgence I've been talking about. They serve as another valuable diagnostic tool to show us whether we are walking with Christ or with our own sinful nature.

> **When self indulgence is at work the results are obvious: sexual vice, impurity, and sensuality, the worship of false gods and sorcery; antagonisms and rivalry, jealousy, bad temper and quarrels, disagreements, factions and malice, drunkenness, orgies and all such things. (Galatians 5: 19 – 21)**

I saw these evidences among myself and the people in my former disciplines. I did not see the positive attributes of godly character, all of which are seen in Jesus in the Gospels. The Bible warns us of the danger of submitting to the sinful nature, regardless of whether one appears to have a power or supernatural gift.

> **Don't delude yourselves: no one makes a fool of God! A person reaps what he sows. Those who keep sowing in the field of their old nature, in order to meet its demands, will eventually reap ruin; but those who keep sowing in the field of the Spirit will reap from the Spirit everlasting life. (Galatians 6: 7 – 8) CJB**

Counterfeit spiritual gifts are not limited to Martial Art people or those involved in New Age religions. The counterfeits are found within the church as well. There are people in the church who feel pride from the power of giving false prophecies and making excuses for when they don't come true. I've known men who are constantly grinning and claiming publicly that the Lord has made them teachers while they preach rather basic or misleading messages to congregations, quoting from saints while they secretly leave multiple girlfriends pregnant and devastated. They naturally cause confusion from their poor examples as Christian leaders and lead others to leave the Church while often crowding out more gifted servants of the Lord because they enjoy the attention. This brings division because the fruits of love and self-control are not present, but rather sexual vice, sensuality and rivalry.

In a recent case, a local fellowship is being disciplined and supervised by the church leadership for unethical fundraising practices and performing idolatrous activities against church approval or knowledge. Among this fellowship was one with the extra sensory ability to detect those people who have reported their activities to the church leadership. A small circle of their members would complain about these "informants" and plot strategies on how to hide their unethical actions, actually crediting this extra sensory ability as coming from the Holy Spirit! This is a lie, for the Holy Spirit does not give people the ability to tear people down or know "who has told on you" through psychic powers. Powers such as these either have demonic sources or some highly developed human sensory ability. Often times it is a combination of both.

Any hidden knowledge revealed by the Holy Spirit is always for the purpose of interceding for others so that they may come to Christ more fully. It is not for secretly knowing who is out to report one's unethical practices to the authorities. We will learn more about the spiritual gift of knowledge in the next chapter. For now it's important to know that hidden knowledge given by the Holy Spirit is always given and used in love.

The particular manifestation of the Spirit granted to each one is to be used for the general good. (1 Corinthians 12: 7)

A preacher came to a local church last year claiming he had a message the Holy Spirit wanted to give a prayer group. He began to give a message that was vague and seemed more focused on attacking certain Christian denominations than anything else. Love was not the emphasis. He even told the group if there was anyone who disagreed with his message, he would be willing to "step outside the church and wait for him". I noticed the sinful fruits of malice, jealousy, bad temper and antagonisms in all this.

The preacher soon began to pray and prophecy over people, telling others to accept Mary into their hearts as a personal savior. He began to repeat the name Mary in a machinegun fashion: "Accept Mary, accept Mary, accept Mary accept Mary, Mary, Mary, Mary, MarMarMarMarMarMary!" From my seat I saw this and immediately prayed, "Spirit of antichrist, I rebuke you! Go to the foot of the holy cross in Jesus name". At the exact moment I said the name Jesus, the preacher reeled back, his head spinning to the side as if he'd been slapped by an invisible hand.

The preacher continued praying and a couple of minutes later, began shouting for people to accept Mary into their hearts as a savior again. Again he yelled out, "Accept Mary, accept Mary, accept Mary accept Mary, Mary,

Mary, Mary, MarMarMarMarMarMary!" Once again I prayed the same way and again his head spun to the side as if he'd absorbed another blow. He no longer continued with his "Mary as savior" emphasis. One choosing to truly honor the blessed Virgin Mary would follow the only command she gave us regarding the Lord Jesus:

'Do whatever he tells you.' (John 2: 5)

For the next month the preacher appeared very uncomfortable whenever he saw me; he would grin nervously and avoid looking me in the eye or saying hello, even when his companions were greeting me. He even refused to enter my house when a young couple came with him to my home one evening for some help in designing a flyer for their business. He waited by himself outside in the dark for about 45 minutes while I worked with the couple. He disappeared from the community a couple of weeks later and never returned. I still pray for him, asking the Lord to draw him into a more complete relationship with Him, using all the details and circumstances of his life to do so.

It's all about love. It's all about glorifying Christ. If we do these things, we will be all the more prepared to be victorious in all that comes our way while serving the Lord genuinely and effectively. Our cause is the expression of divine love in our actions; they are done to edify or build up others. We possess true humility, that which says, "I lack, but I know the Lord will fill me in the areas where I lack."

So the best thing for us to all do is pray regularly to the Lord and ask Him to increase the fruits of the Spirit in us as well as our opportunities to practice them in our community, both Christian and secular, and in doing so, glorify God. In this way we will be better prepared to receive spiritual gifts from the Lord and use them the most effectively:

The particular manifestation of the Spirit granted to each one is to be used for the general good. To one is given from the Spirit the gift of utterance expressing wisdom; to another the gift of utterance expressing knowledge, in accordance with the same Spirit; to another, faith, from the same Spirit; and to another, the gifts of healing, through this one Spirit; to another, the working of miracles; to another, prophecy; to another, the power of distinguishing spirits; to one, the gift of different tongues and to another, the interpretation of tongues. But at work in all these is one and the same Spirit, distributing them at will to each individual. (1 Corinthians 12: 6 – 11)

We are supposed to desire these spiritual gifts. Scripture says so, although it points out emphatically that love is our first aim:

> **Make love your aim; but be eager, too, for spiritual gifts. . . (1 Corinthians 14: 1)**

> **And though I have the power to prophecy, to penetrate all mysteries and knowledge, and though I have all the faith necessary to move mountains – if I am without love, I am nothing. (1 Corinthians 13: 2)**

So we would do well to pray for the fruits of the Spirit mentioned in Galatians 5: 22 – 23. We ask the Lord to increase our ability to love, have His joy, peace and all the other Christ – like characteristics. We ask the Lord to give us more opportunity to serve others by sharing what Christ has done for us and by ministering to their needs. We ask the Lord to bless us with whatever gift necessary to do His work, but we must never forget that the fruit of the Spirit must be present in them. Otherwise, what we think we are doing amounts to nothing and we are deceiving ourselves.

> *Heavenly Father, I ask You in Jesus' name to transform me through the power of your Holy Spirit. Make me more like Jesus, increase me in the fruit of your Spirit. Increase my love for You and others. Increase my joy over knowing You and knowing all You do for us. Increase my inner peace and my patience in waiting for You and others. Help me extend kindness to others more, as well as goodness, gentleness and self control. In all these things I will be obedient to your holy commands. Amen.*

Chapter 20

Gifts of the Holy Spirit I - Wisdom, Knowledge and Faith

About the gifts of the Spirit, brothers, I want you to be quite certain.
(1 Corinthians 12: 1)

Nine "charismata", meaning "supernatural gifts" in the New Testament Greek, are the subject in chapters 12 – 14 of the first letter of Paul to the Corinthians. In chapter 12 Paul deals with the different kinds of charismata, addressing the problem of people having pride in this gift or that one. This is a tendency even today, which is why I first wrote a chapter on the fruits of the Holy Spirit before writing on the charismata.

In chapter 13 of the letter to the Corinthians Paul describes the best way to live the Christian life, that of living in Christ-like love, which is better than possessing the charismata. And in chapter 14, Paul wrote about the problem the Corinthians had with using the charismata in a disorderly way. I encourage you to study these three chapters slowly, meditate upon them and allow the Lord to guide you in the spiritual truths they contain.

As we read in 1 Corinthians 12: 1, our Heavenly Father wants all of us to know about these gifts of the Holy Spirit and He wants all of us in love, to desire them as well. Scripture says:

Make love your aim; but be eager, too, for spiritual gifts. . .
(1 Corinthians 14: 1)

The apostle Paul is addressing the entire church when he says this, not just leaders. The charismata are for everyone to receive, not so we can keep them to ourselves, but so they can be given away to others in love for their good. Paul writes:

> **The particular manifestation of the Spirit granted to each one is to be used for the general good. (1 Corinthians 12: 7)**

How is the Spirit manifested in "each one" (the whole church)? What are these charismata? The next verses explain these things:

> **To one is given from the Spirit the gift of utterance expressing wisdom; to another the gift of utterance expressing knowledge, in accordance with the same Spirit; to another, faith, from the same Spirit; and to another, the gifts of healing, through this one Spirit; to another, the working of miracles; to another, prophecy; to another, the power of distinguishing spirits; to one, the gift of different tongues and to another, the interpretation of tongues. But at work in all these is one and the same Spirit, distributing them at will to each individual. (1 Corinthians 12: 6 – 11)**

So the Lord decides when to give us these gifts, and which ones to give us as the need arises. The charismata are always given in love, for the common good of others, as we've read. In this chapter we'll address the first three charismata, those of wisdom, knowledge and faith.

WISDOM

The first gift, or charisma mentioned in the twelfth chapter of 1 Corinthians is that of wisdom, which lets us know what to do next in a given situation. It's a supernatural wisdom, one given from God for spiritual guidance in a situation where the Lord's wisdom is needed. It is able to solve practical or spiritual problems. It is the "how" and "when" regarding these things. So it reaches beyond the wisdom of experience, training, and study. The Lord Himself gives it to us.

> **Listen, my child, take my words to heart, and the years of your life will be multiplied. I have educated you in the ways of wisdom, I have guided you along the path of honesty. When you walk, your going will be unhindered, if you run, you will not stumble. (Proverbs 4: 10 – 12)**

The charisma of wisdom is the "how" and "when" in prayer intercession for others as well. It answers "How do we solve this?", and "When do we do this?" The charisma of knowledge, which we will discuss after this, may provide us with hidden information needed to solve a problem. Perhaps there will be a prophecy as well, or a spirit discerned. We will be discussing these charismata in Chapter 22. The charisma of wisdom should be used in harmony with any other charismata involved so it can guide us on what to do with the information provided by the other spiritual gifts. The spiritual gift of wisdom brings a proper order in doing things.

It's easy to tell the difference between God's wisdom and the world's wisdom. God's wisdom always works. The world's wisdom doesn't. There are other differences. God says:

> **Anyone who is wise or understanding among you should from a good life give evidence of deeds done in the gentleness of wisdom. But if at heart you have the bitterness of jealousy, or selfish ambition, do not be boastful or hide the truth with lies; this is not the wisdom that comes from above, but earthly, human and devilish. Wherever there are jealousy and ambition, there are also disharmony and wickedness of every kind; whereas the wisdom that comes down from above is essentially something pure; it is also peaceable, kindly and considerate; it is full of mercy and shows itself by doing good; nor is there any trace of partiality or hypocrisy in it. (James 3: 13 – 18)**

So neither self love nor selfish motives, motivate God's wisdom. It's pure, humble and gentle with no arguing or nit picking of any kind. It benefits all who receive it equally; it doesn't play favorites. It doesn't cause a person's head to swell in ego, as intellectual learning can do. God's wisdom brings a humble peace that lasts, regardless of how much chaos may be around.

When praying for someone or something, asking God for wisdom is a good place to start. Confess your need and be willing to be obedient. Put aside our own ideas and agendas. Connect with the Holy Spirit in prayer, asking Him to manifest Himself in the situation. The gift of tongues, which will be discussed in Chapter 23, can be used.

Ask the Lord for the wisdom to know what to do. Perhaps someone needs confession or needs to forgive someone first. Or perhaps a spirit needs to be discerned or rebuked. Maybe healing needs to be prayed for or perhaps someone simply needs to be listened to for a while. Be alert in how you pray and how others are praying. Is there something being suggested from God regarding how you should proceed?

Ask God for the wisdom to know how to proceed in the situation you're in, and He promises to give it generously to you. Have faith in Him to do this. He truly is Adonai Roi (a do NAI row EE), or the "Lord our Shepherd". He guides us wisely in the paths we should take. God says:

> **Any of you who lacks wisdom must ask God, who gives to all generously and without scolding; it will be given. But the prayer must be made with faith, and no trace of doubt, because a person who has doubts is like the waves thrown up in the sea by the buffeting of the wind. (James 1: 5 – 6)**

God promises the wisdom will come to you in your particular situation. You will know the words of wisdom He gives you are from Him because you will feel inner peace as you act on them. The apostle Paul wrote:

> **This is the truth and I am speaking in Christ, without pretence, as my conscience testifies for me in the Holy Spirit. (Romans 9: 1)**

When the wisdom you receive is from God's Holy Spirit, it will be consistent with the Lord's Word and also "fit" with your conscience, your inner voice. You can proceed by obeying God's wisdom and using it in faith, the last spiritual gift we'll discuss in this chapter.

KNOWLEDGE

The gift of knowledge occurs when God provides the Christian with specific knowledge about someone's needs or a certain situation that he or she would not ever be able to know without God's supernatural help. It is diagnostic, whereas the gift of wisdom is more of an ordered plan on how to proceed. The charisma of wisdom is the "how" and the "when", while the charisma of knowledge is the "what" and the "why".

The charisma of knowledge points out the hidden issues the Lord wishes to target in your prayer. This is so a person may receive the restoration, healing or salvation the Lord wishes to give in love. This charisma gives you understanding of the key factors in play in a situation. This spiritual gift allows us to discover hidden things, not simply for the sake of knowing them, but in order to increase our faith and openness to cooperate with God in what He wants to do. Such things could not be discovered easily with our natural senses or possibly would be impossible to do so. In any case, the charisma of knowledge will allow us to be conscious of what really is behind what is going on in a situation. It will also indicate what the Lord is doing in this situation or circumstance as well. Normally the gift of knowledge will manifest itself in words, inner visions or intuitions impressed upon the human spirit. I'll point out examples of these.

On one occasion the Spirit revealed to me that a man visiting our church for the first time was not receiving healing from an illness because of a refusal to repent over having been involved with the occult. This was revealed to me through an inner intuition given to me by the Lord; the man hadn't said much of any words to me, nor was he dressed in any way out of the ordinary. I simply got a strong, inner sense that he was participating in witchcraft, psychic channeling and other similar occult practices.

He admitted his involvement in the occult to me after I shared with him what the Lord had told me. I then explained how the Lord was calling him to repent of this occult involvement so his relationship with God and his health could be restored. The Spirit led me to leave it up to the Lord to deal with the man then. The choice would be his. All God wanted me to do was humbly share the information with the visitor.

On another occasion, a woman suffering from depression and fear was prayed over by several Christians who were given the word of knowledge revealing that she often held onto an object formerly belonging to her deceased mother whenever she needed spiritual comfort. She focused her soul, heart and spirit into this object, breathing into it and accepting it as something that could bring her the peace she needed. She renounced this and great healing came to her as she was no longer bothered by these manifestations. Such information would have not been found out by these Christians even had they questioned her for hours.

A prayer group that meets Monday evenings in San Jose recently received words of knowledge from one of its members during a prayer meeting. The words were a warning; the group needed to stop meeting at the location they had been meeting at immediately. As they prayed and contemplated these words, the group discerned that these words were from the Lord, so in obedience they left that location. The following Monday a bomb exploded in the building they'd left and at the time they would normally have been meeting! Lives were saved from these words of knowledge.

In Chapter 3 I mentioned the words of knowledge the Lord gave me on how to respond to my leg injury as well as revealing the hidden reasons old memories were bothering me so much. In Chapter 14 I described how the Lord gave me words of knowledge guiding me to the prayer fellowship He wished me to go to. In a prayer group I participated in at a Catholic church in Monterey, California recently, the Lord revealed to us certain areas in Mexico where "goddess" idolatry was running rampant through demonic influence. We spent the afternoon in intense prayer, rebuking this evil spiritual influence.

I have heard it said that God rarely gives words of knowledge. If that's true, it's not God's fault. I believe people just don't want to take the time or are willing to put aside their fear and just allow Him to talk to them. Recently I came across a Christian lady who is unable to walk; she needs to use a wheeled walker to go from place to place. I heard her say last week, "I'm not even going to say anything to the Lord about my condition. I'll let Him act upon it if it's His will and when He's ready." It sounds like she's the one that's not ready.

Our God is a loving Father whose nature is to give us all that's good in abundance. He says:

> **"Bring the whole tenth into the storehouse, so that there will be food in my house, and put me to the test," says *ADONAI-Tzva'ot*. "See if I won't open for you the floodgates of heaven and pour out for you a blessing far beyond your needs." (Malachi 3: 10) CJB**

Although God is talking about tithing in the above Scripture, we can see that it is our Heavenly Father's nature to bless us and give us a lot of good things. The Lord describes himself as being the following:

> ***ADONAI* descended in the cloud, stood with him there and pronounced the name of *ADONAI*. *ADONAI* passed before him and proclaimed: "YUD-HEH-VAV-HEH!!! Yud-Heh-Vav-Heh [ADONAI] is God, merciful and compassionate, slow to anger, rich in grace and truth;" (Exodus 34: 6) CJB**

> *(Author's note: In this scripture, the Lord reveals His personal name to Moses. The Bible makes clear it is not to be used casually, which is why no one ever spoke the name but rather used the word "Adonai" meaning "My Lord". In the text above the "Yud-Heh-VAV-Heh" are the four Hebrew consonant letters of God's personal name. [YHVH] The Name itself was not said.)*

Why would such a God not want each of His children to receive the benefits of a word of knowledge as we did in these examples? He does! He truly is "rich in grace and truth"! If words of knowledge aren't being revealed to get at the needed heart of the matter, it's man's fault not His. Man lacks the faith to believe in this gift, is ignorant of its existence, rejects it in disobedience, holds on to unconfessed sin, or is just not willing to be still and listen enough to God's voice.

When you are praying for a specific need, learn to ask the Spirit to give you what is needed in your situation and learn to wait. He will give you the wisdom to know what to do, and if the Spirit leads you to ask for a word of knowledge then do so, believing in faith that you will receive it.

When you receive the word of knowledge, God's wisdom will show you what to do with it, whether it means sharing it with someone present or taking a certain action. In faith, obediently do what the Lord tells you to do.

I have seen other believers receive words of knowledge on things they couldn't possibly know about without God's help, everything from a stranger's injury that needed healing, a future ministry, a hidden sin, the location of a Christian in trouble, a concealed deception in a business situation, and many more. I like how David, "the man after God's heart" went about asking God for words of knowledge. In the following verses he asked God about his safety as Saul (Sha'ul in Hebrew), a determined enemy ruthlessly pursued him:

> Then David said, "*ADONAI* God of Isra'el, your servant has certainly heard that Sha'ul intends to come to Ke'ilah and destroy the city just to get me. Will the men of Ke'ilah turn me over to him? Will Sha'ul come down, as your servant has heard? *ADONAI* God of Isra'el, please tell your servant!" *ADONAI* said, "He will come down." Then David asked, "Will the men of Ke'ilah hand me and my men over to Sha'ul?" *ADONAI* said, "They will hand you over." So David and his men, now around six hundred, got up, left Ke'ilah and went wherever they could. (1 Samuel 23: 10 – 13) CJB

On one occasion I asked the Lord why a couple of church ladies looked so nervous or made snarling faces whenever I passed. "Go to Psalm 119: 74," I heard the Lord say to my spirit. I went there and read the following:

> Those who fear you rejoice at the sight of me since I put my hope in your word. (Psalm 119: 74)

Since those folks weren't rejoicing when one of God's children passed, there was a lack of reverent fear or honor towards the Lord there. 1 John 1: 3 – 11 highly stress that we are supposed to love our brothers in the Lord.

> Anyone who loves his brother remains in light and there is in him nothing to make him fall away. But whoever hates his brother is in darkness and is walking about in darkness not knowing where he is going, because darkness has blinded him. (1 John 2: 10 – 11)

The Lord next led me to passages in the books of 1 & 2Kings and Revelation, where He revealed there was a "Spirit of Jezebel" among the ladies in question. I write a little about this in Chapter 23. I am currently praying for these ladies regularly, rebuking this evil spirit and asking the Lord to bless them with honesty, humility and a teachable spirit. I know the Lord has answered me because they have finally been able to extend love to me. Soon after this, an evangelist trained by them telephoned me. Being aware beforehand of this evil influence, I was able to effectively encourage him and share with him the necessity of being honest with the Lord.

God gives us supernatural knowledge relevant to understanding a certain situation. He does this us in love for the benefit of others and so He can be glorified when people witness His power and tell others of it. So He wishes us to share this knowledge with others in love. Paul writes the following in the "love" chapter addressing the proper use of the charismata:

> **And though I have the power of prophecy, to penetrate all mysteries and knowledge, and though I have all the faith necessary to move mountains – if I am without love, I am nothing. (1 Corinthians 13: 2)**

If we stay close to the Lord in prayer and praise, and a word of knowledge comes to us, we can confidently and lovingly act on it for the good of others and for the glory of our Heavenly Father.

FAITH

According to Nelson's New Illustrated Bible Dictionary, faith is "a belief in or commitment toward God, involving commitment to His will for one's life." When God gives this gift to someone, he or she will comfortably believe in God to do something that many other people would see as impossible. Faith as a charisma is beyond what most believers have on average. It is an intense faith, a trust and confidence in God that produces transformation, miracles and martyrs.

> **Trusting is being confident of what we hope for, convinced about things we do not see. (Hebrews 11: 1) CJB**

You don't need much faith to get started. Jesus says faith as small as a mustard seed will allow you to move mountains for God. And the more you use the faith you have, the more your faith will increase. In speaking about the Christian forefather Abraham, God's Word says:

> **Counting on the promise of God, he did not doubt or disbelieve, but drew strength from faith and gave glory to God, fully convinced that whatever God promised he has the power to perform. This is the faith that was reckoned to him as uprightness. And the word 'reckoned' in scripture applies not only to him; it is there for our sake too – our faith too, will be 'reckoned'. . . (Romans 4: 20 – 24)**

So when we act on what God gives us, such as a word of wisdom or an impression in our spirit to pray about a certain need, our faith will become stronger, as Abraham's did. This will be seen as good and just (righteous) in God's eyes. The increase in faith is given to us when we practice using the faith we already have. Remember what Jesus says about not needing much:

> **'In truth I tell you, if your faith is the size of a mustard seed, you will say to this mountain, "Move from here to there," and it will move, and nothing will be impossible for you.' (Matthew 17: 20)**

Some people ask the Lord for more faith but hesitate to act on something God gives them to do. An example would be a believer who has received a word of wisdom or knowledge from God but won't use it or share it out of fear of making a mistake. If you find yourself in a situation like that, take a step in faith and love, and use what you believe God has given you. He honors this and will bring you back on track if you made a mistake. Remember Romans 8: 28?

> **We are well aware that God works with those who love him, those who have been called in accordance with his purpose, and turns everything to their good. (Romans 8: 28)**

As you practice stepping out in faith, your ability to know the Lord's voice greatly improves. As in the case of Abraham, be obedient in faith, and you will be given more faith. Faith is accompanied by action. The Lord says:

> **Was not Abraham our father justified by his deed, because he offered his son Isaac on the altar? So you can see that his faith was working together with his deeds; his faith became perfect by what he did. (James 2: 21 – 22)**

So you can ask the Lord to give you more faith, but be prepared to take action as God leads you, for your gift of faith to grow and be made complete. Sometimes waiting for the Lord is the action you are to take in faith. Remember when Jesus told his disciples to wait in Jerusalem for the arrival of the Holy Spirit:

> **While at table with them, he had told them not to leave Jerusalem, but to wait there for what the Father had promised. 'It is', he had said, 'what you have heard me speak about: John baptized with water but, not many days from now, you are going to be baptized with the Holy Spirit.' (Acts 1: 4 – 5)**

In faith, the disciples obediently followed the Lord's command and a few days later they were empowered with God's Holy Spirit. Their faith and boldness grew powerfully, and the disciples became transformed from a group of weak, timid, doubting men to powerful witnesses who would transform the world for the Lord.

Your faith will increase when you obey the Lord in faith. Prayerfully, stay close to Him and do what He tells you to do. Remember the one and only command Mary gave us in the Bible:

> **His mother said to the servants, 'Do whatever he tells you.' (John 2: 5)**

Faith and acting in obedience to God go hand in hand. They are inseparable. In fact, the charismata of the Spirit cannot be manifested without them. Their importance is seen clearly in the charismata discussed in the following chapter.

Chapter 21

Gifts of the Holy Spirit II -
Healing and Miraculous Powers

HEALING

When healing is mentioned in scripture, the Lord is referring to total healing from the inside out: spirit, soul, mind and body. Scripture says:

> **May the God of peace make you perfect and holy; and may your spirit, life and body be kept blameless for the coming of our Lord Jesus Christ. He who has called you is trustworthy and will carry it out. (1 Thessalonians 5: 23)**

Your spirit, soul, mind and body are one unit, inseparable in this world. The spirit is that which makes us aware of God and relates us to him. In Genesis 1: 26, God said: "Let Us make man in our own image, in the likeness of ourselves." The Bible book of Genesis was originally written in Hebrew, in which the word "image" referred to moral or spiritual similarity.

Your body reflects your physical being, like your bones, flesh, muscles, organs, etc. Your soul links your spirit and body together; it is your "being." Your soul and mind allow you to be conscious of yourself and includes your thoughts and emotions. Sometimes they are referred to as being the same. At times they are seen as your very life.

What affects one of these parts affects the others. I remember a Vietnam veteran who was paralyzed from the waist down for years. His paralysis was attributed to physical injuries and psychological trauma experienced in combat. He attended a healing worship service and the Holy Spirit revealed to him that he held strong resentment and unforgiveness towards a certain film celebrity who led protests against soldiers returning to the U.S. from Vietnam.

I prefer not to mention the things that were done in the protests; it's enough to say that I could not blame this veteran for being very angered by them. But it is always best to turn whatever it is that angers us over to the Lord. God says:

> **Even if you are angry, do not sin: never let the sun set on your anger or else you will give the devil a foothold. (Ephesians 4: 26 – 27)**

Our bodies were not designed to hold anger inside for long periods of time, and I believe that fact led to the veteran's paralysis. At the healing service the veteran finally, through the strength of the Holy Spirit, was able to forgive this film celebrity and left his wheelchair behind, walking for the first time in many years.

The veteran, by following God's command to forgive in his heart, experienced great healing in his body and mind. I have known adults and even children who have held unforgiveness or bitterness towards someone for months or years and the tell tale signs of such decisions have shown in their bodies and minds: sudden weight gain, depression, lack of energy, bone disease, circulation problems, lung conditions, emotional irritability and more. I met a quiet, angry nine year old once who was already suffering from ulcers!

God's Holy Spirit desires to heal our spirits, souls, minds and bodies. This restoring of wholeness is one of the Lord's charismata. The Lord has been known to heal in many ways. Sometimes it is by laying hands:

> **These are the signs that will be associated with believers: in my name they will cast out devils; they will have the gift of tongues; they will pick up snakes in their hands and be unharmed should they drink deadly poison; they will lay hands on the sick, who will recover. (Mark 16: 17 – 18)**

Other times God heals by casting out Satan.

> **And when Jesus rebuked it the devil came out of the boy, who was cured from that moment. (Matthew 17: 18)**

God's healing can also occur when someone asks the Lord to heal someone from a distance.

> So Jesus went with them, and was not very far from the house when the centurion sent word to him by some friends to say to him, 'Sir, do not put yourself to any trouble because I am not worthy to have you under my roof; and that is why I did not presume to come to you myself; let my boy be cured by your giving the word. For I am under authority myself, and have soldiers under me; and I say to one man, "Go," and he goes; to another, "Come here," and he comes; to my servant, "Do this," and he does it.' When Jesus heard these words he was astonished at him and turning round, said to the crowd following him, 'I tell you, not even in Israel have I found such faith as great as this.' And when the messengers got back to the house they found the servant in perfect health. (Luke 7: 6 – 10)

And sure enough, Jesus said the word and the centurion's servant was healed immediately, even though the ill servant was not physically present. At other times the healing can be gradual, or in steps:

> He took the blind man by the hand and led him outside the village. Then, putting spittle on his eyes and laying his hands on him, he asked, 'Can you see anything?' The man, who was beginning to see, replied, 'I can see people; they look like trees as they walk around.' Then he laid his hands on the man's eyes again and he saw clearly; he was cured, and he could see everything plainly and distinctly. (Mark 8: 23 – 25)

Now could the Lord have healed this man on the first time He laid hands on Him? Of course. I believe He laid hands on the man twice to show that sometimes the Lord heals us in stages. In my instance most of the symptoms of my severe advanced osteoarthritis disappeared on the Palm Sunday weekend of 2007. The rest of the symptoms continued to disappear gradually over the next two to three years.

Some healings can come from "ordinary" prayer as described in the book of James:

> Any one of you who is ill should send for the elders of the church, and they must anoint the sick person with oil in the name of the Lord and pray over him. The prayer of faith will save the sick person and the Lord will raise him up again; and if he has committed any sins, he will be forgiven. So confess your sins to one another

and pray for another to be cured; the heartfelt prayer of someone
upright works very powerfully. (James 5: 14 – 16)

Sometimes we can be required by the Lord to perform a certain action
first for our healing to take place:

'As long as I am in the world I am the light of the world.' Having
said this, he spat on the ground, made a paste with the spittle, put
this over the eyes of the blind man, and said to him, 'Go and wash
in the Pool of Siloam' (the name means 'one who has been sent'). So
he went off and washed and came back able to see. (John 9: 5 – 8)

At times sin can cause our affliction. In John 5: 1 – 19, the account is told
of Jesus healing a man who had suffered from an infirmity for thirty-eight
years. After Jesus healed the man, He found him later in the temple. Jesus
said to the man:

'Now you are well again, do not sin any more, or something worse
may happen to you.' (John 5: 14)

By letting the Holy Spirit lead us, God will choose the best way for a
believer to be healed or minister healing to someone else. The Spirit will
reveal whether forgiveness is needed or a turning away from a sin. Perhaps a
spirit needs to be cast out.

Sometimes the gift of discerning of spirits (to be discussed in the next
chapter) is called for. The Holy Spirit can reveal if someone will be healed
immediately or gradually. Gradually may be so God's glory can be displayed
in the best way at some future time. Jesus, in explaining why the man He
healed had been born blind said:

'Neither he nor his parents sinned,' Jesus answered, 'He was born
blind so that the works of God might be revealed in him.' (John
9: 3)

So the delay in the healing of this man was to glorify God and become a
beloved story of Jesus' love for thousands of years afterwards.

I've seen healing come during praise and worship services. Adoring and
loving God enthusiastically through prayer, dance and song has miraculously
healed people who have injuries and other kinds of health problems.

I believe what happens in these instances is that the believer releases all
emotional attachment and worry over their infirmity (which can bind the

infirmity to you) when he or she begins to praise God, and this frees the Lord to work according to His Word in Matthew 18: 18.

> **In truth I tell you, whatever you bind on earth will be bound in heaven; whatever you loose on earth will be loosed in heaven. (Matthew 18: 18)**

The Lord's gift of wisdom is always good to ask for to know how to proceed regarding healing for us or for others. At times the Spirit may lead us to pray for healing right away. By staying close to the Lord in daily prayer, letting the Spirit lead us, and being obedient to him, we can be more available to be channels of healing for Him, channels to be administered to others in love.

THE WORKING OF MIRACLES

The charisma of the working of miracles refers to the Lord enabling His children to accomplish great things for His glory through abilities that would not be humanly possible. I know of a Christian man who suddenly found himself in a location several miles from his home. He hadn't stepped out the door of his home; he simply found himself next to an injured fellow Christian in need of help without having traveled to him. There are numerous documented occurrences of this taking place among the Church's history. Scripture mentions one:

> **He ordered the chariot to stop, then Philip and the eunuch both went down into the water and he baptized him. But after they had come out of the water again Philip was taken away by the Spirit of the Lord, and the eunuch never saw him again but went on his way rejoicing. Philip appeared in Azotus and continued his journey, proclaiming the good news in every town as far as Caesarea. (Acts 8: 38 – 40)**

There are many other things the Lord can do through believers.   On half a dozen occasions during prayer services He has allowed me to see actual demonic presences in several households in other cities. These visions moved me to pray for these families who had allowed these spirits to enter their families through their acceptance of alcohol abuse, sexual behavior, excessive eating, refusal to seek forgiveness, and more. When I saw these people months after seeing these visions, I learned that the visions had been correct, and they had been in bondage to these things.

I did not ask to be able to see these things, nor are these visions anything to boast about. I see them only as the Spirit lovingly leading me to pray for these people. I don't think about this or any other gift as anything other than the Spirit leading me in ministering love to others in need.

On another occasion, nine men from a local church were moved by the Spirit to pray for a missionary in Africa. At that exact moment, halfway across the world, the missionary was about to be attacked by a gang of bandits in the jungle near a village where he was going to be delivering medical supplies.

As they were about to move in the missionary's camp and murder him for his supplies, the gang saw nine large men standing guard around the missionary who lay sleeping. They decided to call off their ambush, and left instead. The Lord had somehow allowed the praying men to become visible on the other side of the world as a way of scaring off this murderous gang.

One of the gang members later confessed his intended actions to the missionary and how seeing the nine men stopped them from carrying out their murderous attack. The missionary insisted that he had been by himself, but the gang member responded by saying his gang had carefully counted the sentries and came up with nine, a number that presented too much of a risk for following through with their attack.

When the missionary returned to his home church in the United States and shared the story, one of the nine men who had prayed for him stood up and said, "The Lord allowed us to be with you in spirit!" He turned to the members of the church and asked every man in the group who had prayed for the missionary to stand up, and eight others did. The time these nine men prayed corresponded to the exact time the gang intended to attack the missionary back in Africa. This protected the missionary and saved his life.

Christian author and engineer Harold Hill wrote numerous accounts of the Holy Spirit giving him visions of the insides of many malfunctioning machines that confounded expert technicians. The Lord would reveal to him the exact problem with machinery on numerous occasions, and this resulted in several witnesses accepting Christ as Lord and Savior after seeing such intervention from God.

Christian churches in China report of believers being unexplainably lifted over walls to escape pursuing Communist soldiers. Reports of raising the dead have occurred as well.

On another occasion I witnessed seventy people pray over a potluck table having no more than two pizzas, two dozen pieces of chicken, two bowls of salad and a bag of tortilla chips. Everyone had between one to three plates of food!

The wide range of working of miracles would be larger than this book could possibly have room for; the important thing is that we recognize that these miracles are given only by God's will, and are shared by the believer in love as a way of reaching people for God and glorifying the Heavenly Father's name.

It is very important to know that we are not the source of these miracles. It is the Spirit who performs them within us. Anytime one "earns" any kind of supernatural power through one's own effort and "training," it is then Satan's counterfeit, which falls under occult and psychic powers. These powers are encouraged by Satan because they teach man to rely on himself and his own dormant paranormal abilities instead of the Holy Spirit.

Satanic powers never point to Christ. Powers from the Holy Spirit always do. Scripture says:

> **My dear friends, not every spirit is to be trusted, but test the spirits to see whether they are from God, for many false prophets are at large in the world. This is the proof of the spirit of God: any spirit which acknowledges Jesus Christ, come in human nature, is from God. (1 John 4: 1 – 2)**

So anytime a supernatural power comes to you it must point towards sharing the good news of Jesus as Lord and Savior. (As the Holy Spirit and angels of the Lord do) If it does not, it intends to draw you away from Christ and must be rejected immediately. There is no middle ground. The next verse in 1 John says:

> **And no spirit which fails to acknowledge Jesus is from God; it is the spirit of Antichrist whose coming you have heard of; he is already at large in the world,   (1 John 4: 3)**

For Jesus' children, pleading the blood of Jesus causes devilish powers to flee. This is always a good way to test a spirit if you are unsure whether an action is prompting you do is from the Lord or not.

There are all sorts of dangerous problems with occult powers: the serious sin of rejecting the Holy Spirit, the opening up to demonic influence or even possession, mental disorders, the learning of things you aren't prepared or meant to know, serious inaccuracies and deceptions with demonic intelligence, extreme self reliance, pride, and more.

The Spirit of God always gives us the best for us at the best time. As we learned earlier, it comforts, counsels, protects, strengthens us and is our defense. The Spirit always leads us closer to Christ, through ministering to us in love, for the benefit of others and ourselves. The Bible says:

> **On the other hand, the fruit of the Spirit is love, joy, peace, patience, kindness, goodness, trustfulness, gentleness and self – control. (Galatians 5: 22 – 23)**

In the same way, what the Spirit leads us to do always points to Christ. It is Jesus' love in action; Christ-like love in us must always be our foundation in the exercising of the charismata, or anything else for that matter. Christian love is the key element. Scripture says:

> **Though I command languages both human and angelic – if I speak without love, I am no more than a gong booming or a cymbal clashing. And though I have the power of prophecy, to penetrate all mysteries and knowledge, and though I have all the faith necessary to move mountains – if I am without love, I am nothing.**
> **Though I should give away to the poor all that I possess, and even give up my body to be burned – if I am without love, it will do me no good whatever. (1 Corinthians 13: 1 – 3)**

Praise and honor to Jesus who always draws us lovingly to himself through the wonderful things He does for us, and the wonderful treasures He offers us!

Chapter 22

Gifts of the Holy Spirit III – Prophecy and Discerning Spirits

Make love your aim; but be eager, too, for spiritual gifts, and especially for prophesying. (1 Corinthians 14: 1)

'I am the good shepherd; I know my own and my own know me.' (John 10: 14)

At times the Heavenly Father will lovingly impart the charismata of prophecy or the discerning of spirits to His children for the purpose of drawing others to Him. In these, as in all charismata, it is important to take the time to listen to the Holy Spirit of God.

Tragically, the gifts of prophecy and discerning of spirits are seen with much skepticism and disbelief today because of Christians who refuse to listen to the gentle, still voice of the Holy Spirit. They instead try to force this gift upon themselves and others or even put on some kind of rehearsed play. Here is a sadly all too common scenario:

A Christian church holds a "gifts of the Spirit" service in which several leaders call people up to the altar saying that the Holy Spirit wants to speak personally to them, usually while loud, moving music is being played. With loud shouts or emotionally moving voices, the leaders claim that God's Holy Spirit wants to speak individually to each of them and touch them, restore them, and offer them eternal life. Members of the congregation come forward, sincerely desiring to receive a personal, special touch from the Father's Holy Spirit.

As they reach the altar, cries and powerful gestures come from the leaders as they lay hands on the congregation, "prophesying" to them by saying such things like, "God loves you so much and He's doing something wonderful for you" or "The Lord is going to use you greatly", or "Jesus is forgiving and healing you."

When I've attended such services, the same question always comes to my mind. How on earth can any Christian "leader" hear anything from the Holy Spirit with all of the noise and activity going on? They can't! That would explain why whatever words from the "Spirit" they "hear" are so general, they could apply to anyone.

Many Christian leaders will assume that because they asked the Holy Spirit to dwell in them at one point, they can willingly direct the Spirit to people like some kind of energy force that they control and increase with their own emotional intensity.

It is no wonder that the congregation receives nothing more than a few generally encouraging statements and an emotional touch brought about by music and leaders' dramatic flair. Now that's not to say that God can't still touch people through these things. But congregations could be much more powerfully touched by God if they gave Him their full listening ear.

Doesn't anyone remember that the Holy Spirit often comes in stillness? Here's what Scripture says about the Lord's appearance to Elijah:

> **He said, "Go outside, and stand on the mountain before *ADONAI*";**
> **and right then and there, *ADONAI* went past. A mighty blast of**
> **wind tore the mountains apart and broke the rocks in pieces before**
> ***ADONAI*, but *ADONAI* was not in the wind. After the wind came**
> **an earthquake, but *ADONAI* was not in the earthquake. After the**
> **earthquake, fire broke out; but *ADONAI* was not in the fire. And**
> **after the fire came a quiet, subdued voice. (1 Kings 19: 11 – 12)**
> **CJB**

The most powerful healings I ever witnessed were at the Catholic Charismatic Conference in Santa Clara, California I attended years ago. What impressed me about what I saw was that the healings occurred in stillness. Several cripples become completely healed right before my eyes. One adult man whose legs had shrunk to the thickness of a child's arms got up out of his wheelchair and began to walk in the name of Jesus.

I noticed that the leader, a Catholic priest, took the time to listen to the Spirit in silence. At one point members of the congregation started singing Alleluias loudly, but the priest quite forcefully rebuked them and told them to be quiet. He immediately followed up his rebuke by saying, "The Holy Spirit often comes in silence."

The leader was able to describe, in great detail, injuries and health conditions of several people in the audience. Even though there were about five hundred in the congregation, only one would come forward for each description of the health condition the priest gave. The descriptions given to the priest by the Holy Spirit were so specific they only applied to one person in the whole crowd. He would call them forward and they would become completely healed.

What a difference from the general "Jesus is healing someone!" And what a powerful testimony for the skeptical! A woman at the same conference was healed of a chronic knee problem. She attended my church and I saw her about a week later. She shared her surprise with us in our Bible study group at how she had been healed. The pain in her knee was still gone. Seeing all this was enough to make me believe that Jesus still healed.

Now the Holy Spirit does often heal people as they're praising and worshipping the Lord out loud, but in order to hear the Spirit give a prophetic word, word of wisdom or knowledge, one must be willing to wait and listen for the Spirit.

The Spirit acts within us as the Lord pleases, when we invite Him in. We don't control the Spirit's gifts. The Lord directs their use, not us.

PROPHECY

According to the Apostle Paul, prophecy is a gift from the Holy Spirit used for strengthening, encouraging and comforting believers. (See 1 Corinthians 14: 3) Nelson's New Illustrated Bible Dictionary (1986 Thomas Nelson Publishers) defines prophecy as "predictions about the future and the end-time; special messages from God, often uttered through human spokesmen, which indicate the divine will for mankind on earth and in heaven."

In the past, prophecy has come through angelic messengers (See Luke 1: 5 – 38), an audible voice from God (See Genesis 6.), visions and dreams (See Acts 9.), or the Lord's Spirit pressing inwardly upon a believer's spirit to reveal divine information (See 2 Chronicles 20: 13 – 17).

A prophecy can be for an individual or group of individuals (as in a church) and reveals specific information from God revealing His future plan and purpose for them.

An example of a prophecy would be one I received from a Spirit-filled believer four years ago. The Spirit led him to tell me that I would write a special book for the Lord in the future and I would be a doctor for Him. I had little intention of doing so at the time but now as I complete this book and come towards the end of my doctorate training, I see that the prophecy was true and from the Lord.

A leader in my Church prayer group once shared with me a prophecy the Lord gave her. The Lord allowed her to see in a vision, the man who she would marry, even though she had never laid eyes on him before. God also allowed her to see that He would someday powerfully use her in a prayer and praise ministry touching hundreds of lives.

Witnesses were present when she saw her future husband at a social function for the first time and heard her say he would be the one she would marry. She was called crazy for the simple fact that the two of them hadn't met yet, and the gentleman in question was dating another woman at the time.

Both prophecies came true in this prayer leader's life, and she and her husband are both Spirit-filled Christians leading a powerful prayer and praise ministry.

Prophecies like these impact us powerfully because they show the Lord's interest in having wonderful, specific purposes for each and every one of us. The accurate detail in these prophecies reveals their source as being God, not human psyche.

The Apostle Paul encourages us to desire all spiritual gifts, especially the gift of prophecy, for the loving encouragement and the good news of salvation it gives to others. Love must be our motive in humbly asking the Lord to give us this gift as He wills.

When you are in prayer for yourself or someone else and you believe the Lord has given you a prophetic word, it is important to test the spirit of the prophecy to make sure it is from God. Do you remember how to do this from Chapter 14? If not, here's a review:

- The prophecy must not contradict God's Word. For example, it must not encourage someone to break God's commandments or hurt another individual.
- The prophecy must not contradict the wisdom of the Church in issues not specifically covered in Scripture (abortion, cloning, etc.)
- Plead the Blood of Jesus over you to overcome any false spirits that may be trying to mislead you.
- Let God's peace lead your inner conscience regarding your prophecy. You should experience His peace.

Remember that prophecies are given in love and those who receive them grow stronger in their faith and experience comfort from the Heavenly Father. If the prophecy is from God it will contain the fruits mentioned in the letter to the Galatians:

> **On the other hand the fruit of the Spirit is love, joy, peace, patience, kindness, goodness, trustfulness, gentleness and self – control; no law can touch such things as these. (Galatians 5: 22 – 23)**

So you should see these characteristics in prophecies given by the Lord. Prayerfully request the wonderful spiritual gift, discern it carefully, and look for Holy Spirit fruits in it if you believe it comes to you.

DISCERNING OF SPIRITS

On several occasions the Lord may lead a believer to identify a demonic spirits involved in other people's lives. As we can note all throughout the book of Acts, the discerning of an evil spirit always leads to intercessory prayer for the good of the individual/individuals involved. When the Lord has led me to discern such things, I've usually felt them as a force against my own spirit when I pray; on a few occasions I've actually seen them. On still other occasions, the Lord leads me to identify an evil spirit through a scripture His Spirit guides me towards. I don't consider this anything to boast about. In fact I rarely tell anyone outside of the prayer group ministering with me about this because of how unbelievable or "crazy" it sounds. It tends to draw out an unhealthy curiosity in others regarding demonic forces as well. I only see this gift as an urgent command to pray, and I do.

Whenever I have my daily prayer time with God, I always ask Him to make me spiritually sensitive to any deliverance I many need from any demonic interference as I pray. More than a dozen evil spirits are mentioned specifically in the Bible. I list many of them here, along with scripture references to them:

- Spirit of Divination (witchcraft, sorcery, magic, astrology, mythical gods) Hosea 4: 12a; Isaiah 47: 13 – 15; Exodus 22:17; Acts 16: 16

- Familiar Spirit (mind control, ESP, psychic powers, hypnotism) - Deuteronomy 18: 9 – 12; Isaiah 19: 3 – 4

- Spirit of Anger/Jealousy - 1 Corinthians 3: 3; Genesis 4: 4 – 7

- Lying Spirit – Acts 5: 3; 2 Chronicles 18: 22; Proverbs 6: 16-19

- Perverse Spirit (Sex perversions, incest, child abuse) – Romans 1: 18 – 32; Hosea 4: 12b; 1 Corinthians 6: 13

- Spirit of Pride (Too proud, smug, self-righteous) – Luke 18: 11 – 14, Hosea 5: 5; Proverbs 6: 16 – 17

- Spirit of Heaviness/Depression – Isaiah 61: 3; 2 Corinthians 1: 8 – 9

- Spirit of Criticism/Accusation – Zechariah 3: 1; Ezekiel 16: 28; Matthew 11: 18 – 19

- Spirit of Infirmity/Illness – Luke 13: 10 – 16

- Dumb and Deaf Spirit – (Loss of hearing, speech problems, foggy thinking) Matthew 9: 32; Mark 9: 14 – 29

- Spirit of Slavery/Addiction (Drugs, alcohol, porn, video games, workaholic behavior, overeating or any other excess) Romans 8: 15; 2 Peter 2: 19

- Spirit of Fear – Psalm 55:5; Proverbs 29: 25; 2 Timothy 1: 7

- Spirit of Seduction (Commonly goes after Christians by slowly luring them into a sinful behavior) – 1 Timothy 4: 1- 2; 2 Timothy 3: 13; Genesis 39

- Spirit of Anti-Christ (Tries to play down the divinity of Christ and His role as Lord and Savior.) – 1 John 4: 3; 2 John 7

- Spirit of Error (Common in overeducated people, it tries to do away with historical facts in the Old Testament and/or the ministry, death and resurrection of Jesus. E.g. – "God didn't really appear to Moses" or "Jesus didn't really feed 5,000 people with a few loaves of bread and fish. He just showed them how to share.") – 1 Timothy 6: 20 – 21; 1 John 4: 6

- Spirit of Death (Attempts to get people to give in to death prematurely in fear, anguish or spiritual defeat.) – Revelation 20: 13 – 14; 1 Corinthians 15: 26

- Spirit of Jezebel (High religiosity with high disobedience to spiritual leaders while instilling the personal desire to be highly visible and in control; will lead the individual to resist other gifted Christians from growing in ministry; often imparts clairvoyant abilities to the individual so they may combat the servants of the Lord and others who oppose their activities. Attracts many followers involved in sexual immorality.) 1 Kings 18: 4, 13; 1 Kings 19; 2 Kings 9: 30 – 37; Revelation 2: 18 – 25

In Isaiah 27: 1, the Bible also mentions the Leviathan, a serpent-like creature that frequents the sea near coastal areas. Have you ever noticed how the behaviors of the spirits listed above run rampant in coastal cities?

This is not an exhaustive list of all the spirits out there. Don't worry about them or think about them much. We are called to focus on the Lord with all our heart, soul, mind and strength. He is the one we are to be the most conscious of, always listening to His voice.

If the Holy Spirit reveals to us a spirit that needs to be rebuked or tells us about person in need of immediate prayer, we act on this right away. We praise and thank God for calling us to action and we praise and thank Him for the results even before we see them.

If you have asked Jesus into your heart as your personal Lord and Savior, living as one of His humble servants under His authority, you then have authority to plead the blood of Jesus and tell any evil spirit to leave in Jesus' name. Invite the Holy Spirit to come and be present in the situation, that He may fill us instead of anything else.

Please remember to be Jesus conscious, not demon conscious. Our Lord and Savior is to be in our heart and efforts moment by moment. There are times that the Lord would lead us to take overt action against a force of evil; at other times He would have us submit without resistance. How do we know when to do each one?

We must know that in ourselves we have no power to defeat evil. The only One who does is God. God's message to us is that we must learn to focus our attention on Him, the source of overcoming power, and not direct our attention toward the evil confronting us. The Lord will then direct our action moment by moment.

If the Lord allows you to discern spirits in a situation, then plead the Blood and Name of Jesus and send those wicked things away. Pray for the salvation of everyone involved. If the Lord leads you to intercede quietly, then do so. Let Him lead your action.

Chapter 23

Gifts of the Holy Spirit IV – Tongues & Interpretation

1 Thessalonians 5:17 says we are to "pray continually" or "pray without ceasing." We are living this commandment when we praise and thank the Lord in everything, regardless of appearances, as we've learned. Many Christians interpret the commandment as meaning to simply pray often, uttering prayers here and there throughout the day.

Now while we are called to pray in these ways often, there are times, because of our imperfect human nature or a certain situation we have found ourselves in that we fall short of the words to pray with. Other times we may be too tired or overwhelmed, and we cannot pray.

The enemy (Satan) can also distract us, confuse us, or mess with our words while we're praying too. Sometimes we may simply not know what to pray for, or not even know that a certain prayer need exists. At other times we just plainly run out of words.

Is it really humanly possible to pray all day and night long? No it isn't, not by human strength anyway. But if you ask if it is possible through God's power, the answer is yes! The charisma of tongues permits us to pray continually and without ceasing. There are four manifestations of the gift of tongues mentioned in Scripture.

One manifestation of tongues is when it comes as a sign of the Holy Spirit's presence. We see this in Acts 2 and Acts 10: 44 – 46.

> They were all filled with the Holy Spirit and began to speak different languages as the Spirit gave them power to express themselves. Now there were devout men living in Jerusalem from every nation under heaven, and at this sound they all assembled, and each one was bewildered to hear these men speaking his own language. They were amazed and astonished. 'Surely,' they said, 'all these men speaking are Galileans? How does it happen that each of us hears them in his own native language?' (Acts 2: 4 – 8)

This miracle was followed by the Apostle Peter's address to the crowd, and verse 47 of Acts 2 says that 3,000 people became Christians on that day. So hearing people speak languages they could not possibly know can be a powerful sign for nonbelievers to come to Christ. Some time ago, a very learned German language professor watched several Christians pray for someone who was ill. He stood there, grinning in disbelief as he heard them pray in tongues when all of a sudden one of the Christians turned toward him and said in a very high level, classical form of the German language: "Who are you to laugh at my gifts?" The professor heard this rebuke in the language he taught, but at a level that was beyond even his language level skill. He began to cry and repent before the Lord in forgiveness. He came to Christ that day, accepting Him as His Lord and Savior.

In the tenth chapter of the book of Acts we see the gift of tongues come upon a group of non – Jewish believers, and this served as a sign for the Jewish believers present that gentiles, or non – Jews would be filled by the Holy Spirit and become part of the Christian church as well. Peter is preaching the gospel of Christ in verses 36 – 43 of Chapter 10. The gentiles listened and believed in their hearts that Jesus is Lord and the Holy Spirit came upon them before they even had a chance to say a word!

> While Peter was still speaking the Holy Spirit came down on all the listeners. Jewish believers who had accompanied Peter were all astonished that the gift of the Holy Spirit should be poured out on gentiles too, since they could hear them speaking strange languages and proclaiming the greatness of God. Peter himself then said, 'Could anyone refuse the water of baptism to these people, now they have received the Holy Spirit just as we have?' He then gave orders for them to be baptized in the name of Jesus Christ. (Acts 10: 44 – 48)

Another manifestation of the charisma of tongues is when it comes as a special message or announcement to a Christian congregation. When it comes in this way, there must be someone with the gift of interpretation so the tongue's message can be revealed to the assembly. Scripture says:

> **While I should like you all to speak in tongues, I would much rather you could prophesy; since those who prophecy are of greater importance than those who speak in tongues, unless they can interpret what they say so that the church is built up by it. (1 Corinthians 14: 5)**

> **That is why anybody who speaks in a tongue must pray that he may be given the interpretation. (1 Corinthians 14: 13)**

Some Christians will argue that one shouldn't pray in tongues at all unless an interpreter is present. They will list 1 Corinthians 14: 27 which says, "If anyone speaks in a tongue, two or at the most three should speak, one at a time, and someone must interpret."

This scripture however is referring to this second manifestation of the gift of tongues. It was not required during the first manifestation we read about, and as we read about the power it had at converting others to Christ we'll know that it was used correctly. The need for an interpreter is only when a tongue is spoken out loud, directed to the church. When the tongue is spoken publicly before an assembly it must be interpreted otherwise all the people won't understand it.

What does it mean to "interpret" a tongue? Interpretation is to listen to a tongue and receive the meaning of it in ordinary language. The meaning of what was spoken by the tongue can then be given by the interpreter to the assembly in the language they all speak. When a tongue is interpreted, what was spoken in the tongue edifies the church congregation through words of knowledge, a revelation, prophecy or instruction.

> **Now suppose, brothers, I come to you and speak in tongues, what good shall I do you if my speaking provides no revelation or knowledge or prophecy or instruction? (1 Corinthians 14: 6)**

The following verse, 1 Corinthians 14: 28 says, "If there is no interpreter, the speaker should keep quiet in the church and speak to himself and God." This leads us to the next manifestation of the charisma of tongues, which is one of the ways a believer can pray without ceasing. Spiritual sounds, or a hidden language pour out for us in a prayer when our human nature limits us. *This third manifestation of tongues is a perfect prayer going directly to God through the power of the Holy Spirit in a language we can't understand.* Scripture says:

> **And as well as this, the Spirit too comes to help us in our weakness, for, when we do not know how to pray properly, then the Spirit personally makes our petitions for us in groans that cannot be put into words; and he who can see into all hearts knows what the Spirit means because the prayers that the Spirit makes for God's holy people are always in accordance with the mind of God. (Romans 8: 26 – 27)**

> **Those who speak in a tongue speak to God, but not to other people, because nobody understands them; they are speaking in the Spirit and the meaning is hidden. (1 Corinthians 14: 2)**

We, as children of God, have the help of the Holy Spirit to take over our prayer for us. It's a promise; one of God's many gifts for us. You just read it in Romans. The Holy Spirit will pray through us with sounds that intercede for us when our human words can take us no further in praying for a certain need.

As mentioned in the scriptures in Romans, there are also times when we don't even know what to pray for. The Spirit will intercede for us when we pray for someone for whom no one knows what his or her real need is. We can pray in these Spirit led sounds (tongues) and the Spirit can use our prayer for a need we ourselves may not realize we have. Or the Spirit can use our prayer in tongues for a stranger on the other side of the world, for all we know.

We let go of our vocal cords, our voice, and let the Spirit speak through us in a prayer language, or tongue. Here are other scriptures supporting the use of the gift of tongues:

> **So, my brothers, be eager to prophesy, and do not suppress the gift of speaking in tongues. But make sure everything is done in a proper and orderly fashion. (1 Corinthians 14: 39 – 40)**

> **These are the signs that will be associated with believers: in my name they will cast out devils; they will have the gift of tongues; they will pick up snakes in their hands and be unharmed should they drink deadly poison; they will lay their hands on the sick, who will recover. (Mark 16: 17 – 18)**

When you let the Spirit pray through you in tongues, your prayer life will improve tremendously. You will be praying in a heavenly language that only God can understand, one that is completely in His will. Satan cannot penetrate the meaning of the words in your heavenly language and try to exert any influence, and your human nature will not interfere either.

You will be able to pray easily, by praising God or praying in tongues throughout the whole day. You can even pray yourself to sleep this way. Let the Spirit take over for you when you are not sure what to pray for or how to pray about something.

When you pray in tongues, you will not understand what you say, but you will be aware in your spirit that it has been prayer that has occurred in you. Your spirit will experience the peace of prayer.

The last manifestation of the gift of tongues also permits us to pray without ceasing in the form of a song. Scripture says:

I shall sing praises with the spirit and I shall sing praises with the mind as well. (1 Corinthians 14: 15b)

This scripture shows us that prayer can be done with our mind (as have been the prayers we've seen in this book) or we can sing in the Holy Spirit with the gift of tongues. The song may be a new one that comes to you in the Spirit while you pray in the Spirit, or it can be to a tune you already know.

Sing to *ADONAI* a new song, his praise in the assembly of the faithful. (Psalm 149: 1) CJB

"Do I really have to pray in tongues?" is the question that is asked among some Christians. "Why wouldn't you want to?" would be my question back. The answer usually is fear, embarrassment, or some other fleshy reason.

What do I mean by "fleshy"? You probably won't find the word in any Bible dictionary. I am talking about the flesh as I did in Chapter 15. Remember that in Christianity the flesh refers to the inherent desire of people to do things that are evil, or pleasing one's self at the cost of being displeasing to God.

The devil is quite pleased with the controversy and discomfort believers have concerning tongues. Of all the gifts of the Spirit, such as prophecy, healing, wisdom, faith, miraculous powers and knowledge, Satan attacks the gift of tongues more than the rest. You don't see anyone speaking badly of receiving more wisdom, faith, healing or any of the others, do you? It's important to know that the gift of tongues is a base or opening for the other charismata to flow and work in you. In the Biblical examples we covered in Acts 2 and Acts 10, we see that the believers received the charisma of tongues before receiving the other charismata.

The devil doesn't like for Jesus' people to pray too much, and since the gift of tongues permits Christians to pray every minute of the day, it would make sense that he would oppose this gift intensely, especially since he can't understand a word of it!

One thing is for sure, though. By missing out on God's way of allowing you to pray 24/7 you are settling for second best. As God's children, we are called to only settle for THE best, nothing less. Jesus said:

> **I have come so that they may have life and have it to the full. (John 10: 10)**

So tongues are an effective way of praying between God and you. Saint Paul wrote in his letter to the Corinthians:

> **I thank God that I speak with tongues more than any of you; all the same, when I am in the assembly I would rather say five words with my mind, to instruct others as well, than ten thousand words in a tongue. (1 Corinthians 14: 18 – 19)**

Paul was grateful to God for the gift of tongues he received, and as you can see he used it often, but taught that it was not appropriate to use it to instruct members of the church unless an interpreter was present. He also wrote:

> **A person speaking in a tongue does edify himself, but a person prophesying edifies the congregation. (1 Corinthians 14: 4) CJB**

Webster's Dictionary defines the word "edify" as meaning "to improve spiritually." I would say all of us need that! And the Bible says in the last verse that speaking in tongues will improve us spiritually. So then, the gift of tongues will improve our prayer life and spiritual development; we just have to remember that it is not appropriate for instructing the church during a worship service unless an interpreter is present.

The following prayer can help you greatly:

Prayer for receiving the gift of tongues

Heavenly Father You are a great and wonderful God. You always want the very best for us. So forgive me for doubting your best for me in my prayer life. Forgive me for being tempted at settling for second best, which is to pray off and on, and cease often. I want to be obedient and pray to You without ceasing. So send me Your Holy Spirit. I surrender my vocal chords to You. Come Holy Spirit. Intercede and pray through me. Give me my prayer language so I can pray powerfully at all times. I expect to speak in Your heavenly tongues for the glory of Your name. Thank You for the gift of tongues, Lord. Thank You. Praise to You, Heavenly Father! In Jesus name I pray. Amen.

To begin, start out by prayerfully asking for God's help. Start out by releasing your tongue and spirit to Him. A Christian doesn't learn the gift of tongues; rather he releases more and more of his self to the Holy Spirit. Let small sounds pour out of you and over time surrender yourself to the Spirit by letting Him work through you to use more sounds and phrases. I remember reading once about an African tribe whose language consists of only 12 different sounds that they grunt in various combinations. And they are able to communicate with each other about everything they need to! So use the sounds the Spirit gives you. If there aren't many you've received, practice them in faith, so that you may receive more. God says:

> **His master said to him, 'Well done, good and trustworthy servant; you have shown you are trustworthy in small things. I will trust you with greater; come and join in your master's happiness.' (Matthew 25: 21)**

Remember this scripture as you practice your heavenly prayer language, allowing "less of you and more of God" to take over. Don't let your emotions dominate you, but rather allow for the Lord's time in transforming you so more sounds, longer words and phrases will come out of you. Remember what John the Baptist once said of the Lord:

> **He must grow greater, I must grow less. (John 3: 30)**

Pray in tongues whenever you believe God's Spirit leads you, or when for one reason or another, praying in your native language limits you in one way or another. Your mind does not need to work for prayer in tongues to work so you may do it quietly as you work, sleep, or travel from place to place. Prayer in tongues may be done out loud or silently.

You will find that by praying in tongues your whole prayer life will improve and your desire to be in the Lord's presence will grow and grow. Praise God!

> **That is why anybody who speaks in a tongue must pray that he be given the interpretation. (1 Corinthians 14: 13)**

Prayer for receiving the gift of interpretation

Praise and glory to You, oh Lord. Your presence is always among us, and it is a great and holy presence indeed. Thank You for loving us and blessing us abundantly with your love, grace and gifts. Thank You for speaking to us through your Holy Spirit in the charisma of tongues. Open me up to receive the gift of interpretation so that your children may be built up for the glory of Jesus. Through me, interpret this tongue spoken and guide me in the words you wish me to use in giving it to your church. In doing so, your children can be instructed, edified and given knowledge of your perfect will for us. Thank You for all your gifts to us, Lord. Thank You for being the Father who loves to give us good things in abundance. Praise and glory to You, Heavenly Father! In Jesus name I pray. Amen.

Author's Note

I strongly encourage you to be an active member in a Church where Jesus is preached, the Word of God is loved, and people pray often. Surround yourself with Jesus' people. You'll grow much better in your walk with God. Learn from more experienced Christians! There is also strength, safety and encouragement in numbers if the evil one targets you because of all the great changes in your life.

You'll also be blessed with wonderful relationships that can last past this lifetime, forever in other words! As a popular song says, "Friends are friends forever when the Lord's the Lord of them." You'll also learn more about the Lord by sharing experiences and have a lot of fun along the way.

There is no such thing as a "lone ranger" in the Christian walk. Scripture says:

> **Let us be concerned for each other, to stir a response in love and good works. Do not absent yourself from your own assemblies as some do, but encourage each other; the more so as you see the Day drawing near. (Hebrews 10: 25)**

> **Each day, with one heart, they regularly went to the Temple but met in their houses for the breaking of bread; they shared their food gladly and generously; they praised God and were looked up to by everyone. Day by day the Lord added to their community those destined to be saved. (Acts 2: 46 – 47)**

There is more effectiveness in numbers. The Lord works great conversions and many wonderful changes in people who work together as one body for His purposes. They are better prepared for any difficulties that arise along the way.

> **But you must always behave in a way that is worthy of the gospel of Christ, so that whether I come to you and see for myself or whether I only hear all about you from a distance, I shall find that you are standing firm and united in spirit, battling, as a team with a single aim, for the faith of the gospel, undismayed by any of your opponents. This will be a clear sign, for them that they are to be lost, and for you that you are to be saved. (Philippians 1: 27 – 28)**

Even when the church situation is less than ideal, let us remember Jesus' example:

> **He went to Nazara, where he had been brought up, and went into the Synagogue on the Sabbath day as he usually did. (Luke 4: 16)**

Now honestly speaking, Jesus' synagogue (church) left much to be desired. If you read the rest of the fourth chapter of Luke you'll find that the synagogue members tried to throw Him off a cliff out of anger over things they were bothered at hearing Him say after a reading.

If Jesus' congregation was this way and He still went to church regularly, any reasons we may have for not going to church become weak and unconvincing.

In a church you can be helped by having people pray for you, and you can help others by praying for them.

Ask the Lord to lead you to the Christian community He wishes you to be a part of, and He will be faithful to answer your prayer.

Chapter 24

The Eucharist

On the evening of the Lord's Passion, on the eve before His sacrificial death for the sins of the world, He gave us, those who believe in Him, a command for which we are to follow:

> Then he took bread, and when he had given thanks, he broke it and gave it to them, saying, 'This is my body given for you; do this in remembrance of me.' (Luke 22: 19)

> Then he took the cup, and when he had given thanks he handed it to them saying, 'Drink from this, all of you, for this is my blood, the blood of the covenant, poured out for many for the forgiveness of sins.' (Matthew 26: 27 – 28)

So in obedience to the Lord, we carry out His commandment to break bread and eat it, and to take the cup and drink from the fruit of the vine. This we do as a community of Christian brothers and sisters in Him. We eat the bread and drink the wine for various reasons, one of which is to offer to the heavenly Father what He Himself has given us: the gifts of His creation. Scripture says:

> From your high halls you water the mountains, satisfying the earth with the fruit of your works; for cattle you make the grass grow, and for people the plants they need, to bring forth food from the earth, and wine to cheer people's hearts, and to make their faces glow, food to make them sturdy of heart. (Psalm 104: 13 – 14)

We can call this offering the Eucharist. In it we praise and thank the Lord for the work of creation. Christians together can offer the sacrifice of praise in thanksgiving for all the lovely, good and noble things God has made in creation and in humanity.

The Lord's children can express their gratitude to Adonai in the Eucharist for all His benefits, for all that He has accomplished in creation and through the salvation He brings us from sin and death by Christ's sacrifice. We also express our gratitude to Jesus for saving us from God's wrath over our sins and bridging the separation between us and the Father due to these sins. His grace, expressed in His sacrifice on the cross, bridges this gap between us and God, not only saving us from sin and death, but also allowing us to become dedicated to God's service. Jesus is the only Name through whom we can be thankful for these things. Peter, filled with the Holy Spirit, said the following in the book of Acts:

> **'Only in him is there salvation; for of all the names in the world given to men, this is the only one by which we can be saved.' (Acts 4: 11 – 12)**

He alone makes our praise and thanksgiving to the Father for these benefits even possible:

> **So then, as you received Jesus as Lord and Christ, now live your lives in him, be rooted in him and built up on him, held firm by the faith you have been taught, and overflowing with thanksgiving. (Colossians 2: 6 – 7)**

> **And whatever you say or do, let it be in the name of the Lord Jesus, in thanksgiving to God the Father through him. (Colossians 3: 17)**

Jesus unites His children to Himself and to His praises to the Father. Jesus is also our advocate, interceding on our behalf to the Father so this Eucharistic praise to the father can be offered through Him and with Him, to be accepted in Him.

> **Further, the former priests were many in number, because death put an end to each of them; but this one, because he remains forever, has a perpetual priesthood. It follows, then, that his power to save those who come to God through him is absolute, since he lives forever to intercede for them. (Hebrews 7: 23 – 25)**

> **My children, I am writing this to prevent you from sinning; but if anyone does sin, we have an advocate with the Father, Jesus Christ, the upright. He is the sacrifice to expiate our sins, and not only ours, but also those of the whole world. (1 John 2: 1)**

> **For there is only one God, and there is only one mediator between God and humanity, himself a human being, Christ Jesus, who offered himself as a ransom for all. (1 Timothy 2: 5)**

The bread and wine signify the goodness of Adonai's creation and continue on to be a sacrificial memorial of Christ and His Body, the Church. The Eucharist is the memorial of the Lord's sacrifice to us, His Church.

> **This is the revelation of God's love for us, that God sent his only Son into the world that we might have life through him. Love consists in this: it is not we who loved God, but God loved us and sent his Son to expiate our sins. (1 John 4: 9 – 10)**

As a memorial the Eucharist isn't only the remembering of past events but it is the proclamation of the mighty deeds God has done for men. Scripture says:

> **All who prosper on earth will bow before him, all who go down to the dust will do reverence before him. And those who are dead, their descendants will serve him, will proclaim his name to generations still to come; and these will tell of his saving justice to a people yet unborn: he has fulfilled it. (Psalm 22: 29 – 31)**

> **Moshe said to the people, "Remember this day, on which you left Egypt, the abode of slavery; because *ADONAI*, by the strength of his hand, has brought you out of this place." (Exodus 13: 3a) CJB**

(Author's note: "Moshe" is Hebrew for "Moses")

> **Go home to your people and tell them all that the Lord in his mercy has done for you. (Mark 5: 19)**

A special meal is how the nation of Israel understands its liberation from Egypt. The Jewish people understand their liberation from slavery to Egypt through the celebration of the Passover meal. In the book of Exodus, we can read how they were saved from this terrible captivity by the Lord who sent the avenging angel to strike down the first born in every Egyptian family while "passing over" the children of Israel who lived among their captors.

The events of Israel's escape or exodus from Egypt through the Lord's intervention become present to the memory of believers. Every time Passover is celebrated, the events in the book of Exodus are made present to their believers so they may direct their lives according to the praise and thanksgiving taught in those events.

By celebrating the Last Supper with His apostles in the Passover meal, Jesus gave this Jewish Passover a more definite meaning. He too "passed over" through His going to the Father by His death and resurrection. He intercedes for us while He is at God's right hand.

> **Jesus cried out in a loud voice saying, 'Father, into your hands I commit my spirit.' With these words he breathed his last. (Luke 23: 46)**

> **Who can bring any accusation against those that God has chosen? When God grants saving justice who can condemn? Are we not sure that is Christ Jesus, who died – yes and more, who was raised from the dead and is at God's right hand – and who is adding his plea for us? (Romans 8: 33 – 34)**

In the New Testament, the Passover memorial takes on a new meaning. When the Church celebrates the Eucharist, she commemorates Christ's Passover, which is the sacrifice He offered once and for all on the cross.

> **It follows, then, that his power to save those who come to God through him is absolute, since he lives forever to intercede for them. Such is the high priest that met our need, holy, innocent and uncontaminated, set apart from sinners, and raised up above the heavens; he has no need to offer sacrifices every day as the high priests do, first for their own sins and only then for those of the people; this he did once and for all by offering himself. (Hebrews 7: 25 – 27)**

The word "Eucharist" is taken from the New Testament Greek meaning "Thanksgiving". This celebration can also be called "The Lord's Supper" because of the connection it has with the last Passover supper the Lord took with His disciples on the eve of His passion and it also anticipates the future wedding feast, that of Christ feasting with His bride (the Church) in Heaven, the new Jerusalem.

Blessed are those who are invited to the wedding feast of the Lamb. (Revelation 19: 9)

Because of Christ's sacrifice on the cross, the Eucharist is a memorial for us of Christ's body which He gave up for us on the cross and the very blood He poured out for the forgiveness of sins.

> **And as they were eating, he took bread, and when he had said the blessing he broke it and gave it to them. 'Take it,' he said, 'this is my body.' Then he took a cup, and when he had given thanks he handed it to them, and all drank from it, and he said to them, 'This is my blood, the blood of the covenant poured out for many.' (Mark 14: 22 – 24)**

Since we as Christians participate together in this memorial of praise and thanksgiving, the Eucharist is often called Holy Communion. It unites us together as a community set apart in Jesus. The Bible says:

> **The blessing – cup, which we bless, is it not a sharing in the blood of Christ; and the loaf of bread which we break, is it not a sharing in the body of Christ? And as there is one loaf, so we, although there are many of us, are one single body, for we all share in the one loaf. (1 Corinthians 10: 16 – 17)**

The Eucharist brings thanksgiving and praise to the Father, it serves as the sacrificial memorial of Christ and His Body, and by the power of the Lord's Word and Spirit, the presence of Christ is found within the bread and wine. In the Eucharist the Lord Jesus gives us the very body which He gave up for us on the cross, the very blood He poured out for many for their forgiveness from sin. In a way that surpasses understanding, the bread and wine become the Body and Blood of Christ by the power of His Holy Spirit and His Word. The Lord's Supper is a celebration in which Christ is mysteriously made present in the bread and wine for those who believe.

Jesus is present in many ways to His children. He is all seeing, all knowing and all powerful, aware of all our steps. The Bible says:

> **You examine me and know me, you know when I sit, when I rise, you understand my thoughts from afar. You watch when I walk or lie down, you know every detail of my conduct. (Psalm 139: 1a – 3)**

He is present in the poor, sick and imprisoned. In verses 31 – 46 of the 25th chapter of the gospel of Matthew we read how the Lord Jesus will take His place on the throne of glory before all the nations and commend the righteous who gave Him food when He was hungry, drink when He was thirsty, clothes when He lacked them and company when He was in prison.

> Then the upright will say to him in reply, "Lord, when did we see you hungry and feed you, or thirsty and give you drink? When did we see you a stranger and make you welcome, lacking clothes and clothe you? When did we find you sick or in prison and go to see you?" And the King will answer, "In truth I tell you, in so far as you did this to one of the least of these brothers of mine, you did it to me." (Matthew 25: 37 – 40)

The Lord Jesus is also present when two or more are gathered in His name. Scripture says:

> For where two or three met in my name, I am there among them. (Matthew 18: 20)

In the Eucharist, the Lord Jesus is present too, in the actual bread and wine. The whole substance of the bread changes into the substance of the body of Christ and the whole substance of the wine changes into the substance of His blood. Jesus says:

> 'I am the bread of life. Your fathers ate the manna in the desert, and they are dead; but this is the bread which comes down from heaven, so that a person may eat it and not die. I am the living bread which has come down from heaven. Anyone who eats this bread will live forever; and the bread that I shall give is my flesh, for the life of the world.' (John 6: 48 – 51)

This does not mean cannibalism, for if Jesus meant that, it would be a barrier between us and Him that no one could cross. We must not let Satan get us to think that Jesus is trying to get us to practice cannibalism or some other horrible practice. That would take away a special treasure Christ intended for us to have, a treasure that would allow us to experience His life – giving presence within us in a very real and wonderful way.

The Greek word for "flesh" in all the Scripture references in this chapter is "sarx", which refers to the physical, emotional, and mental aspects of human existence as well as the human will. To "eat of the flesh" of Christ is to absorb His entire way of being and living, to receive such a presence in ourselves through the Eucharist. Jesus wishes us to feel, think and act like Him; by the power of His Holy Spirit, He enables us to undergo this transformation:

> **Now this Lord is the Spirit and where the Spirit of the Lord is, there is freedom. And all of us, with our unveiled faces like mirrors reflecting the glory of the Lord, are being transformed into the image that we reflect in brighter and brighter glory; this is the working of the Lord who is the Spirit. (2 Corinthians 3: 17 – 18)**

In the same way, to "drink the blood" of the Lord is to absorb His way of self sacrifice and Holy Spirit – led life motivation and indeed His very life. The Bible tells us the following:

> **'For the life of a creature is in the blood, and I have given it to you on the altar to make atonement for yourselves; for it is the blood that makes atonement because of the life.' (Leviticus 17: 11) CJB**

For the first thousand years of the Church, no one denied that Christ became actually present in the bread and wine. Since then, many churches teach that the bread and wine in Communion merely symbolize Christ. This is not what Jesus taught, however. The Jewish people who listened to Him teach about eating his flesh and drinking his blood would not have become so outraged if he had been speaking symbolically. The gospel of John says:

> **Then the Jews started arguing among themselves, 'How can this man give us his flesh to eat?' (John 6: 52)**

Perhaps the language was shocking for Jesus' listeners or perhaps they were looking for an excuse not to continue with the Lord. At this point, the Bible says:

> **After this, many of his disciples went away and accompanied him no more. (John 6: 66)**

In either case, the Jewish audience listening to Jesus should have known that the words "eating" and "drinking" had a long history of being used as symbols of faith in God and obedience to God. We read the following in Psalm 34:

> **Taste, and see that *ADONAI* is good. How blessed are those who take refuge in him! (Psalm 34: 8)**

This points out the goodness and blessings from following the Lord. In the book of Ecclesiastes, the words "eating" and "drinking" mean the following the Law of the Lord and performing good works:

> **And therefore I praise joy, since human happiness lies only in eating and drinking and in taking pleasure; this comes from what someone achieves during the days of life that God gives under the sun. (Ecclesiastes 8: 15)**

As we read in this verse, this joy, this pleasure from the "eating and drinking" comes after, and as a result of what someone did during the days of life God gave him under the sun. Can someone take "eating and drinking" with them to the grave? Of course not! They refer to obedience to the Lord, following His commands while on the earth. In the preaching Jesus gave to His listeners in the gospel of John, He went on to continue:

> **'Whoever eats my flesh and drinks my blood lives in me and I live in that person. As the living Father sent me and I draw life from the Father, so whoever eats me will also draw life from me. This is the bread which has come down from heaven; it is not like the bread our ancestors ate: they are dead, but anyone who eats this bread will live forever.' (John 6: 56 – 58)**

The Eucharist, when taken with a heart right with God and in faith, allows the believer to consume bread and wine that have become the actual body and blood of Christ. Christ, through this transformation, enters into the very soul of the believer who takes of the Eucharist. A special union takes place between the Lord and the believer in the Holy Eucharist.

The Lord extends many blessings towards us in the Eucharist. His wounded body and shed blood were given for our healing, forgiveness and salvation. The Lord says:

> **He was bearing our sins in his own body on the cross, so that we might die to our sins and live for uprightness; through his bruises you have been healed. (1 Peter 2: 24)**

Communion, then, can bring great healing power in our lives. We can experience healing and release from sickness, inner hurts, addictions, uncertainty, lack of purpose and more. Why is it then that more believers aren't experiencing this kind of healing, transformation and restoration? God says:

Whenever you eat this bread, then, and drink this cup, you are proclaiming the Lord's death until he comes. Therefore anyone who eats the bread or drinks the cup of the Lord unworthily is answerable for the body and blood of the Lord. (1 Corinthians 11: 26 – 27)

When the apostle Paul, directed by the Holy Spirit, wrote this letter to the Corinthians, he was letting them know that Holy Communion was not having its intended effect on them. They were getting sick, becoming weak, and dying. They were also being jealous of one another and quarrelling often. (See 1 Corinthians 3: 3.) Doesn't jealousy occur when you don't see God's wonderful purpose for your life but instead want what another person has?

The Corinthians were partaking of Holy Communion without being aware of what Christ had done for them and what they should be doing, which was to love and forgive each other. They were not recognizing the spiritual reality of what was happening at the Lord's Supper and were acting in a way that dishonored Christ. This brought about discipline from the Lord and serves as an example for us not to enter into the Eucharist lightly.

Everyone is to examine himself and only then eat of the bread or drink from the cup; because a person who eats and drinks without recognizing the body is eating and drinking his own condemnation. That is why many of you are weak and ill and a good number have died. If we were critical of ourselves we would not be condemned, but when we are judged by the Lord, we are corrected by the Lord to save us from being condemned along with the world. (1 Corinthians 11: 28 – 32)

Christ died for their sins; His sacrifice was for their forgiveness as it is for ours. The Corinthians were taking the Eucharist without giving this truth much thought or heart, and undoubtedly, others were taking Holy Communion with resentment or unforgiveness in their hearts towards others.

Anyone who chooses not to forgive another person is not realizing how much God has forgiven them for their own sins and offenses. Matthew 18: 23 - 35 is very clear on how God responds to this. It is a story about a servant who owes his master a lot of money and is about to be sold, along with his wife and family, in payment for this debt. The servant falls to his knees and begs the master for mercy. The master gives him mercy and cancels his debt.

No sooner is this servant freed before he finds a second servant who happens to owe him money too, but a much smaller amount. The second servant begs for mercy also, but the first servant doesn't forgive his debt. Instead the first servant throws the second servant in jail. When the master finds out about that, he becomes very angry. Scripture says:

> 'Then the master sent for the man and said to him, "You wicked servant, I cancelled all that debt of yours when you appealed to me. Were you not bound, then, to have pity on your fellow-servant just as I had pity on you?" And in his anger the master handed him over to the torturers till he should pay all his debt. And that is how my heavenly Father will deal with you unless you each forgive your brother from your heart.' (Matthew 18: 32 – 35)

Please note that the master hands over the unforgiving servant over to the torturers. Who are these torturers? What tortures us when we hold bitterness and unforgiveness in our heart? Things like depression, anxiety, anger, ulcers, headaches, high blood pressure, arthritis, weight disorders and other health problems do. Poor life decisions tend to result from unforgiveness as well. We also lose blessings, the development of our talents, protection and our life purpose in serving the Lord. The devil is behind a lot of that. He is the torturer. The Lord says:

> Even if you are angry, do not sin: never let the sun set on your anger or else you will give the devil a foothold. (Ephesians 4: 26 – 27)

So approach Holy Communion with nothing in between God and your fellow man. Are you harboring unforgiveness in your heart? Is there someone you need to ask forgiveness from? Is there a sin to confess and repent from? Have you been obedient to God? Do you remember Chapter 13? Ask the Holy Spirit to examine your conscience deeply before you partake of the Lord's body and blood in communion. You can pray the following:

Heavenly Father, I thank You for all you've done for me in loving me, forgiving me and offering Yourself to me in Holy Communion. I want the full benefits of what You died to give me. Examine me and point out if I have sinned in my thoughts, words or actions. Lead me to confession and repentance. Also show me if I have any unforgiveness or resentment towards another person. If it's buried so deep I can't find it, please find it for me. In Jesus' name I pray. Amen.

What if the person you need to be reconciled to has died, is too far away, in places unknown or otherwise unable to be found by you? Or what if legal restrictions prohibit you from communicating with them? Speak to the Lord about it. Repent and forgive. God will accept your honest inner willingness to go to this person and will accept your repentance or forgiveness of this person. Then you can partake of Holy Communion with the slate clean in God's sight. God says:

> **So then, if you are bringing your offering to the altar and there remember that your brother has something against you, leave your offering there before the altar, go and be reconciled with your brother first, and then come back and present your offering. (Matthew 5: 23 – 24)**

With nothing between you and God or you and your brother, have faith that the Lord will bless you as you partake of the Eucharist. Isaiah prophesied about Jesus when he wrote:

> **In fact, it was our diseases he bore, our pains from which he suffered; yet we regarded him as punished, stricken and afflicted by God. But he was wounded because of our crimes, crushed because of our sins; the disciplining that makes us whole fell on him, and by his bruises we are healed. (Isaiah 53: 4 – 5) CJB**

So if the Eucharist becomes the body and blood of Jesus for us and within us, and He sacrificed His body and blood to remove our sins, infirmities, and sorrows, we can, in faith, expect to experience great healing and release from these things through Holy Communion. Praise God for His goodness to us!

Please notice that the verse "by his bruises we are healed" is in the present tense. Some people say, "Well Jesus healed back then, but He doesn't anymore." But God says:

> **Jesus Christ is the same today as he was yesterday and as he will be forever. (Hebrews 13: 8)**

Jesus still heals! I am living proof. For 15 years, I struggled with a host of health problems. At this point I've already written about the severe advanced hip osteoarthritis the Lord healed me from. I also had compulsive eating habits and weighed between 210 to 212 pounds. For someone with a height of 5' 7", that was pretty overweight.

In addition to these health problems I also suffered from chronic bronchitis and other lung problems that caused me to lose my voice an average of three or four times a year for up to two weeks at a time. It got to the point where I was coughing out blood. I basically was a mess, in more than ways than one.

I gave these problems to the Lord, thanking and praising him for them, trusting in the goodness He would bring from these things. I began taking the Eucharist a few times a week, making sure to have the belt of truth and the rest of God's armor on me. I approached Holy Communion in faith, love, and forgiveness. The Lord slowly began to heal me of these health problems a couple of years ago.

I now weigh between 150 - 155 pounds. I have no more lung problems nor have I lost my voice even once for the last three and a half years. This is quite a positive health change since multiple voice losses each year had been plaguing me for 30 years. My cough has also been gone all this time as well. I praise God for all the health and healing He has brought to me. He truly is Adonai Rophe (a do NAI ro FEH), "The Lord who heals."

> **Dear friend, I am praying that everything prosper with you and that you be in good health, as I know you are prospering spiritually. (3 John 2) CJB**

Friends and acquaintances say my whole appearance has changed and now has a peaceful, joyful, youthful glow around it. It impresses enough young adults to ask me to teach them to look as fit as I do. "You look great!" people say to me. "The Lord has been good to you." Indeed. Thanks and praise to Jesus! Scripture says:

> **He invigorates the exhausted, he gives strength to the powerless. Young men may grow tired and weary, even the fittest may stumble and fall; but those who hope in *ADONAI* will renew their strength, they will soar aloft as with eagles' wings; when they are running they won't grow weary, when they are walking they won't get tired. (Isaiah 40: 29 – 31) CJB**

So approach Holy Communion with humble reverence, joy and thanksgiving, with a heart that is right with God. After you take the Lord's body and blood, return to your seat with your heart focused on Jesus. Wait upon the Lord. Let Christ quietly speak to you or guide you in praise, thanksgiving, prayer or meditation that is pleasing to Him.

> **May the words of my mouth and the thoughts of my heart be acceptable in your presence, *ADONAI*, my Rock and Redeemer. (Psalm 19: 14) CJB**

So do you see how we give of ourselves by approaching the Eucharist in faith, with our hearts right with God and how God gives himself to us through the presence of Jesus in the bread and wine? That's what a covenant is; an exchange of persons as a living expression of God's love. The Lord says:

> **Give in to God, then; resist the devil, and he will run away from you. The nearer you go to God, the nearer God will come to you. (James 4: 7 – 8)**

So let us allow the Lord use the Eucharist as a way for us to approach Him and as a way for Him to draw closer to us. Let us grow in intimacy with Him and He will bless us!

Lord Jesus, I am hungry and thirsty for many things that do not bring real life. Transform me to become more like You. Use your presence in the bread and wine, your body and blood to satisfy my spiritually and bring me to feel, think and act like You. May I absorb your way of self sacrifice and Holy Spirit – led life through your Eucharistic presence in me. Only your food will enable me to live forever. Nourish and sustain me, oh Lord of lords and Bread of Life, now and at the hour of my death when I go to the beautiful place You have prepared for me. Amen.

Chapter 25

Kingdom Authority

We would do well to study the faith of the centurion found in the seventh chapter of Luke's gospel. The centurion was the one person who impressed Jesus the most in all the gospels, pretty much making Him say "Wow!" We should study this carefully because impressing Jesus isn't easy! Jesus had these words to say after hearing the centurion's message:

> **When Jesus heard these words he was astonished at him and turning round, said to the crowd following him, 'I tell you, not even in Israel have I found faith as great as this.' (Luke 7: 9)**

This gospel account starts with the centurion sending Jewish elders to ask Jesus to heal a servant of his. Jesus left for the centurion's house but was stopped on the way by the centurion's friends. They relayed the following message from the centurion to Jesus:

> **So Jesus went with them, and was not very far from the house when the centurion sent word to him by some friends to say to him, 'Sir, do not put yourself to any trouble because I am not worthy to have you under my roof; and that is why I did not presume to come to you myself; let my boy be cured by you giving the word. For I am under authority myself, and have soldiers under me; and I say to one man, "Go," and he goes; to another, "Come here," and he comes; to my servant, "Do this," and he does it.' (Luke 7: 6 – 8)**

What amazed Jesus about the centurion's faith was that he understood Jesus' authority and he paralleled it to the example of his own humble authority as a centurion.

In these times the centurion submitted to the authority of the Roman emperor. He followed whatever the emperor ordered him to do. The centurion saw that in a similar way, Jesus in His earthly ministry followed the authority of the Heavenly Father. Jesus, the Son of God submitted to the will of the Father and followed it perfectly.

Underneath the centurion's authority were one hundred Roman soldiers and numerous servants. The centurion knew he could command his soldiers and servants with but a word. He knew that whatever he ordered of those under his authority would get done.

The centurion knew that in the same way, Jesus has authority over the world, which had been made through Him. He is the Word of God made flesh and lived among us as a human being. Scripture says:

The Word became flesh, he lived among us, and we saw his glory, the glory that he has from the Father as only Son of the Father, full of grace and truth. (John 1: 14)

And:

For in him were created all things in heaven and on earth: everything visible and everything invisible, thrones, ruling forces, sovereignties, powers – all things were created through him and for him. (Colossians 1: 16)

Because Jesus is the Word of God made human and all things were made through Him and for Him, He has authority to forgive sins (Matthew 9: 1 – 8), heal the sick (Luke 4: 38 – 41), raise the dead (John 11), bring freedom from worldly and demonic oppression (Luke 9: 37 – 43), guide people to the Father (Luke 4: 14 – 21), feed multitudes (Matthew 14: 13 – 21), control the forces of nature (Matthew 8: 23 – 27), defeat death (Luke 24), give eternal life (John 10: 28) and an infinite number of other things (John 21: 25).

The centurion knew that Jesus had authority over the illness of his servant and could command it to leave with just His word, as he himself commanded his soldiers and servants with just his word. He didn't even need to have Jesus come to his house. Jesus could heal his servant from where He was.

It would please Jesus if we too, would have such faith. How can we? By surrendering ourselves to Jesus in every area of our lives and letting Him manage it all. If it seems like a huge sacrifice, think of what each of us will have as authority over us if we refuse Christ: depression, anger, fear, illness, insecurity, demonic oppression, stress, addictions, confusion and anything else that would harm you in any way.

To be over, you have to be under. In order to be over these things, you have to be under the authority of the Savior who is over these things. He died for you, conquering sin and death. Kingdom authority is the authority that assures you victory over the world and along with that, eternal life and an incredible friendship with the Creator of the world who will love you and be with you no matter what.

The exchange is incredibly in our favor. What the Lord asks for is fair, considering what we receive for being His children. You can pray the following:

Heavenly Father, thank You for your goodness to me, and your unfailing love. I surrender this body, mind, soul, and spirit to You. I don't even dare call them mine, for they are yours. Take them, Jesus and may your perfect will be done in this life. Be Lord of all in this earthen vessel, and all that has been entrusted to me. Manage all areas of my life, and send your Holy Spirit to teach me to surrender more to You each day. I am under your holy authority, dear Father. I live in your secret place, oh most high God. In your goodness bless me with victory over anything trying to separate me from your perfect peace. You are the Lord in this so be glorified in the process. Praise be your holy name. I pray this in your holy name, Father, and that of your Son Jesus, and that of your Holy Spirit. Amen.

Chapter 26

Conclusion

Look, I am standing at the door, knocking. If one of you hears me calling and opens the door, I will come in to share a meal at that person's side. Anyone who proves victorious I will allow to share my throne, just as I have myself overcome and have taken my seat with my Father on his throne." (Revelation 3: 20 -21)

How about you, dear reader? Have you been willing to "be victorious", to live in the "secret place of the Most High"? Have you been willing to be a child of the King, a "King's kid"? There's only one way for this to happen! It's by accepting Christ into your heart as Lord and Savior. Have you asked Him in and asked His forgiveness? As you read this book did you begin enjoying the treasures and privileges God has for you as one of His children? Are you overcoming the world as Jesus did? I'm praying for you (and every other reader of this book) to do all these things, if you haven't already.

To those of you who have asked Jesus to come into your heart, I encourage you to pray the following:

Heavenly Father, I have decided that my overriding purpose in life is to be worthy of Jesus and remember whom I represent, You. I'm going to be as committed as I know how to be to please You at all times. I will do this by a life that practically shows what God is doing within me. I will grow to be more like Jesus by surrendering to your Holy Spirit, and in so doing, progressively discover more of You. I will reach this goal because of all your mighty power, that which is inseparable from your glory and majesty.

I pray this in Jesus' name. Amen.

Remember that the Christian life is a process. Scripture says:

> **That is why, ever since the day he told us, we have never failed to remember you in our prayers and ask that through perfect wisdom and spiritual understanding you should reach the fullest knowledge of his will and so be able to lead a life worthy of the Lord, a life acceptable to him in all its aspects, bearing fruit in every kind of good work and growing in knowledge of God, fortified, in accordance with his glorious strength, with all power always to persevere and endure, giving thanks with joy to the Father who has made you able to share the lot of God's holy people and with them to inherit the light. (Colossians 1: 9 – 12)**

You will always need to grow and become more like Jesus but you can take encouragement knowing that you aren't what you were like before. Pray with hutzpah (determination) and practice! You will improve! Scripture says:

> **And all of us, with our unveiled faces like mirrors reflecting the glory of the Lord, are being transformed into the image that we reflect, in brighter and brighter glory; this is the working of the Lord who is the Spirit. (2 Corinthians 3: 18)**

If you are now ready to invite Jesus into your heart, go back to Chapter 2. If you still aren't ready at this point to invite Jesus into your heart as Lord and Savior, you are in my prayers too. Dear reader, I pray that Jesus uses the details and circumstances of your life as part of His perfect loving plan to bring you great blessings and help you realize how much you need Him. May He use these things to draw you close to Him. Amen.

Please pray for me too; I encourage you to visit my website "heyitsallaboutjesus.org" to find out about other books and resources to further help you experience the blessings of living as a King's kid should. By living as the children of the greatest King, we can discover the Lord's perfect will and dream for our lives and live it out beyond our own dreams, and so much so that the word "wildest" can't even describe it. You'll read of more practical applications of how God blesses us and overcomes anything for us when we trust Him in praise and thanksgiving.

May God bless you and keep you. May His face turn toward you and may He be gracious to you. May He give you His lasting peace always and forever. May you live forever in the secret place of the Most High. Adonai Shalom – "My Lord my Peace." Amen.

References

Notes

NOTES

NOTES

Printed in the United States
by Baker & Taylor Publisher Services